MW00851129

Globalization in the 21st Century

Manfred B. Steger
University of Hawai'i at Mānoa

ROWMAN & LITTLEFIELD
Lanham • Boulder • New York • London

Executive Acquisitions Editor: Michael Kerns
Assistant Editor: Elizabeth Von Buhr
Sales and Marketing Inquiries: textbooks@rowman.com
Credits and acknowledgments for material borrowed from other sources, and reproduced
with permission, appear on the appropriate pages within the text.

Published by Rowman & Littlefield
An imprint of The Rowman & Littlefield Publishing Group, Inc.
4501 Forbes Boulevard, Suite 200, Lanham, Maryland 20706
www.rowman.com

86-90 Paul Street, London EC2A 4NE

Copyright © 2025 by The Rowman & Littlefield Publishing Group, Inc.

All rights reserved. No part of this book may be reproduced in any form or by any electronic or mechanical means, including information storage and retrieval systems, without
written permission from the publisher, except by a reviewer who may quote passages
in a review.

British Library Cataloguing in Publication Information Available

Library of Congress Cataloging-in-Publication Data Available

Names: Steger, Manfred B., 1961– author.
Title: Globalization in the 21st century / Manfred B. Steger.
Other titles: Globalization in the twenty-first century
Description: Lanham, Maryland : Rowman & Littlefield, [2024] | Includes
   bibliographical references and index.
Identifiers: LCCN 2023041240 (print) | LCCN 2023041241 (ebook) | ISBN
   9781538179727 (cloth : acid-free paper) | ISBN 9781538179734 (paperback : acid-
   free paper) | ISBN 9781538179741 (epub)
Subjects: LCSH: Globalization—21st century.
Classification: LCC JZ1318 .S742 2024 (print) | LCC JZ1318 (ebook) | DDC
   327.09—dc23/eng/20231214
LC record available at https://lccn.loc.gov/2023041240
LC ebook record available at https://lccn.loc.gov/2023041241

∞™ The paper used in this publication meets the minimum requirements of American
National Standard for Information Sciences—Permanence of Paper for Printed Library
Materials, ANSI/NISO Z39.48-1992.

For Paul James,
friend, intellectual partner, model scholar

Contents

Preface and Acknowledgments

The fate of globalization in the twenty-first century hangs in the balance. Although recent data show that most global integration dynamics have been on the rebound after the devastating impacts of the 2008–2009 global financial meltdown and the 2020–2023 COVID-19 pandemic, public views on globalization remain gloomy and subdued. Even some neoliberal pundits who once framed globalization as "worldwide market integration that benefits everyone" now concede that their turbocapitalist juggernaut may be running out of steam. By contrast, national-populist visions of deglobalization, topped with sprinkles of nostalgic "localism," exert significant mass appeal.

Today's ostensible globalization backlash scenario seems to be confirmed by soaring inflation rates, recurring bank failures, global supply chain disruptions, anti-immigration backlash, accelerating climate change and ecological deterioration, lagging transitions to greener forms of energy, escalating political violence, and rising geopolitical competition among the "great powers, especially the United States–China rivalry and the protracted Russian-Ukrainian war. As UN Secretary General António Guterres reports, the world is enduring its highest number of conflicts since the end of World War II, with 2 billion people living in conflict-affected countries and the highest number of refugees on record seeking new homelands. The UN Secretary General rightly speaks of multiple cascading and intersecting crises that feed a global uncertainty complex never seen before in human history. After all, six of seven people worldwide feel insecure, a twenty-first-century trend that has been intensified by the COVID-19 pandemic and its aftermath. These people are plagued by a nagging sense that whatever control they had over their lives is slipping away. With social norms and institutions crumbling under the onslaught of social media–fanned political polarization, this growing sense of anomie is reflected in the depressing fact that fewer than 30 percent of people worldwide think that most of their fellow humans can be trusted, the lowest value on record. Some public observers of our era of the

Great Unsettling have even gone so far as to suggest that we might be in for a rerun of the Cold-War specter of total nuclear annihilation.

On the flipside, however, such doomsday scenarios reinforce the fact that most of today's problems are *global* in nature. Although they cannot be separated from their concrete local, national, and regional settings, these threatening issues require a synchronized *global* response in the form of innovative ideas and public policies directed at the transformation of our unsustainable socioecological system. This necessary search for comprehensive solutions can hardly afford to indulge the reactionary reflex of glorifying an imagined national greatness of a mythical golden past. Instead, we need to find inspiration from uplifting global success stories such as progress in the worldwide reduction of absolute poverty and new international climate change accords. Although modest and often unenforceable, these agreements suggest that solutions to our global problems lie in more and better, not less, globalization.

For academics, the hard work of envisioning an alternative project of ethical reglobalization begins with a hard-nosed assessment of the current state of globalization. Planning for a better planetary future requires taking stock of the global present. This book, along with my published work on the subject over the last twenty-five years, represents the culmination of my own small contribution to assembling a big picture of twenty-first-century globalization that supports practical efforts of setting the globe on a more equitable and sustainable path.

The vision for this book project originated with Susan McEachern and Michael Kerns at Rowman & Littlefield Publishers. For some years now, these engaged senior editors have encouraged me to bring together in a single volume my appraisal of globalization in the twenty-first century. Following Susan's well-deserved retirement, it has been both a privilege and a pleasure to work closely with Michael Kerns and his assistant, Elizabeth Von Buhr, to bring this long-in-the-making project to completion.

I owe a significant intellectual debt to my colleagues and students at the University of Hawai'i at Mānoa. Nothing is more important in higher education than stimulating discussions with fellow academic travelers, no matter at which stage of their professional careers they find themselves. I especially appreciate my regular conversations with my doctoral student, Margie Walkover, whose knowledge of complexity theory has expanded my own understanding of this vital subject and its links to globalization research.

I am extremely grateful for the steady stream of innovative ideas and feedback provided by Professor Paul James, a dear friend and leading globalization scholar at Western Sydney University, to whom this book is dedicated. Parts of earlier versions of some chapters appearing in this study were co-authored with Paul, who generously allowed me to draw on select passages. I also appreciate Dr. Tommaso Durante's competent academic assistance in designing some illustrations that appear in this book. Tommaso's pioneering "Visual Archive Project of the Global Imaginary" can be found at http://www.the-visual-archiveproject-of-the-global-imaginary.com.

I have been fortunate to have received steady feedback on my globalization scholarship from many other academic colleagues, including nine anonymous external reviewers of the book proposal and manuscript. For many years, numerous readers, reviewers, and audiences around the world have offered insightful comments in response to my public lectures and publications on globalization. I am deeply indebted to them for helping me to hone my arguments.

Most importantly, a deep gasshō goes to my soulmate, Perle Besserman, in recognition and appreciation of her love, understanding, generosity, support, patience, intellectual advice, and expert editorial assistance.

As indicated below, most chapters draw on previous essays published between 2002 and 2021. As I wrote them, it became increasingly clear that they were converging on a common theme: the appraisal of unfolding globalization dynamics in the early twenty-first century. However, the pertinent essays have been significantly revised, supplemented with new ideas, expanded with fresh insights, and woven together in the chapters of this book.

I want to thank the following copyright holders for permission to incorporate previously published materials in both original and revised form:

Brill Publishers: Manfred B. Steger, "Mapping Antiglobalist Populism: Bringing Ideology Back In," *Populism* 2 (2019), pp. 110–36.

The University of California Press: Manfred B. Steger, "Two Limitations of Globalization Theory," *Global Perspectives* 2.1 (2021): DOI: https://doi.org/10.1525/gp.2021.30035.

Taylor and Francis: Paul James and Manfred B. Steger, "On Living in an Already-Unsettled World: COVID as an Expression of Larger Transformations," *Globalizations* 19.3 (2022), pp. 426–38; DOI: 10.1080/14747731.2021.1961460, https://www.tandfonline.com; and Manfred B. Steger and Paul James, "A Genealogy of 'Globalization': The Career of a Concept," *Globalizations* 11.4 (September 2014), pp. 417–34; DOI: 10.1080/14747731.2014.951186, https://www.tandfonline.com.

Oxford University Press: Manfred B. Steger, "What Is Global Studies?" in Mark Juergensmeyer, Saskia Sassen, and Manfred B. Steger, eds., *The Oxford Handbook of Global Studies* (2019), pp. 3–20.

Rowman & Littlefield Publishers: Manfred B. Steger, *Globalisms: Facing the Populist Challenge* (2020).

Many people have contributed to improving the quality of this book; its remaining flaws are my own responsibility.

List of Figures and Tables

FIGURES

TABLES

PART I

Histories and Theories

1

A Genealogy of "Globalization"

The sudden discursive explosion of "globalization" in the 1990s represents an extraordinary phenomenon, especially since the term did not enter general dictionaries until the 1961 *Merriam-Webster Third New International Dictionary*. More than half a century later, substantial dictionaries and encyclopedias of globalization as well as multivolume anthologies on the subject had been published that explore the phenomenon in all its complexities.[1] In addition, thousands of books and articles on the subject were written to cover primarily the objective dimensions of globalization such as transnational economic flows, cross-cultural interactions, and the proliferation of worldwide digital networks.

We can track the burgeoning globalization literature through such big data mechanisms as the Google search engine Ngram, a mammoth database collated from more than 5 million digitized books available free to the public for online searches.[2] The exceptionally rich Factiva database lists 355,838 publications referencing the term. The Expanded Academic ASAP database produced 7,737 results with "globalization" in the title, including 5,976 journal articles going back to 1986, 1,404 magazine articles starting in 1984, and 355 news items reaching back to 1987. The ISI Web of Knowledge shows a total of 8,970 references with "globalization" in the title going back to 1968. The EBSCO Host Database yields 17,188 results starting in 1975. Finally, the Proquest Newspaper Database lists 25,856 articles going back to 1971.

Since the early 2000s, there has been a proliferation of projects seeking to measure objective globalization processes with composite indices such as the A. T. Kearney Foreign Policy Globalization Index, the KOF Index of Globalization, and the DHL Global Connectedness Index.[3] The latter, for example, gauges the depth and breadth of a country's integration with the rest of the world, as manifested by its participation in transnational flows of products and services (trade flows), capital (investment flows), information (electronic data flows), and people (tourism, student, and migrant flows).

Depth refers to the size of international flows as compared to a relevant measure of the size of all interactions of that type, both transnational and domestic. It reflects how important or pervasive interactions across national borders are in the context of business or life. *Breadth* measures how closely each country's distribution of international flows across its partner countries matches the global distribution of the same flows in the opposite direction. The breadth of a country's merchandise exports, for example, is measured based on the difference between the distribution of its exports across destination countries versus the rest of the world's distribution of merchandise imports. These country-level results are aggregated using the overall flows as weights to determine the overall level of depth and breadth of globalization.

Moreover, the DHL Global Connectedness Index is built primarily from internationally comparable data from multi-country sources, with additional data drawn from national statistics. Worldwide depth ratios are calculated using published estimates for the world, rather than being aggregated from individual countries' reported data. Worldwide breadth estimates are calculated using reporting country data on interactions with all partners. In cases where adequate data are not available from a reporting country, but sufficient coverage can be achieved by using flows in the opposite direction as reported by partners, this method is used to calculate breadth. Finally, overall depth and breadth scores are computed using sophisticated weighting schemes.[4]

While quantitative measurements of the material aspects of globalization are certainly important, this opening chapter starts laying the foundation of our assessment of globalization in the twenty-first century by investigating the construction of subjective meanings associated with our keyword. This genealogical inquiry proceeds along the lines of three main guiding questions. When and how, exactly, did the concept "globalization" emerge in people's consciousness? What sorts of meanings were associated with it? Why did some of these meanings drop out over time or become relegated to a secondary status while others leapt to the top? Who were some of the key thinkers who shaped these understandings in various ways? Accepting the genealogical challenge implied in these probing questions, this chapter contributes to the historical and theoretical foundation for our assessment of globalization in the twenty-first century. Directing our analytic spotlight on the conceptual evolution of "globalization," it covers the formative period of the keyword from the 1920s to the 1990s, which constitutes the basis of its ongoing meaning evolution in the new century. The chapter offers a careful genealogical mapping of the concept as an indispensable preliminary attempt to expand our understanding of why and how it came to matter so much by the turn of the twenty-first century.

While paying close attention to continuity in meaning formation, this chapter resists the impulse to construct linear narratives that connect "globalization" to fixed points of a single origin or a straight timeline of meaning accumulation. Rather, it settles for the more manageable goal of presenting readers with some significant "snapshots" of multiple genealogical trajectories that contribute to a better understanding of why certain meanings became dominant at the turn of the twenty-first century and how intellectuals came to use certain keywords as they grappled with the challenges of an increasingly interconnected world. Ultimately, the chapter presents an episodic sketch of continuities, crucial junctures, notable tipping points, and multiple pathways that were involved in the meaning evolution of "globalization."

As the intellectual historian Reinhart Koselleck notes, popular concepts such as "globalization" do not simply depict objective processes but also underpin and inform distinct modes of being and acting in the world.[5] Ideas and material interests continuously interact with each other and are, therefore, interrelated and mutually constitutive. Moreover, influential ideas intermingle with the objective structures of the "real world" into which they are inscribed and thus shape concrete sociopolitical practices. This power of ideas to shape realities on the ground is particularly significant during periods of transition and crisis as reflected in our current era of the Great Unsettling. Echoing Koselleck's insights, the Marxist cultural theorist Raymond Williams refers to pivotal terms and concepts as "keywords," which serve as potent catalysts for the formation of entire vocabularies and narratives of a given historical era.[6] By the turn of the twenty-first century, "globalization" had risen from linguistic obscurity to the status of a keyword, which, for better or worse, had taken the world by storm.

THE FOUR MEANING BRANCHES OF THE FAMILY TREE CALLED "GLOBALIZATION"

While the meanings of seminal keywords such as "economics," "culture," or "modernity" evolved rather slowly and built upon a relatively continuous meaning base, "globalization" has had a rather short and discontinuous history, which involves a multiplicity of intellectual entry points and influences. Perhaps most surprisingly, this complex evolution goes back to meaning constellations and discursive orbits that did not always endure on the long road to academic and public prominence. Like the emergence of *Homo sapiens* as a species where, over many millennia, different kinds of hominids thrived side by side for some time before nearly all of them became extinct, some globalization strains turned out to be evolutionary dead-ends while others thrived. Indeed, the meaning formation of "globalization" was many branched. These

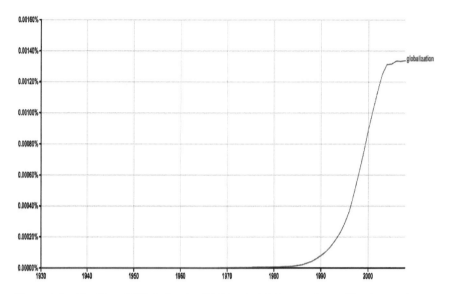

Figure 1.1. The Use of "Globalization" (1930–2010) *Source: https://books.google.com /ngrams/graph?content=globalization&year_start=1930&year_end=2014&corpus=15 &smoothing=3&share=&direct_url=t1%3B%2Cglobalization%3B%2Cc0*

shoots were sometimes fractious and withered. Buffeted by ferocious winds of rapid social change in the twentieth century, they encountered unantici-pated twists and reversals.

As social theorist Philippe Bourbeau observes, the historical evolution of major concepts and issues can best be characterized as "a disparity and diver-sity of meanings; some interpretations are forgotten, set aside, or defeated, while others become integrated into the construction of the dominant narra-tive."[7] This emergent narrative can be broad, meaning two positions at the top of key genealogical lines might be quite distant from each other. Embracing Bourbeau's pluralistic spirit, let us adopt the popular "family tree" metaphor for our genealogical examination. However, we should do so with the afore-mentioned proviso that we envisioned this tree as sprouting diffuse roots and many branches in exceedingly complex patterns.

The early decades of the twentieth century witnessed a clear shift in people's perception of the global as the modern media and communications industries were becoming acutely aware of their own transnational networks serving mass audiences. A number of newspapers around the world, particu-larly in Britain, the United States, and Canada, were using "globe" in their titles, such as the *Boston Globe*, *The Globe* (London), and the *Globe and Mail* (Toronto). From the 1920s forward, some newly constituted commercial airlines featured globes in their advertising projections. Founded in 1927, Pan

American World Airways flew under a blue globe logo until its economic collapse during a very different period of global competition in the 1990s. The *Daily News*—later the inspiration for the *Daily Planet* of Superman fame—proudly displayed a gigantic rotating globe in the massive lobby of its New York headquarters at its opening in 1930.

Already in the 1910s, many Hollywood movie studios had seized upon globes as a vital component of their corporate image. From 1912–1919, the first logo for Universal Films incorporated a stylized Earth with a Saturn-like ring. It was called the Trans-Atlantic Globe or Saturn Globe. In the 1920s, its revised logo was planet Earth floating in space with a biplane flying around it and leaving in its wake a trail of white vapor. Built in 1926, Paramount Picture's New York headquarters was topped by an illuminated glass globe, which was later blackened in response to anticipated perils linked to World War II. In the immediate aftermath of the war—and in the spirit of celebrating the global reach of the communications industry—the Hollywood Foreign Correspondents Association initiated a series of media presentations and receptions they called the Golden Globe Awards.

It was in the critical historical period from the Roaring Twenties to the Revolutionary Sixties that the linguistic shift from "globe" and "global" to the explicit use of "globalization" evolved. The genealogical findings in this chapter reveal the existence of at least four major trajectories in the explicit meaning formation of the concept from the late 1920s to the 1990s. The first meaning branch of the family tree called "globalization" is associated with the academic fields of education and psychology, the second with sociology and cultural studies, the third in politics and international relations (IR), and the fourth in economics and business.

Education and Psychology

The pedagogical-psychological meaning branch appears to be the oldest of the four trajectories and relates primarily to notions of universalization and integration of knowledge acquisition. Its beginnings date back to late 1920s, when a first snapshot shows William Boyd employing the concept throughout his immensely influential work. The Scottish educator associated "globalization" with an innovative "holistic" approach to education: "Wholeness . . . integration, globalization . . . would seem to be the keywords of the new education view of mind: suggesting negatively, antagonism to any conception of human experience which overemphasizes the constituent atoms, parts, elements."[8] In Boyd's usage, globalization had hardly anything to do with the world imagined as interdependent planetary space. Rather, he simply articulated a universal learning process, moving from the global whole to the local particular. It seems Boyd acquired the term by translating the French word *globalisation* as used by Jean-Ovide Decroly. The Belgian educational psychologist had employed the concept in the 1920s in reference to what he called the "globalization function stage" in early childhood development. Within a few years, "globalization" became a more established concept in Decroly's "new education" movement. It was based on a holistic pedagogical method designed to teach children to read and learn—*la méthode globale* ("whole language teaching").

However, over the ensuing decades, this educational and psychological meaning branch of "globalization" declined and withered save for one notable exception. In 1953, C. W. de Kiewiet, president of Rochester University, published a short article that called for the creation of a "globalized curriculum" reflecting the "realities of world conditions."[9] But the author's fervent appeal to "globalize" American universities used the concept only in its verb form, not as a noun. Still, one is struck by the topicality of Kiewiet's demand to globalize the curriculum, especially in light of its sudden reappearance in the 1980s and 1990s. These later initiatives eventually took root in the changing higher education environment of the 1990s and led to significant academic innovations, including the establishment of the transdisciplinary field of global studies.[10] Thus, it would be fair to say that this early pedagogical-psychological branch of meaning formation thinned out and sputtered before mutating into its contemporary discursive field of the "globalization of education." This topical phrase signifies in the contemporary context the study of various objective globalization dynamics such as the transnationalization and rejuvenation of educational systems worldwide. Moreover, "globalization" has also become an important term in the growing pedagogical literature dedicated to the exploration of the dramatic changes that impact higher education as a result of new forms of digital technology, global rankings, and swelling international student flows.[11]

Culture and Sociology

Organized around cultural and sociological meanings, the second branch of the family tree called "globalization" made its appearance in the 1940s. An initial snapshot captures an example remarkable for its isolated occurrence, unusual context, and the mode in which it was delivered. In 1944, Lucius Harper, an African American editor, journalist, and early civil rights leader, published an article that quoted from a World War II letter written by an African American soldier based in Australia. The soldier conveyed his pessimistic impressions of the global dissemination of some racist American views about "Negroes":

The American Negro and his problem are taking on a global significance. The world has begun to measure America by what she does to us [the American Negro]. But—and this is the point—we stand in danger . . . of losing the otherwise beneficial aspects of globalization of our problems by allowing the "Bilbos in uniform" with and without brass hats to spread their version of us everywhere.[12]

"Bilbos in uniform" was a snappy reference to Theodore G. Bilbo (1877–1947), a mid-century governor and US senator from Mississippi, who was an avid advocate of segregation and an openly racist member of the Ku Klux Klan. Bilbo brazenly echoed Adolf Hitler's sentiments expressed in *Mein Kampf* by asserting that merely "one drop of Negro blood placed in the veins of the purest Caucasian destroys the inventive genius of his mind and strikes palsied his creative faculties."[13] At the time, Bilbo and other nationally elected representatives of the segregated South had successfully blocked a series of legislative attempts to clamp down on lynching. These racist Southern politicians sought to complement their obstructionist legislative efforts by spreading anti-Semitic rumors about an "international Jewish conspiracy," aiding what they saw as aggressive Northern interference in Southern political affairs.

By quoting the globalization letter from a Black African American soldier serving his country in the Pacific theater, Harper's article allowed for political mediation that increased the verisimilitude of the passage. Despite Australia's nationally closed and race-based, White-only immigration policy, Black American soldiers in World War II were often greeted abroad with a relative openness that confronted their defensive sensibilities formed in the United States. Harper's article appeared in the *Chicago Defender*, a Chicago-based newspaper primarily for African American readers. At the time, the periodical was probably the most influential newspaper of its kind in the United States, with an estimated readership of one hundred thousand.[14] Overall, though, it appears that the impact of Harper's use of "globalization" on the American press in general and the African American community in particular must have been negligible since virtually no English-language magazines picked up the term for decades after the 1940s.

A second important snapshot corresponding to this sociocultural genealogical branch of the globalization family tree occurred in an academic context that corresponded to the rise of modernization theory and structural-functionalist social systems. These rather abstract approaches in the social sciences were spearheaded by the American sociologists Talcott Parsons and Robert K. Merton. In 1951, Paul Meadows, a notable American sociologist who seems to have been influenced by the rising sociological paradigm, contributed an extraordinary piece of writing to the prominent academic journal,

Annals of the American Academy of Political and Social Science. Although Meadows rarely received mention in the pantheon of globalization pioneers, his article stands out for reasons that will become quickly apparent:

> The culture of any society is always unique, a fact which is dramatically described in Sumner's concept of *ethos*: "the sum of the characteristic usages, ideas, standards and codes by which a group is differentiated and individualized in character from other groups." With the advent of industrial technology, however, this tendency toward cultural localization has been counteracted by a stronger tendency toward cultural universalization. With industrialism, a new cultural system has evolved in one national society after another; its global spread is incipient and cuts across every local ethos. Replacing the central *mythos* of the medieval Church, this new culture pattern is in a process of "globalization," after a period of formation and formulation covering some three or four hundred years of westernization.[15]

This passage is worth quoting at length because it uses the concept in a more contemporary sense. Meadows's interpretation puts "globalization" in a conductive relationship with other pivotal terms of the time such as "industrialism" and "westernization." Moreover, his act of putting "globalization" in inverted commas suggests that Meadows was either uncertain or rather self-conscious about using this new term to illuminate changing social relations. Still, the synergy he formed between such crucial spatial signifiers as "globalization" and "localization" was extended by later globalization researchers like Roland Robertson and Saskia Sassen and suggests that the American sociologist was far ahead of his time.[16]

Another remarkable achievement of Meadows's article lies in its uncanny recognition of the strong nexus connecting "globalization" with "ideology" and "industrial technology" that will be discussed in more detail in the ensuing chapters of this book. As the author points out at the end of his article's introductory section, "The rest of this paper will be devoted to a discussion of the technological, organizational, and ideological systems which comprise this new universalistic culture."[17] Thus, Meadows was one of the first scholars to use "globalization" in a way that would become an enduring meaning a generation later. Still, his pioneering efforts to engage "globalization" in a cultural-sociological mode remained largely dormant until the 1970s and 1980s when other social thinkers started to pick up the term to refer to the "growing interdependence of all humanity" and "the globalization of human culture."[18]

Politics and International Relations

The third genealogical branch of the globalization family tree is rooted in meaning clusters related to politics and international relations (IR). A 1952 snapshot reveals the use of the concept to support the worldwide expansion of the activities of newly established international organizations. Acting as a representative of the United Nations, the international law scholar Sigmund Timberg called for the establishment of a so-called international govcorps, which he envisioned as mediating institutions between the foreign policy strategies of national governments and increasingly globally operating corporations. Evidently, Timberg saw great potential in the development of cooperative structures among nations, which would transform what he called "happenstance globalization" into a deliberate, rational planning process rooted in cutting-edge management techniques. In short, a planned policy form of globalization would not only help to prevent international conflict among nations by means of increasing transborder political and economic activities, but it would also improve the efficiency and productivity of professional bureaucrats working in foreign ministries around the world.[19]

Similarly reflecting on the positive effects of the intensification of international relations, the American political scientist Inis Claude published a widely read article in 1965 on the future of the United Nations. Equating "universalization" with "globalization," the international organizations expert argued, "The United Nations has tended to reflect the steady globalization of international relations."[20] In other words, rather than envisioning the creation of new organizational structures and institutions along the lines of Timberg's international govcorps, Claude considered the United Nations as a whole as the most appropriate model for a rationally planned globalization of international cooperation. Aurelio Peccei, an Italian industrialist, philanthropist, and cofounder of the Club of Rome, picked up on Claude's "movement toward universality" by forging an innovative link between globalization as "mentality" and globalization as "social structure." Thus, Peccei connected the political and sociocultural meaning branches. As he put it, "The important thing, however, in my opinion is that this *process of progressive globalization or planetization* has itself the germ and appeal of an idée-force, because its foundations are cast in the triumphant realities of this age."[21]

Around the same time, and with no reference to Claude or Peccei, an extraordinary article appeared that had the potential of changing the entire field of IR. Penned by the Polish American political scientist George Modelski, the 1968 essay discussed the connection between "globalization" to "world politics" in a comprehensive way:

A condition for the emergence of a multiple-autonomy form of world politics arguably is the development of a global layer of interaction substantial enough to support continuous and diversified institutionalization. We may define this process as globalization; it is the result of the increasing size, complexity and sophistication of world society. Growth and consolidation of global interdependence and the emergent necessities of devising ways and means of handling the problems arising therefrom support an increasingly elaborate network of organizations. World order in such a system would be the product of the interplay of these organizations, and world politics an effort to regulate these interactions.[22]

In the same year his article appeared, Modelski led a team of social science researchers at the University of Washington in drafting a grant application to the US National Science Foundation, which, for the first time, used "globalization" in the title of a comprehensive research project: "The Study of Globalization: A Preliminary Exploration." Unfortunately, this highly innovative project was soundly rejected, thereby halting Modelski's research efforts in this area for two decades. Remarkably, Modelski's sophisticated rendition of the complex process of space-time compression had surprisingly little academic impact, even though the author defined "globalization" in a way that prefigured the heated discussions on its political dimensions during the 1990s.

At the same time, however, Modelski's conceptualization of world order and world politics as "globalization" foreshadowed later challenges to the canonical status of the "international" in IR launched in the 1970s and 1980s by influential political scientists such as James Rosenau, Robert Keohane, and Joseph Nye.[23] These scholars initially employed terms and phrases like "complex interdependence" and "transnationalism" to emphasize the changing dynamics of the international system and the roles played by reconfigured states and a growing variety of non-state actors. Recognizing the rapid transformation of the power and authority of national governments under globalizing conditions, Keohane and Nye eventually argued for a revision of IR's key concept of national sovereignty from a territorially bounded space to a bargaining resource for politics characterized by transnational globalization networks.[24]

Economics and Business

The fourth genealogical branch of the globalization family tree projects economic and business meanings. Here, too, the keyword had a rather tenuous start and was used rarely and intermittently. A snapshot from the early 1960s features the use of "globalization" by François Perroux. A prominent French critic of capitalist financial and economic policies toward the Third World,

Perroux used the concept in a context clearly more akin to its contemporary dominant meaning related to the formation of integrated economic markets on a planetary scale. He referred explicitly to what he called the "*mondialisation de certains marches*" ("globalization of certain markets").[25] Once established, this semantic nexus linking "globalization" to "markets" managed not only to stay alive over the next few decades but began to pick up steam. For example, Michael Haider, CEO of the Standard Oil Company of New Jersey in the late 1960s, argued that there was "no limit to the globalization of American business," which was increasingly "stretching out to developing markets in Africa, Latin America and the Far East."[26]

THE NEOLIBERAL REVOLUTION AND THE "GLOBALIZATION OF MARKETS"

So far, our critical investigation has suggested that, across the middle quarters of the twentieth century, "globalization" generally figured as little more than a "loose descriptor with little analytical shape."[27] It was initially deployed with a surprising variety of meanings and in different social contexts. However, as the popular and academic discourses on the subject converged in the 1980s, "globalization" began to function as a powerful condensation symbol, capable of compressing a whole coterie of economistic ideas and notions into a single keyword. The keyword stimulated a whole host of evaluations, cognitions, and feelings about what people increasingly perceived as a shrinking world powered by free markets and new technologies.

Thus "globalization" became linked to "neoliberalism," a term closely associated with the economic paradigm of Nobel Prize–winners Friedrich von Hayek and Milton Friedman who sought to revive the classical liberal ideal of Adam Smith and David Ricardo, early British advocates of minimal state interference in the capitalist economy. Personified by Anglo-American politicians like Ronald Reagan, Margaret Thatcher, Bill Clinton, and Tony Blair, neoliberalism reached its heyday during the 1980s and 1990s. Known as the "Washington Consensus" and enforced by international economic institutions like the International Monetary Fund and the World Bank, neoliberalism confronted poor countries in the global south with harsh rules and conditions for their economic development. Showing itself to be a remarkably versatile and adaptable doctrine, neoliberalism ate its way into the heart of the Communist world. It managed to charm not only post-Maoist Chinese leaders like Deng Xiaoping but also appealed to the Soviet reformer Mikhail Gorbachev who adopted some tenets under their deceptive slogans "socialism with Chinese characteristics" and "perestroika." Although few political leaders publicly embraced the term "neoliberalism," they all adopted "globalization" as an

appealing label for their neoliberal policies of deregulating national economies, liberalizing international trade, privatizing state-owned enterprises,
downsizing government, and cutting income and corporate taxes. Aiming at
nothing less than overthrowing the dominant postwar paradigm of Keynesian
regulated capitalism, the neoliberal revolution proved to be an important catalyst that helped make the economic and business branch of the family tree the
dominant meaning structure associated with "globalization."

The closing decade of the twentieth century represented a pivotal period
marked by the discursive convergence of "globalization-as-markets" talk. Up
to this point, the use of the concept had occurred largely within the narrow
parameters of the two distinct academic and popular discursive environments.
But with the fall of Soviet-style communism and the rise of Anglo-American
neoliberal economics, "globalization" was leaping into the public limelight
quite suddenly and forcefully, traversing various social fields populated by
academics, journalists, editors, and librarians. For example, the prominent
global studies scholar Mark Juergensmeyer recalled, "A lot of talk about
'globalization' in the immediate aftermath of the fall of the Berlin Wall.
So that would put my first encounter with the concept sometime around
1989 or 1990." Such recognition of the convergence of academic and public
discourses on the subject also characterizes the memory of the globalization
expert Arjun Appadurai. He remembered encountering the concept, "In the
very late 1980s—most likely sometime between 1989 and 1991. I would say
it was after the fall of the Berlin Wall. The context? Most likely, I read about
'globalization' in the press, rather than encountering the term through an
academic route." Similarly, anthropologist Jonathan Friedman recalled, "The
media were starting to use 'globalization' and business got into the act as
well. And I remember a lot of talk about the 'end of the nation-state,' which

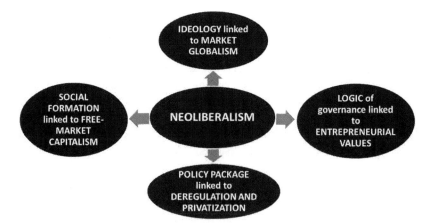

Figure 1.2.   Four Dimensions of Neoliberalism

was very much linked to this new buzzword 'globalization.'"[28] Increasingly understood as an American-led process of "worldwide market integration" following the triumph of deregulated capitalism over socialist planned economies, "globalization" became *the* cornerstone of the emerging ideological constellation of "market globalism" examined in chapter 4.

The most influential early articulation of the neoliberal globalization-as-market narrative appeared as early as 1983 in a *Harvard Business Review* article penned by Theodore Levitt. The Harvard Business School dean imbued the concept with neoliberal meanings that soon escaped their academic business school context and infiltrated the public discourse for good. The description of what Levitt considered "indisputable empirical trends" was inseparable from his neoliberal ideological prescriptions. For example, he insisted that multinational companies had no choice but to transform themselves into global corporations capable of operating in a more cost-effective way by standardizing their products across national markets. Most importantly, the necessary elimination of costly adjustments to various national markets depended on their swift adoption of a "global approach." What Levitt had in mind was the willingness of CEOs to think and act "as if the world were one large market—ignoring superficial regional and national differences. . . . It [the global corporation] sells the same things in the same way everywhere."[29]

Levitt's stated imperative of economic homogenization along the lines of the Anglo-American neoliberal model inspired dozens of similar pieces in high-circulation business magazines and journals. Its authors followed Levitt's lead in seeking to convince large companies to "go global." The advertising industry, in particular, set about creating what they called "global brands" by means of worldwide marketing campaigns. Hence, it seems hardly surprising that the founder of the advertising giant Saatchi and Saatchi was one of Levitt's most fervent disciples.

Levitt's article also had a strong impact on the popular depiction of globalization as an "inevitable" or "inexorable" economic process. Mediated by new digital technologies, globally integrated markets were destined to deliver standardized consumer products on a previously unimagined scale. Among the chief popularizers of Levitt's neoliberal interpretation of "globalization" a decade later, *New York Times* syndicated columnist Thomas L. Friedman stood out. The enormous impact of the journalist's writings was magnified by his personal relationships with political and economic elites on all five continents. Friedman managed to speak to millions of readers in easily digestible sound bites that brought some order to what was often perceived as the threatening complexity and unevenness of the post–Cold War world.

Friedman presented his views on "globalization" in *The Lexus and the Olive Tree*, an international 1999 best-seller lionized by scores of reviewers as the "official narrative of globalization." He argued that the "real character" of what US president George H. W. Bush referred to as the post-1989 "new world order" boiled down to "the one big thing: globalization." He defines the concept as the "inexorable integration of markets, nation-states, and technologies to a degree never witnessed before—in a way that is enabling individuals, corporations and nations-states to reach around the world farther, faster, deeper, and cheaper than ever before, and in a way that is enabling the world to reach into individuals, corporations, and nation-states farther, faster, deeper, and cheaper than ever before.[30]

Friedman's frequent use of the adjective "inexorable" added conceptual weight to his neoliberal interpretation of globalization by suggesting that the liberalization and global integration of markets was an inevitable and perhaps even irreversible process. Indeed, he advocated the restructuring of public enterprises and the privatization of key industrial sectors, including energy, transportation, utilities, and communication: "Globalization means the spread of free-market capitalism to virtually every country in the world. Therefore, globalization also has its own set of economic rules—rules that evolve around opening, deregulating and privatizing your economy, in order to make it more competitive and attractive to foreign investment."[31] Indeed, "market" represents *the* core concept in Friedman's economistic meaning formation of "globalization." He left no doubt as to what he had in mind: "But the relevant market today is the planet Earth and the global integration of technology, finance, trade, and information in a way that is influencing wages, interest rates, living standards, culture, job opportunities, wars and weather patterns all over the world."[32]

For Friedman, such neoliberal globalization was not only destined to generate prosperity and build wealth around the world but also spread American democratic principles that provide for greater political stability in the world. The promotion of liberal democracy through globalization represented a central theme in *The Lexus and the Olive Tree.* The author linked his explanation for the transformation of the Cold War order to democratizing tendencies that allegedly inhere in new technologies like the Internet and the demise of the Bretton Woods system in the early 1970s. He spoke of "three democratizations"—technology, finance, and information—as powerful battering rams breaking down the walls around which the citizens of the old nation-states system communicate, invest, and learn about each other. Enabling the "world to come together as a single, integrated, open plain," these dynamics were depicted as ultimately forcing all nations to integrate into a single global system dominated by the United States.[33]

In short, Friedman saw trade liberalization and global integration of markets inextricably intertwined with the global diffusion of American values, consumer goods, and lifestyles. Thus, *The Lexus and the Olive Tree* closed fittingly with an unapologetic paean to America and its unique role in the globalizing world: "And that's why America, at its best, is not just a country. It's a spiritual value and role model. . . . And that's why I believe so strongly that for globalization to be sustainable America must be at its best—today, tomorrow, all the time. It not only can be, it must be, a beacon for the whole world."[34] Friedman suggested that, culturally speaking, "globalization" was actually "Americanization," that is, the global diffusion of American values, consumer goods, and lifestyles. This American-centered perspective gained steam throughout the 1990s and sparked the proliferation of neologisms such as "McDonaldization" or "McWorldization."[35] Global power brokers eagerly disseminated Levitt's and Friedman's neoliberal ideological perspective of American-led "globalization" as a beneficial economic process driven by the new digital technologies that was destined to lift millions out of poverty while furthering the spread of democracy and freedom around the globe. These elites anchored the term in a conceptual framework that provided the ammunition for the expansion of their free-market oriented political programs and agendas. As genealogical snapshots in this chapter demonstrate, these neoliberal understandings of globalization proliferated in the academic field of economics and business studies.

As advocated in this chapter, critical genealogical investigations of key-words are indispensable for dispelling potent myths of the single-point origins of globalization that are not only historically inaccurate but also serve as ideological tools designed to (re)produce hegemonic neoliberal meanings. Let us consider a final snapshot. In 2006, the *New York Times* featured an article headed, "Theodore Levitt, 81, who coined the term 'globalization,' is dead."[36] The generous obituary that followed was organized around this sin-gular, yet false, origin claim. As demonstrated in this chapter, several global-ization concepts had been in use in the English language in various senses at least as early as the 1920s and possibly even longer. Forced to admit to their error a few days later, the *New York Times* ran a correction that still natural-ized the economistic meaning of the concept:

> An obituary and headline on Friday about Theodore Levitt, a marketing scholar at the Harvard Business School, referred incorrectly to the origin of the word "globalization." While Mr. Levitt's work was closely associated with the idea of globalization in economics, and while he published a respected paper in 1983 popularizing the term, he did not coin the word. (It was in use at least as early as 1944 in other senses and was used by others in discussing economics at least as early as 1981.)[37]

Built on such an uncritical linear narrative of single origins, this *New York Times* snapshot also reflects a reflexive reinforcement of personality cults.

After all, naming the person who first conceived of a significant word or thing has been a crucial feature in the evolution of modern Western public consciousness. At least since the beginning of the European industrial revolution more than two centuries ago, intellectual innovators and technological inventors have been singled out and showered with praise for their Promethean efforts. Over the last century, in fact, this practice has become ever more individualized—as if something as socially and technologically complex as electricity or the computer could be the sudden and single-handed invention of a single genius. Hence, it should not surprise us that this potent individualizing drive to name the "originator" has also been busily in the dominant narrative of the emergence of recent keywords such as "globalization." In fact, this practice has become such a widespread phenomenon that the French sociologist Stéphane Dufoix aptly refers to it as "the religion of the first occurrence."[38]

Conversely, the critical genealogical mapping of "globalization" offered in this chapter excavates the processes indicating how *multiple* meanings initially emerged and how these diverse understandings developed or faded away. Such efforts are predicated upon the renunciation of the religion of the first occurrence. Metanarratives of a single fixed starting point tend to reduce the real-world dynamism of untidy conceptual developments and meaning-making practices to the singularity of frozen positions in space and time. As we noted, Theodore Levitt played an important role in the 1980s by acting as an influential codifier who imbued globalization with economistic meanings centered on the neoliberal signifier "free market." However, he neither invented the term *ex nihilo* nor can its multiple origins be confined to a single meaning cluster associated with the academic fields of economics and business.

Dispelling this influential, yet spurious, *New York Times* story debunks the efforts of neoliberal power to produce truth claims that serve clear political purposes by naturalizing the origins of "globalization" in free market relations. Challenging such claims requires researchers to advance genealogical inquiries in the mode of what Michel Foucault calls "critical analyses of our own condition." Accordingly, the French social thinker describes genealogy as a "method of critique" bearing a strong affinity with histories of knowledge that aim to uncover how the "truth" of a present idea or situation has become established through a series of power moves enveloped in historical contingencies and accidents.[39] In this manner, this chapter tracked the twists and turns in the multiple discourses on "globalization" to underscore how present economistic understandings of "globalization" actually represent a temporary, and rather unstable, victory over a host of other possible meanings.

CONCLUDING REFLECTIONS ON THE MEANING OF "GLOBALIZATION" IN THIS BOOK

Matters of meaning formation look fairly uncomplicated in the public discourse, which has settled on a dominant understanding of "globalization" as early as the 1990s. Although neoliberalism has lost some of its potency in the course of the twenty-first century, its tight association with "globalization" has stuck in the public mind. Thus, if we asked ordinary persons on the busy streets of New York, Vienna, Kolkata, São Paulo, or Melbourne about the meaning of globalization, they would most likely point to economic aspects such as free trade, unfettered investment flows, and globally integrated markets mediated by cutting-edge digital technology.

The reduction of globalization to free-market economics might work in the dominant public discourse, but the meaning structure looks quite different in the academic world. As is the case for most core concepts in the social sciences and humanities, there is not a single, widely accepted meaning of "globalization." In spite of the remarkable proliferation of research on the subject over the last few decades, academic experts are still quarreling over definitional matters. Moreover, they have remained divided on the utility of various analytical frameworks, methodological approaches, the validity of available empirical evidence, and, of course, on the hotly debated normative question of whether globalization should be considered a good or bad thing. Only rarely have globalization scholars managed to strike lasting intellectual accords.

Heeding the voices of discerning critics who have rightfully pointed to these ongoing problems of definitional and conceptual murkiness, let us conclude this genealogical chapter with a full disclosure of the meanings attached to our keyword in this study. For starters, the grammatical breakdown of the keyword yields two constitutive parts: "global" and "-ization." The former is a spatial term, which signifies "worldwide" or "involving and affecting the whole world." The word is rooted in the noun "globe," which, in turn, derives from the Latin *globus* referring to a rounded object such as our planet. The tacking on of "-ization" is a common linguistic practice reflected in similar terms such as "modernization," "industrialization," or "bureaucratization." It signifies a process or series of actions unfolding in discernible patterns across time and space. Thus, "globalization" refers to the dynamic manifestation of the global in detectable configurations and patterns.

We can expand these etymological insights into a definition of "globalization" as a multidimensional set of processes involving the *extension and intensification of social relations and consciousness across world-space and in world-time*. We can conceptualize these globalizing dynamics along three intersecting qualitative variables: *interconnectivity, mobility,* and *imagination.* But we can enhance the analytical precision of our definition by considering some important qualifications.

First, globalization is a geographically uneven and highly contingent configuration. This means that globalization is an incomplete set of processes. While humans have globalized a broad range of social relations, the world is not yet "global" as such. The depth and breadth of globalization processes is routinely overestimated in a world where nation-states still play a significant role. As recent empirical research shows, there are definite limits to the magnitude of globalization processes.[40]

Second, globalization needs to be grasped in its unfolding historicity as a specific set of social practices rather than being fixed or essentialized. This consideration is built into our definition through the proviso that globalization needs to be understood in terms of the world-time in which it occurs. Crucially, different forms of globalization both reflect and are constitutive of different historical configurations of power.

Third, while it is useful to make analytical distinctions between spatial scales running from the local to the global, the world of lived social relations is glocal. This means that the global is always dialectically enmeshed in the local—and vice versa—and that globalization contains homogenization tendencies that coexist and interact with local dynamics favoring "glocal" expressions of cultural diversification and hybridization.[41] In other words, the globalization system constitutes itself not simply through the extension of certain particular social arrangements to all parts of the world, but also through the concomitant particularization and heterogenization of the global through the imposition and diffusion of the local.

Fourth, subjective aspects of globalization such as ideas, ideologies, imaginaries, and ontologies are just as important as its objective, material dimensions reflected in globalized institutional and technological relations such as the transnational mobility of goods, capital, information, and people. At the same time, however, subjective global relations are always constituted in connection to objective social relations.

Importantly, globalization does not always translate into hypermobility. As discussed in more detail in chapter 7, disjunctive movements among major globalization formations can inhibit flows and disable existing links. These formations are *embodied globalization* understood as the worldwide flows and interconnectivities of people, including tourists, refugees, and business travelers; *disembodied globalization* related to worldwide flows and interconnectivities of ideas and information, including images and digital data; *objectified globalization* reflected in worldwide flows and interconnectivities of things, including tradable commodities, greenhouse gases, and viruses;

and *institutional globalization* manifested as worldwide flows and interconnectivities of organizations, including transnational corporations, economic institutions, legal institutions, sports clubs, and so on.

These four formations of globalization provide the periodization framework for our historical examination of globalization in the next chapter.

2

Four Ages of Globalization

Any careful assessment of globalization in the twenty-first century must consider pertinent historical developments. Hence, this chapter assumes the necessary task of offering a bird's-eye view of the evolution of objective globalization processes up to the 1990s. As our genealogical investigation in the previous chapter has shown, globalization as a subjective process has been associated with multiple meanings generated over many decades. By the end of the Cold War, the term entered the consciousness of academics, journalists, and business elites in the global north who welded its meaning to processes of trade liberalization and the worldwide integration of markets. However, globalization dynamics in the "real world" have occurred long before they were named as such by recent actors. As global studies scholar Manuel Castells notes, "Globalization is not new: under different forms, it appears to have happened not only in the 19th century of the common era, but thousands of years ago."[1]

Indeed, *Homo sapiens* became a truly global species as early as 10,000 BCE when small nomadic bands reached the bottom tip of South America. This crowning achievement of human mobility brought to a successful completion a series of terrestrial walkabouts commenced by early African hominins more than 2 million years ago.[2] Since then, globalization has unfolded unevenly across major world regions. As we discuss in this chapter, its long trajectory impacted multiple spheres of human activity, including economics, politics, law, culture, religion, technology, military, and the environment. Specific historical thresholds mark important transitions to new phases of global interconnectedness, mobility, and imagination. In general, the powerful dialectic of historical continuity and change has resulted in the intensification of globalization. But it can also lead to unanticipated slowdowns, stagnations, and reversals.

Instances of such major globalization disruptions abound. Some of them have to do with planetary boundary parameters of human existence that shift independently of social systems and institutions. Consider, for example, the

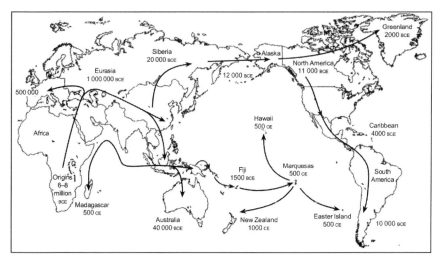

Figure 2.1.   The Global Journey of *Homo Sapiens*

74,000 BCE Lake Toba supervolcano eruption on Sumatra, which triggered a global climate catastrophe that threatened the very survival of our species. Others result from human activities like the twelfth-century BCE collapse of Mediterranean Bronze Age cultures brought about by the onslaught of marauding "sea peoples." Other prominent examples include the fall of the western Roman Empire in the fifth century CE that ushered in the so-called dark ages in Europe; the fourteenth-century bubonic plague known as the Black Death, which killed 75 million people, including 30 to 60 percent of Europe's total population; and the bleak decades from 1914 to 1945 ravaged by global wars, genocides, and economic shocks. Most recently, of course, humanity was hit by a devastating global pandemic. COVID-19 killed millions and brought the fast-paced world of the twenty-first century to a screeching halt. Seen from the bird's-eye view of global history, however, worldwide interconnectivity and mobility has advanced in spite of such periodic disruptions. Still, the volatile and unpredictable historical trajectory of globalization shatters old and engrained Enlightenment beliefs in the inevitability and irreversibility of human progress toward the establishment of a benign world order.

PERIODIZING GLOBALIZATION: PERILOUS PITFALLS

Both the longevity and complexity of evolving global networks beg the central question that frames this chapter: how should contemporary researchers chart the historical development of globalization? After all, it is only through the mapping of its shifting forms that we can identify significant patterns that provide the necessary basis for an informed assessment of its dynamics and overall configuration in the twenty-first century.³ Conventional wisdom in the historical and social sciences suggests breaking up the long and complex story of globalization into more digestible chapters that correspond to distinct "ages" or "epochs." Designing such structured periodization schemes has been central to organizing time and events in more transparent ways that provide people with a better historical understanding of the big picture.

Still, any attempt to demarcate distinct ages of globalization faces formidable perils and challenges. One is the pitfall of "presentism." This term refers to the problematic tendency of focusing too narrowly on fashionable issues of the day and treating them as central to everything at all times. By locking people's attention into a "global now," presentism accentuates current events at the expense of past developments. As sociologist Jan Nederveen Pieterse observes, "Because of its presentist leanings, much research treats globalization unreflexively, may overlook structural patterns, present as novel what are older features, and misread contemporary trends."⁴

Presentism often appears in its related form of "epochalism." This concept applies to the intellectual fallacy of believing that the present time represents an unprecedented new era whose patterns are vastly different from prior epochs. Western modernity has thrived on such claims of novelty by pointing to spectacular human advances in the last two centuries mostly related to technology and economics.⁵ Obviously, it makes sense to argue that innovations like digital technology, global supply chains, or standardized and electronically guided shipping containers have greatly enhanced webs of interconnectivity and clusters of integration across national borders. But the same could be said about many earlier achievements such as the invention of the alphabet, the wheel, the plow, metallurgy, horsepower, irrigation canals, oceangoing ships, long-distance trading routes, bills of exchange, double-entry bookkeeping, the compass, the number zero, the printing press, paper, gun powder, firearms, fossil fuels, the steam engine, the locomotive, the telegraph and telephones, automobiles, airplanes, radio, television, computers, spacecraft, and so on.

Moreover, the dual stranglehold of presentism and epochalism feeds into the still dominant Eurocentric narrative according to which globalization did not start until the "rise of the West" and the Industrial Revolution, conventionally dated between 1500 and 1800. Examples of such short-term perspectives can be found in the claims of influential globalization popularizers like Thomas Friedman, who we encountered in the previous chapter. These writers argue that globalization ultimately boils down to the creation of an American-led world order anchored in the neoliberal market model. Some international relations experts like Michael Mandelbaum go even further by asserting that the "ideas that conquered the world"—"peace, democracy, and free markets"—were "invented" in Great Britain and France in the seven-teenth and eighteenth centuries.[6] Even more discerning global studies pio-neers like Roland Robertson, who developed an innovative historical outline of globalization, largely remained a prisoner of linear stage models and mod-ernization theories that overemphasize the role of Europe and North America as both the sources and drivers of world-historical dynamics and events.[7]

To call such accounts "world history" is a misnomer because they ignore, downplay, or marginalize pertinent nonwestern contributions. And they are based on the demonstratively false assumption that superior concepts, practices, technologies, and capacities were simply diffused from the west to the rest of the world. Moreover, the semantic prominence of terms like "Judeo-Christian values," "European civilization," and "development" in such historical narratives has long served to rationalize, excuse, or assist impe-rialist and colonialist practices. Such perspectives reveal their deep embed-dedness in what historian James Blaut refers to as "the colonizer's model of the world."[8] Hence, periodization schemes of globalization anchored in such limited frameworks do not match the real-world history of multicentered and multidirectional flows of bodies, things, institutions, and ideas.

PERIODIZING GLOBALIZATION: ALTERNATIVE MODELS

How, then, can we periodize the long history of globalization in more careful ways that avoid the pitfalls of presentism, epochalism, and western centrism? Big strides in this direction have already been made by social scientists such as Robbie Robertson, Jan Nederveen Pieterse, Barry Gills, and Jeffrey Sachs, as well as historians like A. G. Hopkins, Kenneth Pomeranz, David Northrop, Philip Curtain, Jerry Bentley, Nayan Chanda, Dominic Sachsenmaier, Akira Iriye, Pamela Kyle Crossley, and others.[9] Reacting against the Eurocentric bias inherent in conventional world history, their critical perspectives have served as important catalysts for the birth of what has become known as "global history."

This new academic field embraces a multicentric and multidirectional model of globalization.[10] It has inspired my own efforts to develop the alter-native periodization outline presented in this chapter, which incorporates insights offered by global historians. Still, my model makes its own inno-vative contribution by delineating historical periods that are linked to the four major globalization formations introduced in chapter 1. Let us recall that *embodied globalization* refers to interrelations and mobilities of bodies across the world. *Objectified globalization* signifies global interconnections and mobilities of objects. *Institutional globalization* corresponds to global interactions and mobilities mediated through organizations such as empires, states, and corporations. *Disembodied globalization* pertains to worldwide interrelations and mobilities of ideas, symbols, data, and other types of information.

Like our planet's massive geological tectonic plates, these globalization formations tend to move at different speeds and levels of intensity. Hyperactive configurations have greater influence in shaping certain historical periods. For example, the earliest age of globalization involved primarily the motion of human bodies, whereas the contemporary era is dominated by digital information flows. Thus, hegemonic globalization formations give specific form and color to the overall spirit of a given era. Others tend to play lesser roles only to return to prominence in future epochs. But the dominance of certain formations at particular times should not detract from the significance of multiple intersections and overlaps. Indeed, the mapping of these interplays among these globalization formations is fundamental to expanding our understanding of their long history and their impacts on present social patterns.[11] At the same time, however, it is important to recognize that all attempts to develop new periodization frameworks of globalization are marred by unavoidable acts of generalization and selectivity. Naturally, such shortcomings are magnified in brief accounts such as my own periodization outline below. Still, I hope that my framework offers a basic mapping of relevant historical dynamics that allows for a better assessment of globalization processes in the twenty-first century.

My historical scheme starts with the age of embodied globalization when nomadic foragers diverged from a single African origin to settle the entire planet. The notion of "divergence" has played a prominent role in the accounts of many global historians. David Northrop, for example, introduced a minimalist periodization scheme, which divides the entirety of global history into just two mega-periods. The first, before 1000 CE, is characterized by forces of divergence that dispersed most human life and allowed for only minimal inter-group relations. The second, after 1000 CE, contains multiple convergences because of increasing contacts and communications. My model acknowledges the significance of this dual dynamic of divergence and convergence but goes beyond the austerity of Northrup's two-age framework.

The second period in my historical periodization scheme is the age of institutional globalization. It covers a long stretch of time in which various polities, states, empires, and other social institutions and organizations emerged, proliferated, and expanded across greater distances. These scale-enlarging institutional dynamics were aided by the intensification of the division of labor, social integration, standardization, and legal codification.

The third period, the age of objectified globalization, saw the birth and rapid evolution of capitalism and colonialism, which facilitated the rise of the world economy at the onset of the Industrial Revolution. A novel political institution—the nation-state—and its associated cultural expressions gradually came to dominate the world. This epoch witnessed vastly enhanced flows of tradable commodities distributed by accelerated means of transportation to every corner of the Earth. Moreover, large numbers of European migrants and enslaved Africans streamed into "new worlds" pried open by colonial violence and subjected to extractive practices of western imperialist powers.[12]

The fourth age of disembodied globalization emerged from the economic chaos and political shocks of the first half of the twentieth century. Benefiting from the new postwar international order and innovative wartime technologies, disembodied globalization accelerated rapidly and culminated in the Information and Communication Technology (ICT) Revolution of the late twentieth century that intensified even further in the new millennium. Yet, neoliberal capitalism turbocharged by digital technology turned out to be a mixed blessing. The flood of cheap consumer goods produced in the low-labor cost regions of the global south and the expansion of embodied mobility in the form of migration and travel were offset by rising levels of inequality, financial volatility, and job insecurity. Thus, this chapter ends with a critical reflection on the nature of global social change in the early twenty-first century, which has led to a condition Paul James and I call the Great Unsettling.[13] Our use of the term "unsettling" has been inspired by David Harvey and Fredric Jameson, two prominent social theorists whose work explores the intersection of western modernity, capitalism, culture, and globalization.[14]

THE AGE OF THE EMBODIED
GLOBALIZATION (10,000 BCE–3000 BCE)

The earliest phase of globalization is exemplified by the dispersion of our species from a single origin in the east African savannahs to all major world regions. Blessed with extraordinary communication capacities that had reached current levels at around 40,000 BCE, Paleolithic hunter-gatherers succeeded in colonizing the entire planet. For some time, they coexisted with our closest relatives, the Neanderthals and Denisovans, who died out not long after foraging groups of *Homo sapiens* made their appearance in Eurasia. "Divergence" is a particularly fitting term to characterize the movement of the 5 to 10 million humans who traversed the planetary landscape in search for food and shelter. Hence, global historians like Peter Stearns rightly emphasize the "decisive quality of dispersion and differentiation of the world's human population on the eve of agriculture."[15]

The human colonization of world space involved primarily physical forms of mobility. Hence, embodied movement represented the dominant globalization formation during this long period. Our nomadic ancestors carried with them only limited supplies of tools and weapons alongside scores of parasitic micro-organisms. Except for domesticated dogs, there were no pack animals that helped ease their burdens or speed up their journey into the unknown. Thus, the movement of things, institutions, and ideas remained at a very basic level.

Social interrelations among these traveling bands were severely restricted and often occurred just by chance. Forms of technology capable of establishing and maintaining durable intertribal connections across long distances were virtually nonexistent. Aside from hunting and foraging, nomadic tribes spent most of their time in seasonally shifting campsites organized around a central campfire.[16] Each clan comprised fifty to eighty members and required a territory of up to 200 square miles to sustain itself. Some scholars have speculated that occasional intergroup encounters elicited at times innate forms of warlike aggression. But such belligerent human behavior directed primarily against out-groups seems to have been balanced by high levels of in-group cooperation and egalitarian forms of solidarity.

Over time, nomadic bands expanded thanks to more efficient food-sharing habits and evolving hunting technologies such as bows and arrows, fish-hooks, nets, and sophisticated traps. Modest population increases put extra pressure on limited resources and eventually forced some members to split off and search for new territories. Out-migrations usually involved only short distances but could accumulate to thousands of miles over longer periods of time. Local environmental degradation because of human overuse also compelled tribal collectivities to move on. There is ample historical evidence that hunter-gatherers arriving in virgin regions were responsible for the disappearance of many large land animals such as mammoths, mastodons, ground sloths, various kinds of horses, flightless birds, and sabertoothed cats. Most scholars agree that these human-induced megafauna extinctions occurred on all continents and were mainly due to the overextension of hunting practices for short-term gains. Such wasteful techniques included, for example, setting bushlands on fire to drive escaping animal herds over steep cliffs.[17]

The age of embodied globalization was devoid of permanent settlements. Citing low levels of interconnectedness and integration, some scholars argue that this early period of human planetary colonization should not count as part of globalization.[18] However, the rationales offered in such arguments are faulty in at least two respects. First, they assume that for globalization to occur, interconnectivities must be fully global. This assumption presupposes a condition of globality, rather than focusing the process of globalization through which globality comes about. As Jan Nederveen Pieterse notes, globalization must not be a global condition in the literal sense because it signifies a processual unfolding toward this condition.[19] This analytic confusion between globalization as a process and globality as a condition is a common mistake made by many scholars.

Second, the claim globalization is not a long-term process exposed an underlying Eurocentric framework, which links the onset of globalization exclusively to western modes of modernity such as the abstract distancing of space and time, the development of critical reflexivity, and the rise of a globally networked civil society.[20] As noted in our previous definition of globalization, however, interconnectivity represents only one of its principal qualities. The other, transworld mobility, was on full display even in the initial age of embodied globalization and irrespective of the slow rate of speed at which human bodies moved across world space.

Starting at around 8000 BCE, the dominant nomadic paradigm was challenged by the Neolithic Revolution. Over the next four millennia, agricultural practices spread from west Asia to north Africa, central Asia, and India. Northern European regions were historical latecomers while the transition to agriculture in the Americas occurred independently as early as eleven thousand years ago. Many factors such as swelling population sizes and the ensuing thickening of social interrelations facilitated the transformation of foraging hunters into sedentary farmers. Another crucial influence over which humans had no control was the warming of the planet that followed the end of the Ice Age, which was the result of changing orbital and tilt relationships between the Earth and the Sun. As the global historian Dipesh Chakrabarty emphasizes, without this extraordinary fluke of nature in the history of our planet, the agricultural and industrial life of our species would not have been possible.[21]

The annual yield of early agricultural crops such as wheat, barley, peas, lentils, and chickpeas was boosted by alluvial modes of farming pioneered in Egypt, Mesopotamia, the Indus Valley, and the Yellow and Yangtze river regions where the rich soils of the river basin was replenished by seasonal flooding. The domestication of sheep, goats, pigs, cattle, and poultry allowed for the dietary addition of nutritious milk, cheese, eggs, and pork. Geographic regions located on or near the vast Eurasian landmass were especially blessed with the natural occurrence of plants and animals suitable for domestication. Hence, global historians emphasize the distinctive role of these temperate east-west zones as catalysts for the intensification and acceleration of globalization processes. These so-called lucky latitudes constituted 28 percent of the Eurasian land mass but became home to more than 60 percent of the total human population. Within these auspicious regions, crucial technological innovations such as Arabic oceangoing ships equipped with lateen (triangular) sails and the metallurgic breakthroughs of copper, bronze, and iron were made and diffused in multiple directions along enduring transport routes. These technological and infrastructure advances outstripped pertinent developments in the Americas, Oceania, and sub-Saharan Africa and gave Eurasians and north Africans a global competitive edge that they never lost.[22]

The steady expansion of agricultural food supply sustained growing populations, which, in turn, facilitated the multiplication and enlargement of social connectivity. On the surface, it seemed that agricultural interdependence came at the expense of embodied nomadic mobility. After all, the new sedentary modes of existence required the establishment of fortified villages and permanent settlements housing several hundred residents. Looking more closely, however, scholars found that farming sparked social and technological practices that were exported on land and extended waterways across significant geographic distances.

Starting around 4000 BCE, the domestication of beasts of burden like donkeys, camels, and oxen also contributed to increasing flows of people, ideas, objects, and institutions. The most consequential case of animal domestication involved the taming of the Eurasian wild horse at around 3500 BCE. This feat was accomplished by farmer-herders pushing north from Mesopotamia into the steppes near the Black Sea and the northern Caucasus. As Jeffrey Sachs points out, "Only the horse offered the speed, durability, power, and intelligence to enable deep breakthroughs in every sector of the economy: farming, animal husbandry, mining, manufacturing, transport, communications, warfare, and governance."[23] In contrast, native American nomads hunted their immense wild horse herds to extinction, which meant these regions fell behind Eurasia and North Africa, whose inhabitants made this unique animal an indispensable part of their daily lives. Finally, the cultivation of this crucial human-horse relation might have sparked the invention of the wheel at around 3000 BCE in Southwest Asia. The combination of domesticated horses and wheeled carriages of all sorts—including lumbering carts carrying humans and trade objects and speedy chariots made for organized warfare—provided a significant jolt to the expanding networks of social interrelations, mobility, and imagination.

THE AGE OF INSTITUTIONAL GLOBALIZATION (3000 BCE–1600 CE)

It took several millennia for the widely dispersed agricultural communities within favorable geographic regions around the world to develop multiple and enduring interconnections necessary for the formation of populous states. Decentralized and egalitarian hunter-gatherer bands slowly gave way to centralized, highly stratified, and patriarchal "temple-palace conglomerates" headed by nobles and priests.[24] These ruling groups exempted themselves from hard manual labor while claiming the lion's share of taxes and tributes collected from domestic subordinate groups and conquered peoples outside their territory. Agriculture-based polities spearheaded the division of labor, which created two additional social classes that did not fully participate in food production. One class consisted of permanent craft specialists who directed their creative energies toward the production of tradeable goods and innovative technologies. The other group comprised experts who safeguarded the power of the ruling classes. Agricultural bureaucrats oversaw the precise accounting of food surpluses necessary for the growth of the centralized state. Military specialists were given responsibility for the raising and training of professional armies. Commercial administrators oversaw the establishment and maintenance of long-distance trade routes while leaving the physical exploration of promising regions to entrepreneurial merchants and itinerant state agents. The crucial role of state bureaucrats and professional soldiers highlights the significance of institution-building and war-making for the creation and expansion of global networks. Unfortunately, these pivotal integrating dynamics are often neglected in the pertinent literature.[25]

The increasingly complex organization and stratification of expanding human societies owed much to the rise of a disembodied force linked to the remarkable language capacity of *Homo sapiens*: the written word. The momentous invention of writing occurred between 3500 BCE and 2500 BCE in multiple geographical locations including Mesopotamia, Egypt, and central China. Around 1750 BCE, the first extensive written codification of law was accomplished by court bureaucrats of the Babylonian king. In the following centuries and millennia, the *Codex Hammurabi* served a model for numerous legal frameworks in different societies. But it was only with the perfection of the vowel-containing Greek alphabet in 800 BCE and the classical Chinese script in 500 BCE that written information about all sorts of things could be disseminated more easily and quickly across long distances. This interplay between the institutional expansion of imperial states and their enhanced communicative capacities, contributed, in turn, to swelling flows of tradable goods and people.

The communication revolution wrought by writing also enabled budding intellectuals in Eurasia and North Africa to provide posterity with enduring historical accounts centered on imperial expansion and competition. Their critical examination of cosmologies, stories, mythologies, and traditions linked to various cultural contexts was rooted in their universalizing inclinations and their recognition of large cultural clusters as "civilizations." However, as Robbie Robertson reminds us, what made civilizations such as classical Greece, Persia, or China integrated social wholes endowed with enduring meaning and significance was not their imagined distinction from "barbarism" but their interconnectedness and overlap across multiple cultural zones.[26] But the understanding that the historical formation of large cultural entities depended on myriads of cross-cultural contacts and exchanges is already reflected in exceptional early world histories, such as the comprehensive narrative produced by the Hellenistic writer Polybius in the second century BCE:

> Now, in earlier times, the world's history had consisted, so to speak, of a series of unrelated episodes, the origins and results of each being as widely separated as their localities, but from this point onwards history becomes an organized whole: the affairs of Italy and Africa are connected with those of Asia and of Greece, and all events bear a relationship and contribute to a single end.[27]

To be sure, universalizing empires like Rome and China were not "global" in the contemporary usage of the word. As Polybius's insight demonstrates, a thin layer of Roman intellectuals and bureaucrats developed a universalizing ethos and common cultural framework that perceived their world as "globalized." Hence, globalization is not a process that started with European modernity or industrial capitalism. Rather, it represents an unfolding dynamic that includes major imperial expansions in the premodern world undertaken by the Egyptian Kingdoms, the Persian empire, the Macedonian empire, the Arabian empires of the Umayyads and Abbasids, the Mongol empire, the Aztec and Inca empires, the Holy Roman Empire, the African Empires of Ghana, Mali, and Songhay, and many others.[28]

Once again, Eurasia and North Africa took a leading role in the unfolding story of institutional globalization. Between 1000 BCE and 1500 CE, this large region contained roughly 80 percent of humanity. The lucky latitudes, home to 60 percent of this population, succeeded in accommodating their growing numbers through the rapid spread of crops, domesticated animals, and new technologies.[29] The Eurasian east-west axis also expedited the multicentered and multidirectional diffusion of new religions, particularly Buddhism, Christianity, and Islam. Supported by well-resourced institutions such as churches, temples, and mosques, itinerant preachers displayed a high degree of courage and mobility in their zealous efforts to establish new communities of faith in far-flung places. Indeed, their export of novel religious institutions was just as important as their spread of new religious ideas.

The making of these world religions benefited greatly from the creation of world maps, which also facilitated the expansion of trade and warfare.[30] For example, Chinese cartographers fashioned printed atlases that included phonetic designations for European place names as well as skillful sketches of the shape and continental orientation of Africa. Similarly, their counterparts in classical Rome produced imperial maps that stretched from its westernmost province of Britannia to Mesopotamia and the Indian river Ganges in the east. One of these surviving maps, the highly stylized and spatially distorted Peutinger Table, provides holistic sketches of roads, ports, and settlements that linked the Eternal City to the farthest known reaches of the Roman world.

Imperial expansion and the ensuing soaring levels of interaction within and among vast territories pushed ruling elites to devise more systematic means of population control through the synchronizing of everyday social life. Standardization measures of all kinds served as a crucial driver of intensifying objectified globalization dynamics that would come to dominate the coming historical period.[31] For example, the civil service state assembled by the Chinese Han dynasty (206 BCE–220 CE) promoted an extensive codification of law together with the fixing of weights, measures, and values of coinage. The standardization of the size of cart axles and road widths allowed Chinese merchants to make precise calculations as to the desired quantities of imported and exported goods. Such large-scale coordination measures exploded during the trade-friendly Sung dynasty (960 CE to 1279 CE), which led not only to the further extension of imperial institutions, but also to the expansion of market arrangements through the activities of independent merchants and entrepreneurial financiers.

The significance of the interplay between institutional and objectified globalization during this period was further reflected in the growth of major long-distance trade networks, especially in three geographic regions: China, Arabia, and, toward the latter part of the age of institutional globalization, Europe. Until the sixteenth and seventeenth centuries, Australia, America, and Oceania remained separate from this expanding web of Eurasian institutional and objectified interrelations. Still, it should be noted that the Aztec and Inca empires, for example, succeeded in developing major regional trade networks in their own hemisphere.

The most expansive of the Eurasian trade routes was the Silk Road, which linked the Chinese Empire to the Roman Empire via the intermediary Parthian domain and other Asian and African trading communities. An amazing variety of goods and people traversed this vast transcontinental highway: silk, porcelain, gold, silver, jewelry, linens, precious woods, spices, oil, merchants, missionaries, warriors, and slaves. More than a millennium after the Silk Road first reached the Italian peninsula, a truly multicultural group of Eurasian and African globetrotters—including the Moroccan merchant and explorer Ibn Battuta and his famous Venetian counterparts of the Marco Polo family—traveled this splendid highway to the imperial court of the thirteenth-century Mongol Khans in Beijing. Their forcible unification of consecutive territories linking the East China Sea to the Hungarian plains had opened up a short century of relatively safe land travel across 5,500 miles. Remarkably, eight hundred years later, the Chinese Communist government attempted to reconstitute the ancient Silk Road in the form of its massive One Belt, One Road initiative, which is designed to spread the global influence of China and link its urban centers to multiple locations around the world.

The social networks in the age of institutional globalization expanded and intensified as a result of further population increases linked to growing food production, greater institutional security, and multiplying trade exchanges. During this era, the world's population grew from 15 million to 500 million. This demographic upswing translated not only into denser networks of interconnectivity and mobility, but also into the enhanced flow of human bodies from the countryside to urban centers and across continents. In particular, globalization processes received a significant boost with the capture of the Americas by European maritime powers at the end of this epoch, most notably imperialist Spain and Portugal. The Earth's vast oceans served as the new highways for imperial expansion. Notable improvements in shipbuilding and navigational devices allowed sixteenth-century European "explorers" like Ferdinand Magellan and his crew to circumnavigate the planet. This impressive display of European navigational power had benefited from the sudden and unexpected collapse of China's maritime superiority less than a century earlier. Surprisingly, the inward-looking rulers of the Ming dynasty had decided to suspend the successful trade voyages undertaken by their vast fleets operating in the South China Sea and the Indian Ocean.

The sixteenth-century European conquest of the Americas—and subsequently the entire Pacific region—created geographies and geopolitics of genuinely "planetary" dimensions. Previously isolated communities in the new worlds suddenly found themselves dangerously exposed to the transcontinental invaders aided by superior gun-based military technologies. In particular, oceangoing vessels equipped with naval cannons as well as smaller gunboats were decisive in breaking indigenous coastal resistance through devastating bombardments from the sea. Land-based wheeled cannons proved to be equally effective in forcing interior local populations to accept the violent imposition of alien European institutional and cultural arrangements. As a horrified Aztec witness reported to his illustrious overlord Motecuhzoma, the Spanish *conquistador* Hernando Cortés and his ruthless band of plunderers possessed shocking weapons capable of discharging "a thing like a ball of stone [which] comes out of its entrails; it comes out of shooting sparks and raining fire. If it is aimed against a tree, it shatters the tree into splinters. This is the most unnatural sight, as if the tree had exploded from within."[32]

Higher population densities and enhanced interrelations over greater distances also eased the global spread of micro-organisms, which caused widespread human infectious diseases. Traveling viruses and bacteria had periodically decimated human populations before, such as the bubonic plague of the fourteenth century, which killed up to one-third of populations in

China, the Middle East, and Europe. But the globalization of pandemics did not reach its most horrific manifestations until the fateful sixteenth-century collisions between populations of the old and new worlds. Although the precise population size of natives on both American continents before European contact remains a contentious issue, it is estimated that the deadly germs carried by resistant imperialist invaders might have killed up to 56 million people. This toll amounts to an inconceivable 90 to 95 percent of the total indigenous population. Their Great Dying was so massive that it impacted the global ecosystem. The sudden drop of global atmospheric carbon dioxide because of rapid reforestation of formerly human-cultivated habitat contributed to a lowering of global air temperatures by at least 0.15°C.[33] The ensuing Little Ice Age in Eurasia corresponds to a period of global cooling between the thirteenth and seventeenth centuries that froze European rivers, triggered crop failures and famine in Asia, and expanded glaciers on all continents.

The brutality of European westward expansion toward the end of the age of institutional globalization was also reflected in systematic, large-scale human trafficking practices developed by imperial states and their commercial agents. Launched in the early 1500s by Portuguese merchants and intensifying over the next three centuries, the transatlantic slave trade transported tens of millions of Africans to the Americas and the Caribbean to toil on plantations, in mines, the construction industry, and various domestic settings.

But the sixteenth century Columbian exchange involved not only slaves and pathogens, but also numerous plants, animals, and minerals.[34] For example, horses, cattle, sheep, goats, and pigs entered the new world, in the process changing native lands and peoples in profound ways. Moreover, the Americas provided the old world with such important good staples as maize, potatoes, cacao, vanilla, and tomatoes while receiving wheat, rice, sugarcane, and cotton in return. Finally, the lucrative export of American tobacco to the old world made smoking pipes, cigars, and cigarettes a global obsession for centuries until the damaging health effects of this popular habit received full public attention in more recent times.

THE AGE OF OBJECTIFIED GLOBALIZATION (1600–1910S)

Having contributed relatively little to objectified globalization between about 500 CE and 1200 CE, the rise of Europe north and south of the Alps benefited greatly from the diffusion of technology from Islamic, Chinese, and African cultural spheres. Pertinent innovations include the spinning wheel, the compass, mechanized printing, gunpowder, the stirrup, paper, clocks, sophisticated wind and water mills, extensive postal systems, revised maritime technologies, and advanced ocean navigation techniques.[35] The emerging configuration of "modernity" in Europe has become widely associated with this singular model rooted in the Enlightenment project of objective science, generalizing codes of law, and rational modes of thought and social organization divorced from the perceived irrationalities of myth, religion, and political tyranny. By contrast, less Eurocentric historical perspectives have acknowledged the emergence of multiple strains of modernity that emerged during this historical period in various parts of the world—both independently and in resistance to the expanding and invading European model.[36]

It would go far beyond the scope of this chapter to identify and discuss in sufficient detail the many impacts and manifestations of intensifying globalization processes during this critical era. In keeping with our historical bird's-eye view of globalization, let us narrow our focus to three related dynamics: the growth of commerce and long-distance trade intertwined with the expansion of European imperialism and colonialism; the emergence and spread of the nation-state; and the origin and development of industrial capitalism.

The successive rise of Italian, Dutch, and English metropolitan centers and their affiliated merchant classes before and during the age of objectified globalization was an important factor in the growing volume of long-distance traded goods. Vying for the task of supplying the ruling classes with a growing list of luxury objects, European economic entrepreneurs laid the foundation of what later scholars would call the "world economy."[37] However, it is important to bear in mind that profit-oriented forms of merchant and finance capitalism first arose in China, Arabia, and Southeast Asia—centuries before they became significant forces in the west. Still, Europeans proved to be fast and adroit learners.[38] Once small footholds of merchant capitalism were established in predominantly feudal environments, they grew steadily and in innovative ways. This commercialization of social life is reflected, for example, in the formation of enduring and extremely successful merchant unions such as the Germanic Hanseatic League or the Great Ravensburg Trading Company.

With the capture of the Americas, a worldwide trading system centered in Europe came into existence, soaked in the blood and brutality of imperialist expansionism. Karl Marx famously referred to such ruthless forms of "pacification" and plunder as the "primitive accumulation of capital."[39] Gold and silver extracted from American mines by the forced labor of natives and imported slaves flowed into Europe, where its minted end products paid for imported Asian spices, cotton fabrics, silks, and porcelains. By the 1600s, newly founded joint-stock trading companies, including the Dutch East India Company, the Dutch West India Company, the Hudson's Bay Company, the British East India Company, the British South African Company, and the

Russian American Company, set up profitable posts outside Europe. Until 1900, when these giant companies had lost their edge to superior industrial production systems, they served as the primary agents of European trade and global colonial expansion. Engaging entrepreneurial shipowners and skilled sea captains, these corporations developed a triangular Atlantic trade that brought products for mass consumption from Europe to ports along the African West Coast. From there, they transported African captives as slaves to the Caribbean and the Americas to work in vast plantation complexes that transported coveted raw materials such as sugar, tobacco, and cotton back to Europe where they were sold for a hefty profit, processed into finished goods, and consumed.[40]

The establishment and profitable growth of these commercial enterprises depended on their ability to acquire from states the monopoly to regulate most intercontinental economic transactions, set up their own police forces, and, in some cases, maintain sizable standing armies. Granting monopoly trading and political enforcement rights to these corporations was a convenient way for European states to bankroll the astronomical costs of colonial expansion. It also allowed for the commercial extension of endemic European national wars aimed at achieving cultural and economic superiority.[41] Occupying a gray zone between political and mercantile power, these trading companies created the authoritarian social institutions and practices that eventually enabled colonial governments to place these foreign regions under their direct political rule. By the eighteenth century, the great southern continent of Australia and numerous Pacific islands were slowly incorporated into the European-dominated flow of goods, institutions, and bodies. The European takeover of the new worlds involved primarily the interplay of objectified and institutional globalization. As historian Jürgen Kocka suggests, it was reflected in "the dynamic symbiosis between ambitious holders of political power, calculating financiers, and daring or perhaps unscrupulous adventurers. Here we see an irritating amalgamation of trade and warfare, an aggressive jumble of lust for power, capitalist dynamism, and lawless violence."[42]

On the discursive level, the global expansion of European empires proceeded in the name of pursuing noble "civilizing missions" that included forced religious conversion campaigns. The frequent resistance of native peoples to such Christianization efforts tended to be interpreted by their colonizers as proof for the "blackness of their souls" and their "ignorant" attachment to their "inferior" and "primitive" cultural traditions. But even the reluctant adoption of alien religions did not protect indigenous peoples from the nefarious political and cultural effects of imposed racial categories that naturalized social forms of white superiority and thus cemented the place of Europeans and their North American descendants on top of fixed power hierarchies. Moreover, the imposition of the colonizers' languages, modes of education, dress, and manners became a convenient way of universalizing their particular European cultural forms and practices.

Following the end of multiple and protracted religious conflicts between Catholics and Protestants, which was finally codified in the 1648 Peace Treaty of Westphalia, new scientific, cultural, political, and commercial currents in Europe and its American colonies culminated in what came to be known as the Enlightenment or the Age of Reason. Threatened by critical rationality, the previously dominant feudal structures began to crumble. Factors in their demise include rising literacy rates that originated with Gutenberg's perfection of East Asian technology—the printing press and paper—and the Protestant Reformation's emphasis on the individual interpretation of scripture absorbed in the vernacular.

Millennia-old traditional social imaginaries linked to the Church no longer secured and reproduced divinely sanctioned power hierarchies in the form of dynastic states and empires. Although the republican experiments of classical Greece and Rome had been short-lived in Renaissance Italy, they were partially resurrected in the trade-based Dutch Republic, which became a pre-eminent world power in the seventeenth century. Between the 1770s and the 1840s, there arose on both sides of the Atlantic the now familiar template of the "nation." It inspired revolutionary forces in the British colonies of North America, France, Haiti, and the Spanish territories of South America, as well as the embryonic labor movements in Europe. However, the concept of the nation no longer referred to an aristocratic state hierarchy supported by clerical elites, but to an abstract "general will" operating in ordinary people. The political implications of nationalism were as clear as they were audacious: henceforth it would be "the people" (albeit only males) who exercised legitimate authority in political affairs in the name of reason and its underlying natural law. But who really counted as part of "the people" and what constituted the essential elements of the nation became the subject of fierce political debates and social struggles.

Nationhood found its concrete political expression in the transformation of feudal subjects into free citizens who laid claim to equal membership in the cultural nation, which institutionalized its autonomy in the form of the territorially based nation-state. Over the next two centuries, this European nation-state framework spread to all corners of the earth and eventually became the standard form of political organization around the world after World War I. Indeed, nation-states served as the foundation of an "inter-national order" reflected not only in the proliferation of new political and economic institutions but also in multiplying civil society organizations ranging from the Universal Postal Union to the International Red Cross. Still, the emergence of nationalism as a global transformative force constituted a mixed blessing. While it inspired millions to throw off the yoke of feudalism and colonial servitude, it also acquired a murderous political potency in combination with invidious "scientific" race theories built on imagined biological essences and hierarchies.

These crucial decades witnessing the birth of nationalism also saw another major change that would weave an even more intricate worldwide human web. Capitalism was now transformed from a commercial system of profit-taking through the trade of objects into an industrial system based on maximizing profits through the development of the forces of production. Explanations of the origin and early evolution of this momentous socio-economic transformation that took the world by storm fall into two competing frameworks. The first amounts to a "commercialization model." It emphasizes historical continuity between age old trading practices and industrial capitalism by claiming that commercial activities gradually matured through a series of technological and political advances into their modern form. Escaping the economic regulations of feudal and absolutist governments in the wake of the Enlightenment revolutions, industrial capitalism unleashed the full potential of the allegedly innate human tendency to trade and barter. Adam Smith celebrated the unlimited accumulation of capital at the outset of the Industrial Revolution in his social philosophy based on individualism, rational self-interest, free trade, accelerated division of labor, and the providential workings of the market's "invisible hand."[43]

The second explanation of capitalism's rise amounts to a "specificity model," which highlights the significance of a momentous social transformation that occurred in a specific geographic location. It was in England and Scotland where the unique establishment of a market-based system of property relations known as "agrarian capitalism" opened the door to a fully commodified form of capitalism based on industrial production. In order to gain access to the means of life, British people had no choice but to enter this newly emerging social environment as either self-interested owners of the means of production or dispossessed sellers of labor power. Once industrial capitalism had taken root in Britain, the productive power of the new economic system guaranteed its imposition on the rest of Europe, and ultimately, the whole world. To locate the origin of industrial capitalism in a single country, however, does not mean that the specificity model denies the emergence of different national or regional forms along uneven development trajectories. In fact, the next two centuries witnessed the proliferation of variations on the industrial capitalist theme. At the same time, however, all these capitalist variants were structurally bound to reproduce, in Ellen Meiksins Wood's words, "effects that it had at the beginning within its country of origin: dispossession, extinction of customary property rights, the imposition of market imperatives, and environmental destruction."[44]

Marxist economic historians like Wood argue that it makes a significant difference which of these two models of the origin and evolution of industrial capitalism win out in the pertinent scholarship. If the commercialization model prevails, then the role of technology and industrialization must be afforded a prominent place in the explanatory framework. But if the specificity model is adopted, then technological improvements will have to take a backseat to the series of prior transformations of social property relations. In this case, the key factor in the rise of industrial capitalism would be profound social change, not just the power of technological innovation.

Either scenario, however, acknowledges the significance of the Industrial Revolution as a major force behind the rising power of northwestern Europe to shape globalization. It facilitated the birth of an economic system capable of per-capita productivity and mass production of commodities beyond the wildest dreams of the agriculturally based age of institutional globalization.[45] Indeed, industrial capitalism was already recognized very early in the nineteenth century as a phenomenon that crossed state borders, becoming a global reality.[46] But why did the Industrial Revolution occur in Europe and not in East Asia where people enjoyed comparable living standards at the time?

According to the global historian Kenneth Pomeranz, it was the fortunate location of northwestern European coal reserves combined with Europe's access to American resources that powered the rapid industrial transformation along resource-intensive and labor-saving paths. Thus, the Industrial Revolution initiated what Pomeranz calls the "great divergence" between Western Europe and North America and the rest of the world in terms of incomes, industrial production, and military power. It gave Euro-American societies the upper hand in determining the worldwide expansion of social relations until the rise of the East Asia region in the late twentieth century.[47] Other world historians like Sven Beckert insist that the Industrial Revolution owes much of its vitality to the growing significance of key commodities in world trade. For example, large-scale commodity production systems such as the British "empire of cotton" linked thousands of spinners, weavers, and manufacturers of the Lancashire cotton industry to distant growers and consumers around the world.[48] Such global production chains organized and mediated by digital technology became the key to the global division of labor in the second half of the twentieth century.

Despite their intellectual differences, however, both global historians point to enhanced industrial production in factories as a major factor in the transition to a new phase of global interconnectedness, mobility, and imagination. While technological inventiveness might not have been a sufficient condition for the emergence of industrial capitalism, it certainly was a necessary ingredient. Powered by coal-produced energy, and, later, petroleum, globalization processes benefited greatly from the invention of new technological objects

usually known as "machines." For example, James Watt's 1776 rotative steam
engine was designed to drive all kinds of machinery and thus accelerated the
transportation of goods and people over land and sea. The resulting shrinkage
of distance was achieved by huge steamships like Germany's SS *Kaiserin
Auguste Victoria* or Britain's RMS *Olympic*. These floating giants could carry
hundreds of passengers while cutting the transatlantic crossing time from a
month in the early nineteenth century to less than a week in 1912.

Indeed, the steam engine and the associated switch to high-energy fossil
fuels unleashed not only advances in factory production and manufacturing, but also set off a chain reaction of further discoveries.[49] Trains began to
steam along increasingly standardized railroad tracks, transporting growing
volumes of goods and record numbers of people to their ever-expanding geographic destinations at ever-increasing speeds. The Trans-Siberian Railroad,
the longest railway in the world, was constructed between 1891 and 1916. It
connected Moscow with the Pacific city of Vladivostok over a record distance of 5,772 miles. Between 1906 and 1914, it facilitated the permanent
migration of 4 million Russian farmers to Siberia. The proliferating technologies of industrial capitalism reached a dizzying apex in the early 1890s and
1900s with the invention of motorcars and airplanes. What came to be known
as the belle époque unfolded in the privileged regions of the global north.
This "beautiful epoch" exuded general optimism, regional peace, economic
prosperity, and technological as well as scientific progress. At the same time,
however, it was sustained by continuing colonial subjugation and exploitation, as reflected in the 1885 Conference of Berlin, which divided up Africa
among competing European powers. Similarly, the United States fashioned a
takeover of Hawai'i, Cuba, and the Philippines in the 1890s.

Thanks to the free trade movement that expanded rapidly from the early
1800s to the outbreak of World War I in 1914, the volume of international
trade quintupled, as did European financial investment in the United States.
By 1910, the British Empire comprised a quarter of the land surface of the
world, which included more than a quarter of its population. Supported by
international bankers who had made the City of London the world's first
major financial center, industrialists celebrated their defeat of domestic
agricultural interests that had sought to maintain protectionist controls on
foreign trade. Objects and bodies flowed smoothly across national borders.
International lending and investment boomed as governments and businesses
eagerly embraced the world markets. The sterling-based gold standard, which
guaranteed the exchange of a country's currency for gold at a pre-established
rate, made possible the worldwide circulation of leading national currencies
like the British pound and the Dutch Guilder. Likewise, standardized global
pricing systems facilitated trade in important commodities like grains, cotton, and various precious metals. Increasingly spearheaded by the surging

United States, the integrating world economy grew at its most rapid rate in recorded history, which included previously underprivileged regions in South America and Asia. As economist Jeffry Frieden notes, "The opening years of the twentieth century were the closest thing the world had ever seen to a free world market for goods, capital, and labor."[50]

But trade liberalization did not mean that industrializing countries completely abandoned the use of tariffs. In fact, most economic internationalists also supported a system of social protection for the purpose of the continued industrial development of their nation. Indeed, the world economy operated within the nation-state system of world capitalism. In other words, pre-1914 economic integration was achieved through trade in goods and services between nationally-based production systems. Nationally based capitalists organized national production, and a national working class produced commodities within their own borders. As will be shown in the next section, this relatively shallow integration of the nation-based world economy in the age of objectified globalization differed markedly from the deep integration of the global economy in the age of disembodied globalization, which involved the transnationalization of the production of goods and services and the creation of global supply chains.

Moreover, most international trade occurred within Europe and between Europe and North America and Australia. In the early 1900s, Japan emerged as the lone Asian industrial power. Still, the factory-driven expansion of world trade also stimulated the growth of international and multinational companies like Germany's Singer Sewing Machine Company or America's US Steel. It also enabled the rise of industrial titans like John D. Rockefeller, powerful financiers like Nathan Mayer Rothschild, and newspaper magnates like William Randolph Hearst. Brand name packaged goods like Coca-Cola drinks, Campbell soups, and Remington typewriters made their first appearance.

On the eve of World War I, merchandise trade output reached a level unmatched until the 1970s, driven not only by a massive increase in the world's population to 1.8 billion but also by the ability of industrial capitalism to provide affordable products for mass consumption. Colonial goods like cocoa, rice, sugar, and tobacco imported from the European overseas territories ceased to be the privilege of the upper classes and became readily available to the average consumer in Berlin, Vienna, or Paris. The retrospective account penned wistfully by John Maynard Keynes, the preeminent economist of the twentieth century, best describes the apex of the age of objectified globalization:

> The inhabitant of London could order by telephone, sipping his morning tea in
> bed, the various products of the whole earth, in such quantities as he might see

> fit, and reasonably expect their delivery upon his doorstep; he could at the same
> moment and by the same means adventure his wealth in the natural resources
> and new enterprises of any quarter of the world. . . . He could secure forthwith,
> if he wished it, cheap and comfortable means of transport to any country or
> climate without passport or other formality.[51]

To keep up with growing volumes of supply and demand, the expanding
world economy promoted the migration of skilled and unskilled laborers
within and across continents. In 1910, global labor migration reached 3 million people per year. Hailing mostly from Europe and Asia, more than 1 million immigrants were bound for the United States, Canada, or Australia. The
migrants were drawn to these regions of the new world by the promise of a
brighter economic future as well as greater political and religious freedoms.
Moreover, these enormous waves of transcontinental migration intensified
cultural exchanges and transformed existing social patterns.

The culmination of the age of objectified globalization in the belle époque
also intersected with a sharp increase in the mobility of ideas, images, data,
and information. Disembodied globalization received a major boost with the
invention of the telegraph, which revolutionized the means of communication and stimulated the globalization of commerce and the news media. In
1866, the first commercially viable transatlantic cable enabled almost instant
transcontinental communication, albeit at the very high cost of $100 for
ten words. Only twenty years later, the rate had fallen to twelve cents per
word, which allowed millions of consumers and producers to take advantage of the new medium. In 1903, US president Theodore Roosevelt tested
the recently completed global telegraph infrastructure by sending himself a
round-the-world telegram, which arrived in less than nine minutes.

New applications of electricity proved to be an important conduit for the
intensification of disembodied globalization. The 1890s and 1900s witnessed
the electrification of "world cities" like London, Paris, and New York, whose
inhabitants enjoyed their enhanced mobility by means of trams, underground
trains, and escalators. The development of mass communication and the
international dissemination of news was taken a step further with the advent
of international telephone connections and the first successful wireless radio
signal transmissions. In 1914, there were 10 million telephones in operation
in the United States alone. In order to raise the global visibility of the newly
established corporations, international advertising agencies launched the first
full-blown, transborder commercial promotion campaigns. For example,
AT&T coined snappy advertising slogans in celebration of a world "inextricably bound together."[52]

The spread of mass-circulation newspapers, magazines, photography, and
film further enhanced the global awareness of a rapidly shrinking world in

which mass consumption, violence, risk, poverty, and aspiration all converged at dizzying speeds. Japanese, African, and Polynesian art began to exert a powerful influence on cutting-edge European Impressionist and Cubist painters like Paul Cezanne and Pablo Picasso. And the enticing photographic images of exotic and unspoiled "paradises" in the colonial world that appeared in high-circulation newspapers and illustrated magazines spawned the beginnings of an organized international tourism industry.

As the new networks of railways, steamships, and telegraphic communications brought distant places into closer proximity, previously minor discrepancies in local time-telling became a global problem. The solution represented a crucial spatial achievement related to the intensification of disembodied globalization: the synchronization and standardization of clock times. This was accomplished at the 1884 Prime Meridian Conference in Washington, DC, where astronomers, observatory scientists, geodesists, surveyors, mathematicians, and railway engineers exchanged ideas about worldwide timekeeping.[53] Their newly devised global temporal order linked the entire planet by counting twenty-four hours around the globe. Each hour was aligned to a "time zone" marked by prime longitudinal meridians east and west of London's Greenwich Observatory. In addition, this successful globalization of time into spatially distinct planetary zones arrayed around the center of the dominant British Empire allowed for the standardization of national time within most industrialized countries.

Finally, time also underwent important personal uses as it shrank to the size of an individual accessory adorning people's clothes. Millions of pocket watches snatched up by eager consumers in the 1890s and 1900s changed their sense of time to shorter and shorter intervals. "Minute-long phone conversations" or "fifteen-minute coffee chats" became commonplace phrases that measured social interactions in shrinking time. The rapid diffusion of pocket watches—and later wristwatches—not only accelerated modern life but also solidified the industrial norms of punctuality, calculability, and exactness. The mechanical compression of time also facilitated the rise of Taylorism—a production efficiency methodology that broke every factory job or task into small and simple segments. Such new forms of "scientific management" offered industrial workers incentives for good performance and punished shirkers, thus contributing to soaring levels of capitalist productivity and economic efficiency.

THE AGE OF DISEMBODIED
GLOBALIZATION (1945–PRESENT)

The collapse of the buoyant international order at the start of the Great War demonstrated that globalization was neither inevitable nor irreversible. The resurgent forces of nationalism and protectionism favored social systems based on economic autarky and national self-sufficiency. From the 1920s to the mid-1940s, the vast majority of the world's population was plunged into misery and dislocation by such catastrophic events as two world wars; an influenza pandemic that killed 40 million people worldwide; the terror of a genocidal German Nazi dictatorship and a brutal Soviet communist regime, both of which pulled away from most institutional arrangements; the Great Depression of the 1930s, which accelerated the shrinking of the world economy in addition to producing soaring unemployment rates; and worldwide immigration restrictions and other obstacles to the movement of people, save for millions of soldiers fighting in the global wars.[54] To make things worse, the end of World War II saw the detonations of two powerful American atomic bombs that killed more than two hundred thousand Japanese civilians. The dawning nuclear era raised the very real threat of total annihilation and reminded people around the world of their intertwined fates as a planetary species. And yet, this horrifying possibility of global nuclear war eventually became normalized during the Cold War by its fitting acronym MAD (Mutually Assured Destruction).

Still, one major globalization formation largely escaped the disruption of worldwide social interrelations and mobilities during these challenging interwar decades: disembodied globalization. Newly emerging media such as radio, movies, and mass circulation newspapers flooded people with information, impressions, and ideas about local events as well as faraway places. As historians J. R. McNeill and William McNeill point out, this information avalanche, combined with rapid population increases especially in urban areas, had the additional political effect of allowing skilled speakers like Adolf Hitler or Franklin D. Roosevelt to reach millions of people in an attempt to attract them to their political agendas.[55] TV broadcasting, pioneered in the 1930s and 1940s, further amplified the global social impacts of these new disembodied modes of communication. By the 1960s, the TV set became an essential item in most homes located in the privileged global north.

The two world wars not only accelerated the crucial shift from a coal-based framework of industrial development to a worldwide energy infrastructure run on petroleum, but it also proved to be a significant factor in the creation of digital electronic machines. Harvard University's Mark I computer, for example, was initially used by the US Navy for gunnery and ballistic calculations.

The invention of magnetic-core memory and transistors in the 1950s made commercial computers viable. The 1960s witnessed a dramatic increase in the number of such computers, with deliveries tripling every year. One of the earliest solid-state commercial computers, the IBM 1401, entered the market in the 1960s as the world's most widely used data processing system. The ensuing decades saw an explosive growth of personal computers. In the early 1970s, Steve Jobs and Steve Wozniak exhibited their first Apple II machine at the First West Coast Computer Fair in San Francisco. Equipped with built-in BASIC programming language, color graphics, and a 4,100-character memory, the Apple II model went on sale in 1977 for $1,298. Even the Internet—the most celebrated hallmark of disembodied globalization—originated in secret US war communication projects that underwent further development in the Cold War era in response to path-breaking Soviet satellite technology.

By the 1980s, the rapidly growing stature of disembodied globalization was finally given a name: The ICT Revolution. This enormous digital leap manifested in a series of innovations that included not only the rapid development of desktop and laptop computers and the Internet, but also the emergence of cable television, wireless phones, electronically guided shipping containers, fiber-optic cables, electronic barcodes, and global commodity chains. To be sure, the Internet played a pivotal role in the rise of disembodied globalization to dominance, especially through the creation of the World Wide Web that brought individuals, civil society associations, and governments together in mushrooming online communities. The total number of websites exploded to 17 million in 2000 and the number of Internet users worldwide reached over 400 million that same year. Most of these consumers were located in the global north, which spawned the fitting neologism "digital divide."

Insightful social thinkers like Manuel Castells referred to the age of disembodied globalization as a new "information age." He wrote about the rise of a global "network society" built on the "flowing spaces" and the "timeless time" forged by the new "information superhighways."[56] For the first time in human history, the electronic compression of space and time opened up immaterial spatial and temporal dimensions: "cyberspace" and "real-time." Powerful microelectronic technologies connected multiple "virtual worlds" to the physical world in ways that made geographic space part of cyberspace and vice-versa. Proliferating "dotcom" enterprises offered consumers personal and instant access to cyberspace in conflicting ways that both sustained and undermined people's identities, interests, and needs. Constituting real-time markets for the exchange of information and knowledge, these autonomous virtual spaces also transformed the operation of stock markets and globalized higher education by enrolling "distant learners" in new "online courses."

The postwar rise of disembodied globalization intersected with and stimulated the rebound of the other three formations, resulting in the accelerated shrinkage of geographic distance and the increasing porosity of national boundaries. Embodied globalization benefited greatly from the invention of jet engines, which made their first appearance as Messerschmitt Me 262 turbojet aircrafts in the German Air Force in 1944. During the 1950s, improved jet aviation technology enabled the construction of commercial wide-body airliners capable of transporting soaring numbers of objects and bodies to distant destinations in record time. In 1958, Pan American World Airways ushered in the commercial jet age by starting its regular transcontinental service. Each of its Boeing 707 aircrafts could carry more than one hundred passengers and eleven crewmembers. The flight from New York City to Paris took only 8 hours and 41 minutes and was affordable even for middle-class consumers at a relatively modest round-trip ticket price of $489. Less than two decades later, French and British Concorde supersonic airplanes cut the trans-Atlantic crossing time to just under 3 hours and 30 minutes. Wealthy passengers holding Concorde tickets could enjoy lunch in a fine brasserie on the Seine and take friends out to dinner in a Manhattan steakhouse the very same day. By the mid-1970s, hundreds of jet airlines served nearly 500 million passengers annually. Many of them experienced new physical problems connected with such extreme forms of space-time compression. The most obvious effect was the body's inability to cope with swiftly changing time zones. This unpleasant side-effect of accelerating embodied globalization introduced new terms into the English language: "jet lags" suffered by "jet-setters."

Another crucial World War II–related invention that allowed for the movement of bodies beyond Earth's atmosphere—rocket technology—initially applied to long-range guided missiles like the German V-2 rocket. At the end of the war, Wernher von Braun, Nazi Germany's leading rocket engineer, was brought to the United States to head up its burgeoning space program. After the establishment of NASA in 1958, von Braun and his large team of technicians and scientists successfully developed the Saturn V rocket, which launched the three-man crew of Apollo 11 on their historic mission to the moon in July 1969. The pictures of our "Blue Planet" snapped from outer space during the Apollo missions in the 1960s created in billions of people the first stirrings of a global imaginary. More than anything, the new space age gave physical concreteness to our borderless "global village"—a popular phrase coined by the Canadian communication scholar Marshall McLuhan that sought to capture the complex dynamics of spatial stretching, thereby making geographic distance much less of an obstacle in human interaction. Observing that the "mechanical age" of the industrial revolution was rapidly receding, McLuhan predicted correctly that the "electric contraction" of space and time would eventually make the entire globe as open to instant and direct communication as small village communities in previous ages had been.[57]

Institutional globalization also made a successful comeback under the auspices of expanding American postwar hegemony. A new international architecture characterized by a steep rise of intergovernmental organizations starting with the founding of the United Nations (UN) in 1945, headquartered in New York City. Committed to resolving conflict and assuring peace through its permanent Security Council, the UN created sub-agencies dedicated to assisting political refugees, working for global disease control, promoting international economic development, and supporting children's welfare. Far from functioning as a world government, the new organization nonetheless served as a crucial catalyst for institutional globalization. In particular, the setting of international humanitarian standards such as human rights exerted tremendous global influence. To some extent, the UN also stimulated the explosive growth of international non-governmental organizations such as Doctors Without Borders and Greenpeace from several hundred, in 1945, to nearly one hundred thousand in the 1990s.

Moreover, the accelerating process of global decolonization in the 1950s and 1960s created new nation-states in the global south while at the same time intensifying global flows and international exchanges. The new political order of sovereign but interdependent nation-states anchored in the UN charter raised the prospect of global democratic governance. However, such internationalist hopes quickly faded as the Cold War divided the world for four long decades into two antagonistic spheres: a liberal-capitalist First World dominated by the United States, and an authoritarian-communist Second World controlled by the Soviet Union. Both blocs sought to establish their political and ideological dominance in what came to be known as the "Third World." The stark reality of the Cold War rivalry forced these developing nations in the global south to choose sides. Hence, intensifying institutional globalization processes operated in a bipolar geopolitical environment in which the hostilities between the two superpowers played themselves out in hot proxy-wars in the Third World—such as the Korean War (1950–1953) and the Vietnam War (1955–1975).

These institutional dynamics unfolded in tandem with the globalization of a rather uniform western "culture industry" largely based in the United States. Hollywood movies, French Fries, McDonald's-style fast food, blue jeans, chewing gum, rock 'n' roll music, American-English idioms like "OK" or "showtime," and iconic American cars like the Ford Mustang or Harley Davidson motorcycles took the three worlds by storm. Even the Liverpool-based sensation band the Beatles only gained global superstar status after their record-breaking 1964 North American tour was kicked off by their first live US television appearance on *The Ed Sullivan Show*. Yet, the consumerism and materialism of intensifying "Americanization" also created a powerful cultural backlash in the form of alternative social movements and a spiritual yearning for a "New Age." The American Civil Rights movement of the 1950s and 1960s and the anti–Vietnam war demonstrations in the 1960s and 1970s served as catalysts for the growth of global counterculture. Unlike the prewar labor movements that had embraced primarily class politics, these new social movements often coalesced around identity positions opposed to racism, sexism, homophobia, and war. The same logic applied to the budding environmentalist movements of the 1960s and 1970s.

The rising fortunes of objectified globalization originated in 1944 in the sleepy New England town of Bretton Woods. Led by the United States, the major economic powers of the west jettisoned the protectionist policies of the interwar period and struck a compromise that combined international economic integration with national policy independence. Their renewed commitment to the expansion of trade and economic cooperation reflected a shared belief in the effectiveness of global commercial interdependence as a bulwark against another devastating economic crisis or a new world war. The successful establishment of binding rules on international economic activities resulted in the creation of a stable currency exchange system and new international economic organizations. The International Monetary Fund (IMF) was established to administer the global monetary system. The International Bank for Reconstruction and Development, later known as the World Bank, provided loans for Europe's postwar reconstruction. In the late 1950s, its purpose was expanded to fund major industrial projects in the developing world. The General Agreement on Tariffs and Trade (GATT) became the first global trade organization charged with fashioning and enforcing multilateral trade agreements.

In operation for almost three decades, the Bretton Woods regime contributed greatly to the establishment of what has been called the "golden age of controlled capitalism." States pledged close economic cooperation but maintained control over their economic policies and money flows. Existing mechanisms of state control over international capital movements made possible full employment and the expansion of the welfare state. State-regulated capitalism delivered spectacular economic growth rates, high wages, low inflation, and unprecedented levels of material wellbeing and social security. High taxation on wealthy individuals and profitable corporations led to the expansion of the welfare state. Rising wages and increased social services in the wealthy countries of the global north offered workers entry into the middle class. More than half of the workers in the First World belonged to a union. An increasing number of people in the First World could afford to spend vacations abroad or even escape in "charter planes" to distant tourist zones that sprang up in the Third World.

By the early 1970s, however, controlled capitalism ground to a halt. In response to profound political changes in the world that were undermining the economic competitiveness of US-based industries, President Richard Nixon abandoned the gold-based fixed rate system in 1971. This new world of floating currencies increased economic unpredictability and financial volatility. To make matters worse, a major energy crisis hit the world in the form of two "oil shocks" in 1973 and 1979. Reflecting the growing ability of the Organization of Petrol Exporting Countries (OPEC) to control a large part of the world's oil supply, the price of petrol at the pump quadrupled overnight and contributed to a condition of "stagflation"—the simultaneous occurrence of runaway inflation and rising unemployment. During the next ten years, the world economy tanked as it remained haunted by chronic price instability, soaring public sector deficits, and falling corporate profits.

Home to a quarter of the world's population, the Third World remained economically dependent on their former colonial masters. In return for supplying much-needed loans to developing countries, the increasingly neoliberal countries of the global north demanded from its creditor nations, as early as the 1980s, the implementation of so-called structural adjustment programs. Their official purpose was to reform the internal economic mechanisms of debtor countries in the developing world so that they would be in a better position to repay the debts they had incurred. In practice, however, structural adjustment programs rarely produce the desired result of economic development because mandated cuts in public spending translate into fewer social programs, reduced educational opportunities, more environmental pollution, and greater poverty for the vast majority of developing countries. Given the dominant role played by the United States in this process, it was no coincidence that this program became known as the Washington Consensus.

The collapse of the Soviet Bloc in 1991 shattered the bipolar postwar order and kicked globalization into an even higher gear. The world witnessed a changing world order in which the global hegemony of the United States began to be challenged by multiple rising powers such as China, India, and Brazil. Alongside this incipient political configuration, a "New Economy" of global reach was rapidly unfolding, driven by the deregulated market forces of neoliberalism. By the turn of the twenty-first century, post-Mao China emerged as the world's fastest rising economic power and leading manufacturer. The total export volume of world trade exploded from $876 billion in 1975 to an astonishing $6 trillion in the late 1990s. As discussed in chapter 1, when "globalization" emerged in the public discourse of the 1990s as *the* buzzword, its meaning had already been shackled to the dominant neoliberal framework.

The internationalization of trade benefited greatly from falling transportation costs linked to dramatic advances in shipbuilding and container technology. Once the standardization of shipping containers was agreed to in 1965, the 8-foot-wide, 8½-foot-high, and 10-, 20-, or 40-foot-long boxes could be handled by ports around the world and rolled straight onto flat-bed trucks. Facilitated by accelerating processes of global standardization mediated by digital technology, the explosion of global trade went hand in hand with the liberalization of financial transactions. Key components included the deregulation of interest rates, the removal of credit controls, the privatization of government-owned banks and financial institutions, as well as the explosive growth of investment banking. The globalization of financial trading allowed for increased mobility among different segments of the financial industry, with fewer restrictions and greater investment opportunities. The number of transnational corporations (TNCs) skyrocketed from 7,000 in 1970 to about 50,000 in 2000. The largest TNCs in 2000—giant firms like General Motors, Exxon, and IBM—maintained subsidiaries in several countries. Rivaling nation-states in their economic power, these corporations began to control much of the world's investment capital, technology, and access to international markets.

The ICT revolution also transformed personal finance and banking routines and accelerated significantly during the twenty-first century. The first globally linked credit cards such as American Express, MasterCard, Diners Club, and Visa expanded across the 1960s. Electronic cheque-clearing systems were developed in the 1970s and electronic funds-transfer systems (EFTPOS) and automatic teller machines (ATMs) came into regular use in the 1980s. Electronic banking through global browsers such as Netscape, Internet Explorer, and Google took hold in the 1990s, as did new schemes for electronic marketing, merchandizing, and computer-assisted share trading such as through the NASDAQ system (1971), London Stock Exchange Automatic Quotation system (1986), and the Hong Kong Automatic Order Matching and Execution System (1993).

Thus, the age of disembodied globalization witnessed the rise of transnational capital, which moved the capitalist system from a world economy to a global economy. As William Robinson explains, during the belle époque each country developed a national economy which was linked to other national economies through trade and finances in an integrated international market. But global capital mobility in the late twentieth century allowed capital to reorganize production worldwide into new globalized circuits of accumulation. Hence, the determining distinction between the world economy of the age of objectified globalization and the global economy of the age of disembodied globalization was the digitally mediated globalization of the production process itself.[58]

This transformation of capitalism also involved its change from a primarily industrial form to its current twenty-first century financial configuration. This shift was reflected in the turn of the finance world toward traded derivatives. These esoteric contracts specified future outcomes based upon the relative performance of another instrument or investment. It is hard to say when the threshold was passed, but post-risk options as a primary way of accruing value developed quickly from the 1970s and grew exponentially from the mid-1980s. By the turn of the century, electronically traded derivatives amounted to an estimated US$70 trillion or eight times the annual GDP of the United States. Hedge funds increased significantly over the first years of the new century, growing annually at approximately 15 to 20 percent. Derivative exchanges began to be conducted "over the Counter" on private digital networks as the exchange of the temporally projected value of value-units that did not yet exist except as projections. While these new derivative exchanges serve as remarkable examples of the increasing compression of space and time, they also became the basis for economic disasters such as the 1997 Asian Financial Crisis or the 2008 Global Financial Crisis.

The dramatic acceleration of worldwide interdependencies and mobilities that occurred in this age represented yet another quantum leap in the history of globalization. As noted in the preface of this book, political leaders of different ideological persuasions praised in unison what they saw as the beneficial outcomes of this turbocharged era of worldwide space-time compression. In 1998, UN Secretary Kofi Annan managed to capture this widespread spirit of optimism in a widely publicized speech at Harvard University: "Globalization is commonly understood to describe the advances in technology and communications that have made possible an unprecedented degree of financial and economic interdependence and growth. As markets are integrated, investments flow more easily, competition is enhanced, prices are lowered and the living standards everywhere are improved."[59]

CONCLUDING REFLECTIONS

The accelerating compression of world-space and world-time of the age of disembodied globalization resulted in greater technological and economic productivity that made for a more interdependent world. As discussed in more detail in chapter 7, it also ushered in a new phase of global instability that intensified in the twenty-first century. To call the contemporary phase the Great Unsettling means that the rapid development of abstracted and disembodied connectivity has come to relativize—and thus unsettle—relations between people, machines, regimes, objects, and nature. Today, the Great Unsettling stretches into every aspect of social life.

In ecological terms, the Great Unsettling stands for the proliferation of unsustainable social practices driven by the economic imperative of accumulating capital and extracting profits. New interventions into nature radically degrade and alter the planetary environment in ways that go far beyond the familiar ecological exploitation and manipulations engendered by the Industrial Revolution. Similarly, genetic scientists are struggling to work through the implications of mapping and manipulating the basic building blocks of life. What began as a project that linked all of life on earth, turned into a global scramble for control of exploitable genes. As Donna Haraway observes, a new kind of "species is technically and literally brought into being by transnational, multibillion-dollar, interdisciplinary, long-term projects to provide exhaustive genetic catalogs."[60]

As illustrated in more detail in later chapters in this book, the social consequences of the Great Unsettling have become the macro-context of globalization in the twenty-first century. The phenomenal world of producing and moving bodies, objects, information, and institutions around the world has now been framed by a new digital layer of the economy. Ironically, it has been ushered in through the legislation of nation-states, which frequently operate beyond the reach of democratic influence. Across the world, concepts of "freedom" and "liberty" have been claimed by both the political Left and Right as their own, and yet, the data-surveillance of people's lives has become more and more intrusive and incompatible with individual freedom. Neoliberal attempts to remake the global market still involve deregulating its older integrating mechanisms while increasing the intensity of multiple corporate centers of interconnected control, usually through algorithm-driven data-logistics. In turn, these digital structures, most prominently in the form of Meta, Twitter/X, TikTok, and other proliferating social media platforms, have become the new management tools for both selling commodities of all sorts and conducting electoral politics.

The Internet, wireless communication, digital media, and online social networking sites overlay and remake older forms of social interchange, thus highlighting the dominance of disembodied globalization in the current age. The unprecedented and encompassing digital networks of communication tightly connect the local and global in new, and often productive, ways. Still, these interactions often elicit contradictory experiences as well. They offer individualized and relativized portals onto a world of apparently open possibilities—even as these social interrelations are carried by an intense global integration of a corporate-controlled platform of tools and services that seek to harness and channel those possibilities. As we will discuss in the ensuing chapters, we live today in an unsettling and volatile era characterized by disjunctive and disjointed dynamics involving the four major formations of globalization.

3

A Critical Appraisal of Globalization Theory

Turning to matters of theory, this chapter completes the task of establishing a firm historical and conceptual foundation for our assessment of globalization in the twenty-first century. Over the past decades, globalization theories of all sorts have flourished. Fashionable deglobalization talk notwithstanding, this academic boom suggests that the compression of world-space and world-time continues to be a major topic deserving of serious reflection. At the same time, however, the proliferation of theoretical research on the subject has turned out to be a mixed blessing.

On the upside, globalization theories have brought fresh perspectives and insights to our understanding of contemporary social change. As global studies scholar Jan-Aart Scholte observes, the early decades of the twenty-first century have witnessed a significant expansion of the 1990s globalization debates, resulting in a "substantial library of explanatory and normative global theory."[1] Most importantly, globalization scholars have successfully challenged the analytical hegemony of "methodological nationalism" associated with the academic disciplines of International Studies (IS) and International Relations (IR). The term refers to the conventional IR view that nation-states are the principal actors on the world stage and thus should serve as the basic unit of analysis. By contrast, globalization thinkers place transnational interconnections and mobilities at the center of their methodological attention. Finally, as discussed in later chapters of this book, globalization theories have also provided vital conceptual frameworks for addressing pressing global problems such as economic inequality, terrorism, ecology, national populism, digitization and electronic surveillance, and of course the emergence and worldwide spread of new pandemics like COVID-19.[2]

On the downside, globalization theory continues to struggle with some of its long-standing limitations. These include shallow attention to spatial dynamics involving complex processes of digitization, thin transculturalism, underdeveloped integration of postcolonial and ecological perspectives, and scarce examinations of certain global issues like poverty and gender disparities.[3] One should add two further limitations to this list: conceptual murkiness and spotty transdisciplinarity. As for the former, several key concepts of globalization theory still lack definitional precision and clear analytical delineation.[4] As discussed in chapter 1, this shortcoming applies even to the basic term "globalization," which is often employed without the conceptual sharpness and historical specificity required for innovative research.[5]

With regard to insufficient transdisciplinarity, many globalization theorists have been slow to expand their core vocabulary to include pertinent themes and keywords outside their familiar literatures. Their apparent reluctance to forge new conceptual linkages and associations and their unwillingness to expand beyond conventional themes indicate deeper problems of deficient reflexivity and narrow knowledge hierarchies. The obvious remedy would be to make systematic efforts to incorporate relevant insights generated in cognate fields such as environmental studies, postcolonial and indigenous studies, and computer science. After all, if globalization theorists want to engage in a genuinely global analysis of globalization, they must contribute to a markedly more diverse polylogue across disciplinary boundaries, which are drawn and monitored by dominant academic players in the global north.[6]

Finally, the mushrooming of globalization theories has made it much harder to maintain a general overview of the literature on the subject. In addition, theoretical debates have often become abstruse and cacophonous, demonstrating that reflections on the global tend to be geared toward academic insiders. Students and non-experts who stand to benefit most from gaining greater insights often perceive "global theory talk" as too dense and arcane. To be sure, the dynamics involving worldwide interconnectivity, mobility, and imagination defy easy explanations. Paradoxically, however, increasing social complexity and accelerating social change only amplify the need to bring more clarity and precision to the study of globalization.

Responding to some of these limitations of globalization theory, this chapter combines the task of providing a clear and informative overview of influential intellectual currents with a critical appraisal of conventional analytical frameworks that are of great significance in the twenty-first-century academic context. In particular, my criticism is directed against antiquated classification models. It seeks to break down its entrenched typology of globalization theory centered on reductionistic and antagonistic perspectives. Challenging this rigid oppositional "camp" mentality, my alternative analytical framework offers a more accessible and fluid overview of globalization theories that relies on intersecting modes or styles of thinking.

GLOBALIZATION THEORY: THE BASICS

How should we understand *theory* in "globalization theory"? The concept is derived from the classical Greek word *theoria*, which means "contemplation" or "gaze." These terms carry both philosophical and religious connotations. A theorist is a person who reflects on the world to gain rational knowledge of its objects or initiate mystical encounters with the divine. Placed into the context of modern science, theories are broad analytical frameworks for grasping and explaining phenomena in the natural and social world. In turn, empirical research depends on theory to construct coherent frameworks of analysis and specify objects of inquiry. At their core, then, theories are systematic ways of recognizing and analyzing shifting patterns and regularities. In short, theory is just another word for *pattern analysis*.[7]

For globalization theorists, the central patterns to be analyzed are those related to the "compression of world-space and world-time."[8] The terms "globalization theory" and "global theory" are often used interchangeably in academic discourse.[9] Indeed, there exists considerable thematic and methodological overlap. Both frameworks are designed to theorize global dynamics unfolding within and across contemporary societies. But there are also some differences. Most importantly, globalization theory focuses on the flows of people, ideas, objects, and organizations across intertwined spatial scales running from the local to the global. Thus, it places "glocal" connectivities and mobilities at the center of analysis. By contrast, global theory attends primarily to global-scale dynamics such as global governance, global supply chains, global security, global civil society, and global capitalism.

THE DOMINANT FRAMEWORK OF GLOBALIZATION THEORY

Since the turn of the twenty-first century, overviews of theoretical approaches to globalization have been organized around a conceptual model that postulates the existence of three competing approaches. Usually presented as "waves" or "phases" in the evolution of globalization theory, three intellectual "camps" are said to be inhabited by "hyperglobalizers," "sceptics," and "transformationalists."[10] Each wave/camp in this dominant model of globalization theory is alleged to have generated a distinct set of arguments that puts it at odds with its competitors.

The relatively small, but influential, camp of hyperglobalizers is portrayed as making up the bulk of the first wave of globalization theory starting in the early 1990s. These thinkers are said to have elevated globalization to the status of primary driver of contemporary social change. According to this interpretation, first-wave accounts postulate an epochal shift in interconnectedness and mobility. Many of the hyperglobalist writers associated employ sweeping economistic narratives that predict the eventual denationalization of economies through the rapid expansion of transnational networks of production, trade, and finance.

The influential Japanese management guru Kenichi Ohmae serves as one of the prime examples of first-wave thinkers. His influential books celebrate new forms of techno-economic interconnectivity as the indispensable central nervous system of an ultracompetitive "borderless world."[11] Ohmae portrays transnational investment and commodity flows as the slayers of antiquated trade protectionism. He expresses the hope that "archaic" nationalist sentiments at the core of crucial modern legal notions such as "state sovereignty" will soon be eclipsed by global capitalism. Offering a more nuanced and politically sophisticated account, scholars like Susan Strange argue that intensifying globalization processes undermine many of the traditional functions of nation-states, but without making them obsolete. As she puts it, "Where states once were masters of markets, now it is the markets which, on many crucial issues, are the masters over the governments of states."[12]

This first wave of hyperglobalizers is said to have lost much of its momentum at the turn of the twenty-first century. Two successive waves corresponding to the camps of skeptics and transformationalists materialized quickly thereafter. Committed to the production of less polemical and more empirically oriented globalization theories, skeptics are presented as a relatively united camp emphasizing the continuing significance of nation-states and geographic regions. Paul Hirst and Grahame Thompson represent the prime example of skeptical second-wavers. Building on the work of earlier theorists, the British political scientists argue that the world economy has never been a truly global phenomenon. At best, it amounts to just another wave of internationalization in the form of a limited regional dynamic confined to North America, Europe, East Asia, and Australia. Without an integrated worldwide economic system, there can be no such thing as "globalization." Thus, Hirst and Thompson summarize their skeptical case against the existence of economic globalization: "As we proceeded [with our economic research], our scepticism deepened until we became convinced that globalization, as conceived by the more extreme globalizers, is largely a myth."[13]

Similarly, neo-Marxist critics like Immanuel Wallerstein, Justin Rosenberg, Leo Panitch and Sam Gindin, and Clyde Barrow are often mentioned as examples of second-wave skeptics committed to the view that globalization represents hardly an epochal transformation.[14] They see the concept as amounting to little more than a trendy signifier given to the latest phase in the evolution of capitalism. Hence, they reject the generalizing force of the concept of "globalization" as "meaningless." Another group of academics cited as exemplars of the skeptical approach includes thinkers who take hyperglobalist economists to task for downplaying the looming threat of social disintegration as a result of unfettered neoliberal globalization.[15]

The third camp of "transformationalists" is associated with theorists who consider globalization as a powerful set of deterritorializing processes that move societies toward greater global interconnectivity.[16] Unlike hyperglobal-izers, however, these thinkers hold more moderate expectations about the pace and future trajectory of social change. As Global Studies scholar David Held explains:

> In comparison with the sceptical and hyperglobalist accounts, the transforma-tionalists make no claims about the future trajectory of globalization; nor do they seek to evaluate the present in relation to some single, fixed "globalized world," whether a global market or a global civilization. . . . Such caution about the exact future of globalization is matched, nonetheless, by the conviction that contemporary patterns of global economic, military, technological, ecological, migratory, political, and cultural flows are historically unprecedented.[17]

Transformationalists accept the skeptical claim that globalization should not be seen as a single, monolithic process but as a complex, often contradic-tory, and uneven set of processes involving sub-global scales as well. Hence, they sympathize with the skeptical insight that globalization involves regional and local dynamics. In the same vein, James Rosenau uses the term "frag-megration" to describe the "pervasive interaction between fragmenting and integrating dynamics unfolding at every level of community."[18] Moreover, transformationalists resist the hyperglobalist reduction of globalization to economics. Instead, they divide their research attention among what they consider three equally important dimensions of globalization: economics, politics, and culture.

To its credit, the dominant model based on the three-wave/three-camps template served the important purpose of creating a much-needed typology of the theoretical perspectives on globalization. It became an influential clas-sification scheme for organizing the proliferating ideas and approaches on the subject. But there are also some serious problems with this model. First, it draws sharp boundaries around each camp. However, a careful perusal of pertinent writings shows that overlaps and intersections among various glo-balization theories are just as common as divisions. Models that emphasize stark differences minimize these connections across camps and thus miss out on important processes of overlap and cross-fertilization. Second, the claim that three successive waves of globalization theories followed each other in neat diachronic fashion is belied by the messiness of various camps engaging each other in real time. For example, significant skeptical accounts emerged roughly simultaneously with hyperglobalist narratives. Similarly, the writings of pioneering globalization thinkers such as Roland Robertson and Arjun Appadurai show clear transformationalists elements. Finally, the theoretical frameworks developed by influential globalization theorists are conceptually much richer and more complex than reflected in the rather rigid and reductionistic categories of hyperglobalizers, skeptics, and transformationalists.

AN ALTERNATIVE FRAMEWORK OF
GLOBALIZATION THEORY

Recognizing the virtues of the dominant framework, my alternative framework for analyzing globalization theories seeks to overcome some of the identified limitations of the dominant model by organizing globalization theories according to three intersecting "modes" or "styles" of thinking.[19] The *generalizing mode* approaches globalization as an integrated, holistic process cutting across all spatial scales and applying to all major social domains. Its thinkers often draw on the insights of classical social thinkers to foster comprehensive understandings of globalization. The *domain mode* is utilized by thinkers who inquire into specific dimensions of globalization such as economics, politics, culture, and ecology. Over the years, new domains and subdomains have been rapidly added to this expanding list. Lastly, the *complexity mode* appeals to theorists who approach globalization as a changeable and highly contingent set of phenomena, which requires deep explorations into multiple forms of complexity and differentiation. What is common to all three modes is that they share forms of critical reflection, which include both class-based approaches and identity-centered forms of social critique such as cultural theory, feminist theory, queer theory, psychoanalytic theory, and others.

 Based on simultaneous and intersecting styles of theorizing rather than successive waves and distinct camps, my alternative analytical framework holds many advantages. First, the modes of thinking correspond to the internal characteristics of globalization dynamics themselves rather than creating intellectual positions made to conform to topics imposed by the author. Second, it breaks down the antagonistic camp mentality inherent in the dominant model. While affirming the particularity of each mode, it also emphasizes synergies among these genres that stimulate mutually reinforcing insights. I argue that the three styles of theorizing developed their profiles over three decades in a complex interplay of both contrasting ideas and overlapping perspectives. Third, my approach challenges the simplistic linearity of three separate theory waves washing across time. While acknowledging that globalization theories are always evolving, my framework also captures the simultaneity of interactions across these three styles of thinking. There is little evidence that hyperglobalizers preceded skeptics, who, in turn, were followed by transformationalists. Rather, different perspectives emerged simultaneously and in constant interaction with each other at all stages of the unfolding globalization debate during the 1990s and beyond.

Each of the following three sections elucidates a particular style of thinking about globalization with reference to the works of one or two exemplary theorists. To be clear, most of these thinkers have engaged in research that reaches across several modalities. This suggests that the three analytic styles are neither mutually exclusive nor incompatible. Rather, their overlap reflects the intertwined evolution of globalization theory as a collective enterprise which brings to bear multiple modes of theorizing to produce knowledge of the global. At the same time, however, most of the theorists usually show a special affinity for one particular genre. Their mastery of their chosen primary mode pervades the selection of their key themes, their choice of methodologies, and the presentation of their findings.

THE GENERALIZING MODE

"General theory" refers to any conceptual framework that attempts an overall explanation of social or natural phenomena. Unlike domain theory, which studies particular dynamics, general theory delineates overarching patterns and answers fundamental questions. Constructed at the top level of generality, such theories aim for a high degree of internal consistency and coherence of their propositions. Furthermore, they seek to grasp relationships and linkages spanning the entire spectrum of reality ranging from the micro-level to macro-structures. Moreover, general theories cover a large number of phenomena that reach across multiple domains of inquiry and involve extended timeframes. Such comprehensive models allow for a greater degree of conceptual integration. The ultimate research goal of general theorists is to present research findings that support claims to universal validity and applicability.

Accordingly, globalization theorists adopting a generalizing mode approach their subject as a comprehensive phenomenon cutting across all spatial scales and applying to all major dimensions of social life. They seek to gain an integrated understanding of the role of globalization in generating social change across national borders. Aiming for nothing less than the construction of a systematic theory of globalization, their efforts are associated with conceptualizations of the global as the worldwide interactions among relatively stable structures such as political institutions, systems of economic production, networks of communication, and cultural practices. Generalizing thinkers recognize globalization as an extremely intricate and differentiated set of processes, but they also show some affinity for the complexity style of thinking.

Moreover, generalizing thinkers like to situate their macro-approaches within major currents of Western social thought, claiming that some of these classical insights have withstood the test of time. In particular, they connect their global analyses to traditional themes such as modernization, industrialization, capitalism, the division of labor, solidarity and social cohesion, class and social stratification, secularization, and historical stages of social development. Thus, generalizing theorists construct their globalization frameworks in the "grand theory" style of pioneering European social thinkers such as Karl Marx, Max Weber, and Émile Durkheim.

There are only a handful of contemporary thinkers who accept the formidable challenge of constructing a comprehensive analytical framework of globalization. These include Anthony Giddens, Roland Robertson, David Held and his collaborators, and, to a lesser extent, Jan-Aart Scholte.[20] To illustrate the workings of the generalizing mode, let us consider one of the most successful attempts to produce a holistic and historically grounded model of globalization. Its primary features can be found in the work of the late British political theorist David Held, especially in his co-authored study titled *Global Transformations*. This massive five-hundred-page tome introduces readers to a collaborative and transdisciplinary research project stretching over the entire decade of the 1990s. Serving as the lead author of the volume, Held was joined by Anthony McGrew, an international relations scholar who interpreted domestic politics as a product of powerful interstate forces; David Goldblatt, a social theorist with a strong background in ecology and environmental policy; and Jonathan Perraton, an noted economist and international finance expert. These authors promise to deliver "a distinct account of globalization, which is both historically grounded and informed by a rigorous analytical framework."[21]

Their generalizing mode of inquiry unfolds in a series of five conceptual steps that yield the key components of their comprehensive globalization theory. The first step starts with their firm rejection of influential accounts of globalization as a singular dynamic anchored primarily in the economic domain. Instead, the authors describe the compression of world-space and world-time as a highly differentiated set of processes unfolding across six distinct domains of social activity: economics, politics, culture, military, migration, and ecology. This multidimensional approach makes it easier for them to present globalization as a multicausal product of a combination of social forces including technological innovation, market dynamics, ideology, and political decisions. In other words, Held's generalizing mode of theorizing globalization aims at overcoming monocausal explanations that point to particular aspects of social activity—usually economics or politics—as the source of global transformation. Finally, this initial step also underscores the significance of interconnectivity and mobility as key qualities of globalization.

The authors' second move involves the location of their approach within the academic context of the globalization debates of the 1990s. To that end, they present the dominant model of globalization theory characterized by the antagonistic camps of hyperglobalizers, skeptics, and transformationalists. Since we are already familiar with this conventional framework, there is no need to go into further detail here. While Held and his collaborators show some sympathy for the transformationalist camp, they reject overly deterministic depictions of global transformation toward a fixed historical destination such as a single world society or a globally integrated market. Instead, they subscribe to a more contingent version of transformationalism that casts globalization as an uncertain and open-ended set of processes susceptible to unanticipated setbacks and outright reversals.

The third step entails the identification of four spatio-temporal forms of globalization: the *extensity* or width of global networks; the *intensity* or depth of global interconnectedness; the *velocity* or speed of global flows; and the *impact* propensity of global interconnectedness. While breadth, depth, and speed appear to be straightforward criteria for evaluating globalization, "impact" is trickier and thus requires further elaboration. Ultimately, the authors distinguish between four types of impact: *decisional*, understood as the impact of globalization on policy options and social choices; *institutional*, referring to the impact of globalization on organizational agendas and designs; *distributive*, defined as the impact of globalization on the distribution of power and wealth within and between countries; and *structural*, understood as the impact of globalization on major political and economic structures such as states and capitalist markets.

In addition to the four spatio-temporal dimensions—extensity, intensity, velocity, and impact—Held's fourth step is the introduction of four *organizational dimensions*. Physical, legal, and symbolic *infrastructures* are necessary for facilitating global connections and flows. The *institutionalization* of global networks requires the regulation and routinization of global patterns of interconnectedness in terms of trade pacts, defense alliances, sports events, and so on. Globalization is also organized through patterns of *social stratification* that reflect uneven and asymmetrical power relations. Finally, dominant *modes of interaction* ranging from coercion to cooperation are responsible for the rise and fall of specific globalization regimes across various historical epochs. Comprised of eight key components—four spatio-temporal dimensions and four organizational dimensions—Held's sprawling analytical framework constitutes the basis for both a qualitative and quantitative assessment of historical patterns of globalization that can be measured empirically. Moreover, the systematic evaluation of how these dynamics have played out across time allowed for a historical comparison of distinctive forms of globalization and a sharper identification of their key attributes.

Held and his co-authors are now ready to put the finishing touches on their theoretical edifice. Their fifth and last conceptual step involves the construction of a comprehensive typology of globalization. It consists of four discrete types of globalization that reflect different patterns of worldwide flows, networks, and interactions. Type 1 corresponds to *thick globalization* characterized by an extensive reach of global networks that is matched by their high intensity, high speed, and high impact across all domains and organizational dimensions of social life. A deregulated capitalist world imagined by market globalists in which national borders have become largely irrelevant represents one possible manifestation of Type 1.

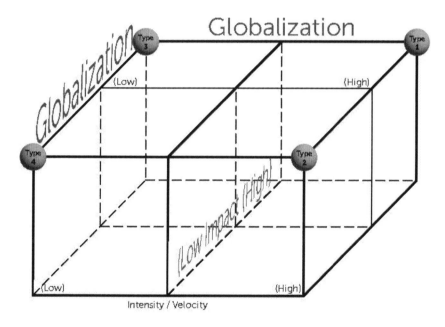

Type 1 = thick globalization
    (high extensity, high intensity, high velocity, high impact
Type 2 = diffused globalization
    (high extensity, high intensity, high velocity, high impact
Type 3 = expansive globalization
    (high extensity, high intensity, high velocity, high impact
Type 4 = thin globalization
    (high extensity, high intensity, high velocity, high impact

Figure 3.1. **David Held's Typology of Globalization** *Credit: Dr. Tommaso Durante*

On the opposite end of the spectrum, we find Type 4, which qualifies as *thin globalization* because it contains global networks that rank low on all eight key components of globalization. A deglobalized world of rein-vigorated, sovereign nation-states invoked by national populists would be an example of Type 4. Located between these thick and thin models are Types 2 and 3, which correspond to diffused and expansive forms of globalization. *Diffused globalization* ranks high on the scale of extensity, intensity, and velocity, but its impact is highly mediated by national or global institutions. This type resonates with the vision of justice globalists who embrace the idea of a highly interconnected world whose social impacts are tightly regulated by egalitarian institutions of global governance. *Expansive globalization* scores high on the criteria of extensity and impact but low on intensity and velocity. This type is exemplified in the bygone world of gradual western imperial expansion in which the worldwide reach of European empires nega-tively impacted indigenous civilizations.

Employing a generalizing style of theorizing globalization, Held and his collaborators also show some affinity for the complexity mode. But they insist that the extremely intricate and differentiated set of globalizing processes be grasped in their totality only through an overarching framework attentive to the specific dynamics operating in multiple dimensions. Thus, their research aim is to "develop a more comprehensive explanation of globalization which highlights the complex intersection between a multiplicity of driving forces, embracing economic, technological, cultural and political change."[22]

The generalizing mode of theorizing globalization possesses the virtue of seeking to develop a general and systematic framework for understanding the compression of the world in its full complexity. Scholars writing in this mode keep alive the possibility of assembling the big picture of what globalization is and how it unfolds across a wide range of domains and geographical and historical contexts. Moreover, generalizing styles of thinking situate scholar-ship on the global within currents of social thought whose insights have with-stood the test of time. In particular, this mode connects globalization theory to some of the enduring categories and issues of classical social thought.

On the downside, however, the generalizing mode often remains overly attached to these key concepts—and thus some major problems—of nineteenth- and twentieth-century European social theory. The writings of most generalizing globalization theorists rarely engage with crucial con-temporary identity categories such as race, gender, and sexual orientation. References to postcolonial theory and non-western philosophical frameworks are sporadic and often underdeveloped. If they do occur, these engagements are usually confined to defensive responses to legitimate demands for the greater incorporation of knowledge produced outside the Euro-American academy. As noted in the previous chapter, Anthony Giddens, for example, limits "modernity"—which he uses in the singular—to specific European historical contexts and geographic origins.[23]

An additional weakness of the generalizing mode is that it requires the preliminary task of mapping out in much detail the various domains of the phenomenon, which then are brought back together in highly abstract overarching models. As reflected in Held's framework, the attempt to tame multidimensionality within an analytical meta-framework ultimately leads to a confusing welter of analytical categories and typologies like "social domains," "spatio-temporal dimensions," and "organizational dimensions." Unable to stop their sprawling abstractions, generalizing thinkers often find themselves bogged down in lengthy explanations of how these multiple components fit together. Similarly, when applied to concrete global problems like climate change or economic inequality, the distinctions between these proliferating categories became blurred, thus inviting conceptual confusion. Hence, the generalizing mode of theorizing of globalization is vulnerable to criticism concerning the capacity of any grand theory to adequately explain global interconnectivity, mobility, and imagination.

THE DOMAIN MODE

Much to their credit, some early globalization pioneers writing in the 1990s did recognize the difficulty of developing a comprehensive theoretical framework. Hence, they presented the compression of the world-space and world-time as a differentiated set of processes, which unfolded in specific aspects of social life. Hence, the gist of the domain style of theorizing global-ization lies in breaking up the enormous proportions of the phenomenon by identifying its most pivotal dimensions and then focusing pertinent research on one or two of these aspects. The decoupling of distinct domains under the signifier "multidimensional" serves two important objectives. First, it makes it easier for globalization thinkers to accomplish their analytical task of gain-ing a better understanding of clearly demarcated parts of the whole. Second, it allows them to engage in collaborative projects along the lines of multidis-ciplinarity, with each individual researcher bringing their academic expertise to bear on larger conceptual mappings of globalization.

The domain mode of theorizing attracts scholars trained in conventional disciplines and entices them to explore particular aspects of globalization nestled under the fledgling transdisciplinary umbrella of Global Studies. The most frequently researched dimensions include the *economic*, referring to the intensification and stretching of economic connections across the globe;[24] the *political and governmental*, dealing with expansion of political, governance, and citizenship interrelations across the world;[25] the *cultural*, exploring the intensification of cultural flows across the globe;[26] and the *ideological*, tackling the worldwide expansion of political belief systems.[27] Over the years, new domains and subdomains were added to this list, including ecology, technology, communications, media, art, law, religion, democracy, education, military and war, race and ethnicity, gender, human rights, diplomacy, social movements, citizenship, postcolonialism, urbanization, security, migration, and many more. The acceleration of climate change, in particular, spawned the publication of major globalization studies after the turn of the twenty-first century.[28] Indeed, the two most visible academic book series on globalization now contain dozens of volumes covering a broad spectrum of dimensions.[29]

One of the most unorthodox and innovative examples of domain-thinking can be found in Michael Hardt and Antonio Negri's study of the political dimension of globalization. Hailed by sympathetic reviewers as "*The Communist Manifesto* for our time," their unexpected best-selling book, *Empire*, focuses on the emerging political world order at the turn of the twenty-first century. Hardt and Negri's analysis of the political domain of globalization is characterized by their remarkable ability to paint in transdisciplinary strokes, in the process drawing on a plethora of materials from legal studies, politics, economics, philosophy, anthropology, cultural studies, comparative literature, and critical theory.

At the core of the study, one finds the authors' insistence that "Empire" represents a radically new paradigm of political authority and control—a "new global order" composed of a series of national and supranational organisms that supersede old, nation-state-centered forms of sovereignty. "Empire" is not merely a metaphor but a theoretical concept signifying a "political subject that effectively regulates these global exchanges, the sovereign power that governs the world."[30] In their view, this single logic of globalization is no longer opposed by an extra-systemic "outside," thus constituting a new form of sovereignty that effectively encompasses the "spatial totality" of the entire globe. Wielding enormous powers of oppression and destruction, Empire neither establishes a territorial center nor relies on fixed boundaries, but "manages hybrid identities, flexible hierarchies, and plural exchanges through modulating networks of command. The distinct national colors of the imperialist map of the world had merged and blended in the imperial global rainbow." As a regime "with no temporal boundaries and in this sense outside of history or at the end of history," Empire thus dwarfs any particular imperialist project previously undertaken by single nation-states.[31]

After a descriptive analysis of the present features of Empire and a long interpretation of the historical transition from imperialism to Empire, Hardt and Negri conclude on an optimistic note, suggesting that the creative forces of the exploited and subjugated producers that sustain Empire were also capable of autonomously constructing a "counter-Empire"—an alternative political organization of global flows and exchanges fueled by "the multitude" and its "will to be against." Struggling for global mobility, global citizenship, a guaranteed social wage, and the right to the reappropriation of the means of production, this subjugated multitude is said to invent new forms of democratic expression as well as novel manifestations of constituent power.[32]

In this context, Hardt and Negri offer an insightful discussion of the subversive effects of a political demand for global citizenship. A direct response to a globalizing world, mass migration and increasing mobility are alleged to contain the revolutionary political potential to undermine economic inequalities and asymmetrical power relations that are rooted in an anachronistic defense of fixed boundaries and spatial divisions separating the northern and southern hemispheres. Calling for subversion, insurrection, and biopolitical self-organization, the authors end their political analysis of globalization by introducing the heroic figure of the "militant"—depicted as somewhat of a cross between Saint Francis of Assisi and an anarchistic union organizer—as the figure who best expresses the revolutionary potential of the multitude.[33]

Hardt and Negri's unorthodox, yet sophisticated, approach demonstrates both the strengths and weaknesses of domain thinking. On the upside, their attention to shifting forms of political sovereignty in a globalizing world gives their analysis the sort of precision and focus that is sorely lacking in Held's generalizing thinking. Another virtue of Hardt and Negri's domain mode of theorizing lies in its ability to explore the political aspects of globalization by incorporating a more manageable set of insights taken from relevant social thinkers, especially Karl Marx, Gilles Deleuze, and Felix Guattari. Yet, their theoretical approach also manages to draw on multiple intellectual currents associated with anarchism, existentialism, poststructuralism, critical theory, critical race theory, subaltern studies, and feminist theory.

Hardt and Negri's approach also exemplifies one of the main shortcomings of domain thinking: the difficulty of reassembling a big picture of globalization that integrates other domains, thus giving them the same analytical weight. On one hand, Hardt and Negri suggest that a single political logic of globalization manifested as Empire also operates in all spheres of social life, such as instructions of social control, the formation of global markets, the creation of new technologies, the expansion of vast circuits of material and immaterial production, and the generation of gigantic cultural flows. On the other, their political discussion of the decline of national sovereignty takes precedence over the related explanation of their systemic totality whose dynamics are said to affect all domains. In other words, their exploration of an evolving global space of authority and control portrays globalization both as a political project of superseding old, nation-state-centered forms of sovereignty and as a universal logic that pertains to the phenomenon of globalization in general. Domain approaches, then, face the immensely difficult task of fusing their specific insights into a bigger picture without falling prey to the generalizing move of integrating all major dimensions of globalization into a single analytic framework.

THE COMPLEXITY MODE

The complexity mode of theorizing approaches globalization as an intricate, changeable, and highly contingent phenomenon whose study requires close encounters with multiple forms of complexity and differentiation.[34] Complexity theory is an analytical framework developed to recognize and address the limitations of western scientific thinking's reliance on linear dynamics. Its evolution has followed two distinct paths. First, complexity science emerged from a form of complexity thinking that focuses on the reproduction of complexity dynamics as mathematical and computational models. Second, social complexity is a nascent effort by sociologists and contemporary social philosophers to construct an epistemic framework for complexity theory that is relational. This form of complexity thinking uses qualitative and quantitative logics to account for the emergent multiple relationships whose mutually constitutive dimensions generate complex social patterns.[35] As applied to globalization theory, "complex connectivity" captures, as John Tomlinson notes, in a "simple and relatively uncontentious way" a basic understanding of globalization as a "rapidly developing and ever-densening network of interconnections and interdependencies that characterize modern social life."[36]

From the beginning, globalization thinkers writing in the complexity style sought to connect their analytic focus to the elusive ideals of transdisciplinarity and multidimensionality.[37] Since global complexity appears in many forms and pervades different social arenas, globalization thinkers have approached it from different angles and through multiple levels of analysis. Early research efforts often involved empirical mappings of complexity that drew heavily on the cybernetic discourse of "networks" and "flows," which intensified at the turn of the twenty-first century as a result of the ICT Revolution.

The Spanish sociologist Manuel Castells represents an intriguing exemplar of combining two styles of thinking. On one hand, he could be seen as a domain theorist focusing on the dimension of communication, but on the other, he relies on complexity thinking as his primary mode of analyzing globalization processes. In particular, Castells plays a pivotal role in the academic attempt to situate technological complexity discourse centers on "electronically processed information networks" within the emerging globalization debate configured around social interdependencies. Examining complex globalization processes operating in economic, social, and cultural domains, he offers an empirically grounded account capable of explaining changing social and organizational arrangements of what he calls the "global network society."[38] Castells presents digital communication and information networks as open structures capable of infinite expansion and integration of a large number of new nodes and ties. He claims that a global Information Age—embedded in interconnected networks of production, power, and experience—has replaced the Industrial Age and its centrally organized, vertical chains of command and control geared toward the production and distribution of power. As Castells explains:

> [D]igital networking technologies, characteristic of the Information Age, powered social and organizational networks in ways that allowed their endless expansion and reconfiguration, overcoming the traditional limitations of networking forms of organization to *manage complexity* beyond a certain size of the network. Because networks do not stop at the border of the nation-state, the network society constitutes itself as a global system, ushering in the new form of globalization characteristic of our time.[39]

In particular, Castells seeks to unlock the complexities of the global network society by concentrating on "flows"—purposeful and repetitive sequences of exchange and interaction involving such things as language, data, money, or drugs—that pass through nodes along the ties of the network. However, under conditions of increasing complexity, flows can assume many different forms, characteristics, and qualities. Recognizing this difficulty, Castells introduces his influential notion of the "space of flows," which applies to microelectronics-based digital communication, advanced telecommunication networks, and computerized information systems. These flowing spaces transform conventional forms of social space by "introducing simultaneity, or any chosen time-frame, in social practices, regardless of the location of the actors engaged in the communication process." Unlike the conventional "space of places"—bounded space linked to specific locations such as delineated suburbs, villages, towns, and the nation-state—space of flows describe a new inter-relationship of knowledge, power, and communication that "involves the production, transmission, and processing of flows of information." To be sure, the space of flows on the Internet still relies on the production of localities as nodes of expanding communication networks, but the primary function of such "places" consisted of providing "material support of simultaneous social practices communicated at a distance."[40]

Building on Castells's notion of "space of flows" as well as Zygmunt Bauman's similar idea of "liquid modernity," John Urry, too, seizes on the transformative impact of globalization to connect social inquiries into the nature of the global with the "complexity sciences" and "chaos theory" in order to capture new transnational dynamics. In particular, he argues that concepts and methods borrowed from physics and biology have the capacity to expand our understanding of the global as a complex system or series of interdependent systems. Appreciative of Castells's innovative examination of intersecting global networks as the new framework for studying globalization, the British social theorist nonetheless criticizes his colleague for lacking a sufficiently broad range of theoretical terms necessary to illuminate the intensification of global complexity. As he sees it, Castells's notion of "network" is "too undifferentiated a term" to capture the dynamic properties of global processes and worldwide interconnectivity and mobility. Hence, Urry's basic premise is to overcome the "limitations of many globalization analyses that deal insufficiently with the *complex* character of emergent global relations."[41]

As his starting point, Urry proposes that emergent global systems should be conceptualized as interdependent and self-organizing "global hybrids." Combining both physical and social relations in curious and unexpected ways, these formations can evolve toward both disorganization and order. Teetering "on the edge of chaos," global hybrids often move away from points of equilibrium and stability, thus exhibiting the qualities of unpredictability, contingency, nonlinearity, irreversibility, and indeterminacy that have long been described and analyzed in natural sciences devoted to the study of complexity such as quantum physics, thermodynamics, cybernetics, ecology, and biology. Urry cites informational systems, automobility, global media, world money, the Internet, climate change, health hazards, and worldwide protests as examples of such global hybrids.[42]

Next, Urry introduces the concept of "globally integrated networks" consisting of "complex and enduring networked connections between peoples, objects and technologies stretching across multiple and distant spaces and times." Their purpose is to manage global complexity by inserting regularity and predictability into the chaotic multiplicity of emergent globality. For example, global enterprises like McDonald's, American Express, or Sony are organized through globally integrated networks that interweave technologies, skills, texts, and brands to ensure that the same service or product is delivered more or less the same way across the entire network. This makes outcomes predictable, calculable, routinized, and standardized. Under conditions of advanced globalization, however, globally integrated networks often exhibit insufficient flexibility and fluidity to implement appropriate modes of organizational learning.[43]

Finally, Urry introduces another key concept for the purpose of advancing our understanding of globalization as complexity: "global fluids." While these highly evolved manifestations of global hybridity undoubtedly involve networks, Urry insists that the term "networks" does not do justice to the "uneven, emergent and unpredictable shapes" that global processes might take. Structured by the various dimensions and domains of global order, global processes traveled along network ties from node to node, but their movements were much less stable and predictable than Castells suggested when he introduced the notion "space of flows" within global networks. Urry argues that "global fluids" is a better concept because their properties allow them to "may escape, rather like white blood corpuscles, through the 'wall' into surrounding matter and effect unpredictable consequences upon the matter." For example, powerful "fluids" of traveling people or health hazards such as global pandemics tend to travel across national borders at changing speeds and "at different levels of viscosity with no necessary end state or purpose." Hence, Urry considers his notion of global fluids—possessing different viscosities—superior to the "networks" metaphor in explaining how the "messy power of complexity processes" impacted the global age.[44]

For all its virtues—such as its insistence that globalization is neither unified nor presented as a linear and orderly set of processes unfolding in separate domains—the complexity mode of theorizing exemplified in the works of Urry and Castells suffers from at least four weaknesses.

First, like generalizing theories, it relies on multiple and overlapping concepts to describe complexity in abstract ways that make it extremely difficult to understand how metaphors like "globally integrated networks" and "global fluids" are related.

Second, these rather dense and abstract set of concepts are employed in the service of arguments that provide little by way of real-world illustration and specification, thus obscuring the connection between theory and practice that is vital for the engagement of global problems. For example, the very different mobilities of commodities and refugees crossing national borders demonstrate that the metaphors of "flows" and "liquids" can only serve as partial descriptors of the real-life complexity of globalization dynamics. Moreover, such metaphors also tend to diminish vital questions of structural power, including the power to stop people and objects moving across borders.

Third, the poststructuralist emphasis on fluidity overemphasizes discontinuities, contingency, and surface flows at the expense of paying sufficient attention to existing continuities, determinations, and deeper structures.

Finally, the investigation of globalization through the prism of growing complexity demands from researchers the acceptance of the impossibility of coming to closure in the analysis of the global. The resulting imperative of intellectual modesty that comes with the recognition of limits to knowledge tends to be obeyed by only the rarest of academics—complexity globalization thinker not exempted.

CONCLUDING REMARKS

After an initial overview of influential mappings of globalization theories, this chapter introduced an alternative framework based on modes of thinking to critically analyze major theoretical currents. The generalizing mode of theorizing globalization facilitates macro-level inquiries with reference to traditional themes of social theory such as modernization, industrialization, the division of labor, social stratification, secularization, stages of social development, and capitalism. Thus, generalizing theorists tend to construct their globalization discourse with reference to the grand theories of classical social thinkers. The domain style of thinking attracts theorists seeking to go beyond the confines of conventional academic disciplines. Eager to explore significant globalization dynamics that correspond to their area of expertise, they are united in their recognition of the value of transdisciplinarity. Lastly, the complexity mode appeals to theorists who approach globalization as a changeable and highly contingent set of dynamics. Thus, they engage in close encounters with multiple layers of networks, systems, flows, fluids, and interdependencies. Complexity theorists also favor the design of new research tools and innovative methodologies that can illuminate the rich and intricate patterns of global social change on both the macro- and micro-level.

The alternative modality framework guiding our journey through the landscapes of globalization theory responds more effectively to the dual challenge of enhancing accessibility to these difficult writings while retaining intellectual sophistication. Most importantly, it makes it easier for readers to discover their own affinity for certain modalities—and the corresponding contributions of leading theorists—and thus plant their own flag, knowing how various ways of thinking about globalization relate to the larger body of literature on the subject.

The opening three chapters of part I of this book served the purpose of laying the necessary historical and theoretical foundations for our assessment of globalization in the twenty-first century. We can now turn to specific aspects starting with an exploration of the changing ideological landscape of our time.

PART II

Ideologies and Movements

4

Contending Globalisms

Our young twenty-first century has witnessed a profound transformation of the familiar ideological landscape dominated by liberalism, conservatism, and socialism. That these conventional "isms" have come under full-scale attack in recent decades is demonstrated by what could be called a proliferation of prefixes that adorn ideologies. The attachment of "neo" and "post," in particular, has created popular compounds such as "neoliberalism," "neo-conservatism," "neofascism," "post-Marxism," and so on. These semantic additions reflect people's growing sense that something new has happened to the grand ideologies of European modernity and that they are moving past their familiar meaning orbits.

What, then, is "neo" about political thought-systems in the twenty-first century? Engaging this question, this chapter points to the rising global imaginary as a major force driving the current ideological transformations. Thus, the discussion starts with a short examination of the crucial connection between changing political ideologies and shifting social imaginaries. The bulk of the chapter presents the ideational makeup of the three contending "neo-isms:" market globalism, justice globalism, and religious globalism. However, this conceptual mapping exercise does not occur in the abstract but is linked to concrete political events and social movements that have impacted the globalizing world of the twenty-first century.

POLITICAL IDEOLOGIES AND SOCIAL IMAGINARIES

The modern political ideologies of liberalism, conservatism, and socialism emerged in the wake of the great eighteenth-century revolutions in Europe and the Americas. From the start, these new ideational constellations competed with religious belief systems over what norms and values should guide specific societies. And yet, these self-consciously secular ideologies resembled religious doctrines in their totalistic desire to shape all aspects of social life. Codified by power elites and embraced by significant social groups, these budding isms became key drivers in the evolution of modern industrial societies.

Playing both integrative and fragmenting roles, ideologies are neither mere justifications of economic class interests nor impractical metaphysical speculations. Rather, they function as shared mental maps designed to help people navigate their increasingly differentiated social worlds.[1] Their primary function is to simplify the complexity of the political sphere by means of potent truth-claims that "lock in" the meaning of key ideas such as "freedom," "equality," or "security." As political theorist Michael Freeden explains, "An ideology attempts to end the inevitable contention over concepts by *decontesting* them, by removing their meanings from contest. 'This is what justice means,' announces one ideology, and 'that is what democracy entails.'"[2] Such interlinked truth-claims give each thought-system its unique conceptual fingerprint or "morphology." Vying with other ideational configurations for the control of authoritative meanings, ideologies provide justifications for making political decisions regarding "who gets what, when, and how."[3]

To adequately grasp the fundamental changes that are transforming the ideological landscape of the twenty-first century, it is necessary to examine the crucial link between political ideologies and social imaginaries. Social philosopher Charles Taylor argues that the latter constitute implicit "background understandings" that provide the most general and deeply engrained parameters within which people imagine their communal existence. Thus, social imaginaries serve as commonsensical frameworks for how "we"—the members of a particular community—fit together, how things go on between us, and what kind of expectations we have of each other.[4] The dominant social imaginary of the last two centuries has been deeply colored by the "national" as reflected in namable communities such as France or Colombia.[5] As discussed in chapter 2, the eighteenth-century social revolutions in Europe and the Americas served as the midwives for the birth of a national imaginary, which was exported to the rest of the world through colonial and imperialist practices. The national imaginary, then, refers to a background understanding in which the "nation"—plus its affiliated or to-be-affiliated "state"—constitute the legitimate container for modern political communities. This definition corresponds to Benedict Anderson's notion of modern imaginings of the nation as a limited and sovereign community of individuals whose knowledge of each other is, in most cases, not direct, but mediated through abstract linear time and the rise of "print capitalism."[6]

Emphasizing the overarching stature of the national in the dominant social imaginary, Benedict Anderson and other critical social thinkers reject the commonplace notion that nationalism is just another ism such as liberalism or socialism. Following their intuition, I treat the national not as a distinct ideology but as a substantive component of the modern social imaginary. Ideologies, on the other hand, occupy the surface layer of social consciousness. Crucially, they function as the translators of the implicit social imaginary into explicit political doctrines. While each ideology deploys and assembles its chosen core concepts in specific and competing ways, they are all "nationalist" in the sense of performing the same fundamental task of articulating the dominant background understanding into concrete political agendas. In so doing, grand ideologies like liberalism and conservatism normalize national territories, speak in recognized national languages, construct national histories, and appeal to national audiences. These dynamics apply equally to socialism and communism, whose proclaimed "internationalism" has remained a distant ideal whereas its concrete political configuration took the form of *German* social democracy, Soviet *Russia's* "socialism in one country," and "socialism with *Chinese* characteristics."

For two centuries, then, the partisans of the grand ideologies of western modernity clashed with each other over such important issues as the purposes and forms of government, the roles of the state and the economy, the extent of civil rights, the significance of race and gender, and so on. Clinging to their specific political programs, the ideological competitors passed over their common embeddedness in the national imaginary. By the early decades of the twentieth century, ideologies had been such successful translators that the national became "banal," that is, the ubiquitous and taken-for-granted template for all modern communities.[7]

However, as noted in chapter 2, new ideas and social practices emerging after World War II produced in the public consciousness a sense of rupture with the past similar to the break that had occurred in the late eighteenth century. The intensification of worldwide interconnectivities and mobilities occurred hand in hand with the growing subjective recognition of an increasingly interdependent world. As Roland Robertson emphasizes, the compression of the world into a single place made the global the new frame of reference for human consciousness and social action.[8] Thus, globalization involved not only changes in the objective macro-structures of society but extended deeply into the subjective micro-structures of the individual self and its dispositions.[9]

IDEOLOGICAL STRUGGLES OF THE TWENTY-FIRST CENTURY

Erupting with great intensity from within and onto the national, the rising global imaginary unsettled engrained notions of the nature and status of the national community. Something "neo" was happening that moved the twenty-first-century world "post" the essentialized framework of the "international" order. Consequently, the reconfigured political ideologies of the new century no longer represent exclusive articulations of the national imaginary. Rather, they manifest as three contending globalisms equally capable of translating the waxing global imaginary into competing political agendas and programs. Therein lies the genuine novelty of the twenty-first-century ideological landscape and its move past an exclusive association with the national.

Market Globalism

The first of these novel globalisms, market globalism, rose to dominance in the late 1990s with the help of transnational power elites. They shaped its ideological pattern by fastening on to the new buzzword "globalization" as the central keyword for their neoliberal agenda of globally integrated markets and the worldwide spread of consumerist values. Market globalists discarded, absorbed, and rearranged large chunks of liberalism and conservatism while at the same time forging new ideas into a global political vision. The outcome was a coherent ideational configuration situated around five central truth-claims: (1) globalization is about the liberalization of trade and the global integration of markets; (2) globalization is inevitable and irreversible;

Figure 4.1.   Globalisms in the Twenty-First Century

(3) nobody is in charge of globalization; (4) globalization benefits everyone; and (5) globalization furthers the spread of democracy in the world. In chapter 1, we discussed parts of these claims in the writings of Theodore Levitt and Thomas Friedman. Thus, we can confine our current discussion of market globalism to some critical observations about the veracity of these foundational assertions.

Regarding claim 1, the message of liberalizing trade and integrating markets around the world serves to solidify as fact what is actually a contingent political initiative. After all, this neoliberal project was realizable only through the political power of national governments willing to break with the postwar Keynesian compromise of regulating their economies. In other words, national governments legally engineered deregulated markets and zero-tariff trade zones. The common neoliberal assertion that governments can best contribute to the process of market deregulation by simply getting out of the way of business represents, therefore, a clear example of ideological distortion. After all, the state-activist character of neoliberal administrations in the United States, the UK, Australia, New Zealand, and others during the 1980s and 1990s attests to the importance of strong governmental action in bringing about "free markets."[10]

Hence, neoliberal governments served as the core drivers of what critics began to call "corporate globalization" or "globalization from above." In their state-imposed pursuit of trade liberalization and global market integration, the combination of pro-market political elites and corporate interests violated their own principles of decentralization, limited government, and negative liberty. Moreover, their economistic perspective on globalization reduced ecological, cultural, and political dimensions of globalization to mere appendices of the primary dynamics of global markets.

Claim 2—"globalization is inevitable and irreversible"—projects a teleological belief in the historical inevitability of neoliberal globalization, which makes for a poor fit for a market-globalist ideology. After all, throughout the twentieth century, liberals and conservatives consistently criticized socialism and communism for their deterministic claims that devalued human free agency and downplayed the ability of noneconomic factors to shape social reality. However, a close study of the utterances of influential market globalists at the turn of the twenty-first century reveals their reliance on a similar reductionistic narrative of historical inevitability. While disagreeing with Marxists on the final communist goal of historical development, market globalists nonetheless share with their ideological opponents a fondness for an economic determinism. Their narrative essentializes the spread of irreversible market forces driven by technological innovations that claims to make the global integration of national economies "inevitable" and "irreversible." This portrayal of economic globalization as some sort of natural force, like bad weather or gravity, makes it easier to convince ordinary people that they have to adjust to the discipline of the market if they are to survive and prosper.

Claim 3—"nobody is in charge of globalization"—downplays the geopolitical fact of western domination. If the "natural laws" of the market have preordained a neoliberal course of world history, then globalization does not reflect the arbitrary agenda of a particular social class, group, or country. People are not in charge of globalization; markets and related technologies are. Human actions might accelerate or retard globalization, but in the last instance, the invisible hand of the market will always assert its superior wisdom. Thomas Friedman puts it succinctly: "And the most basic truth about globalization is this: No one is in charge. . . . We all want to believe that someone is in charge and responsible."[11]

While there may be no conscious conspiracy orchestrated by a single evil force, it is not difficult to identify asymmetrical power dynamics behind the global integration and deregulation of markets. Backed by powerful states in the global north, international institutions such as the WTO, the IMF, and the World Bank have enjoyed a privileged position of making and enforcing the rules of the global economy. In return for supplying much-needed loans to developing countries, these economic organizations demanded from their creditors in the global south "structural adjustments" in return for much-needed development loans. This Washington Consensus spelled out a new form of colonialism based on neoliberal principles of deregulating national economies, privatizing state-owned enterprises, and cutting trade tariffs.

Claim 4—"globalization benefits everyone"—lies at the very core of market globalism because it provides an affirmative answer to the crucial normative question of whether globalization represents a "good" or a "bad" phenomenon. Market globalists frequently connected their arguments in favor of the integration of global markets to the alleged benefits resulting from the liberalization and expansion of world trade. For example, former US Secretary of the Treasury Robert Rubin asserted that free trade and open markets provided "the best prospect for creating jobs, spurring economic growth, and raising living standards in the United States and around the world."[12] While some market globalists acknowledged the existence of unequal global distribution patterns, they nonetheless insisted that the market itself would eventually correct these "irregularities" and "imperfections."

The final market-globalist claim—"globalization furthers the spread of democracy in the world"—is anchored in the neoliberal assertion that freedom, free markets, free trade, and democracy are reciprocal terms. The compatibility of these concepts hinges on a limited understanding of democracy as involving formal procedures such as voting at the expense of the direct participation of broad majorities in decision making. This thin definition of democracy is part of what William Robinson identifies as the Anglo-American neoliberal project of promoting "polyarchy" in the global south. For the global studies scholar, the concept of polyarchy differs from the concept of "popular democracy" in that the latter posited democracy as both a process and a means to an end—a tool for wrestling political and economic power from the hands of elite minorities to the masses. Polyarchy, on the other hand, represents an elitist and regimented model of "low-intensity" or "formal" market democracy. Polyarchies not only limit democratic participation but also require that those elected be insulated from popular pressures so that they may govern "effectively."[13] Their promotion of polyarchy makes it easier for market globalists to advance their neoliberal project in an idiom that ostensibly supports the democratization of the world.

Justice Globalism

Market globalists experienced little discursive pushback throughout much of the 1990s. Moreover, major political parties on both the center-left and center-right around the world embraced their ideological vision. But no single ideational system ever enjoys absolute and enduring dominance. Battered by persistent gales of socioeconomic change and political dissent, the small fissures and ever-present inconsistencies in all political ideologies threaten to turn into major cracks and serious contradictions. Growing gaps between the assertions of the ideologues and the lived experience of ordinary people usher in long-term crises for hegemonic ideas. At the same time, however, such systemic crises also represent a golden opportunity for disadvantaged social groups to propagate new ideas, beliefs, practices, and institutions.

During the first decade of the new century, arguments critical of market globalism began to receive more play in the public discourse on globalization. This development was aided by a heightened awareness of how global corporate profit strategies were leading to widening global disparities in wealth and wellbeing. Thus, market globalism encountered a serious challenger on the political Left in the form of justice globalism. Aware of the power of discourse, its codifiers opposed "globalization-from-above" with their own vision of globalization-from-below. Hence, their ideological vision was hardly "anti-globalization" as market globalists claimed but favored a different mode of global interdependence. Crucially, there were multiple geographical origins of their "alterglobalization" stance such as the anti-free trade agenda stitched together by the Mexican Zapatista Army of National Liberation. Engaging in effective global framing—a flexible form of global thinking that connected local or national grievances to the larger context of global justice—Zapatista leader Subcommandante Marcos announced to the world that their local struggle in the southern Mexican state of Chiapas was of global significance: "[W]e will make a collective network of all our particular struggles and resistances. An intercontinental network of resistance against neoliberalism, an intercontinental network of resistance for humanity."[14]

This potent combination of growing global activism and spectacular market failures in parts of the global south and Europe created larger discursive and political openings for a fledgling alterglobalization movement (AGM), which had become confident enough to call on its mass membership to organize protests at official international meetings of high-profile market-globalist institutions like the IMF, the World Bank, the G-8, the World Economic Forum (WEF), or the WTO. The first large-scale confrontation between the forces of market globalism and its challengers on the left came in late 1999, when fifty thousand people representing labor, human rights, and environmental groups took part in the anti-WTO protests in Seattle, Washington. These disparate groups learned a crucial lesson: the best way of challenging the established framework of market globalism was to build a broad transnational support network.[15] In spite of the predominance of North American participants, there was also a significant international presence. In fact, the global character of the Seattle demonstrations was a central feature that distinguished it from other mass protests in the recent past.[16] Clearly articulating justice-globalist concerns, this eclectic alliance criticized the WTO's neoliberal position on agriculture, multilateral investments, and intellectual property rights. The ensuing street clashes between demonstrators and with the police—dubbed the Battle of Seattle—was the first in a series of similar demonstrations around the world in the early 2000s.

Ultimately, the alterglobalization demonstrations at the turn of the twenty-first century also served as a vital catalyst in the 2001 creation of the World Social Forum (WSF) in Porto Alegre, Brazil. This global platform soon became the central organizing space for tens of thousands of justice globalists who delighted in their annual counter-summit to the January meeting of the market-globalist WEF in the exclusive Swiss ski resort of Davos. Designed as an open meeting place, the WSF encouraged and facilitated a free exchange of ideas among scholars and activists dedicated to challenging the neoliberal framework of globalization-from-above. Their organizations represent different interests, possess distinctive structures, pursue various projects, and are based in different geographical regions. They include labor unions such as the Australian Council of Trade Unions (ACTU) and the American AFL-CIO, environmental groups such as Greenpeace, agricultural co-ops such as the All Arab Peasants and Agricultural Cooperatives Union, think-tanks and educational organizations such as Focus on the Global South; indigenous peoples' assemblies such as Congreso Nacional Indigena de Mexico, financial watchdog groups such as ATTAC, feminist and women's networks such as World March of Women, human-rights organizations such as Oxfam International, religiously affiliated groups such as Caritas International, migration associations such as the Forum des Organisations de Solidarité Internationale Issues des Migrations, peace networks such as Peace Boat, alternative public policy organizations such as Global Policy Network, global democracy advocacy groups such as the Network Institute for Global Democratization, North-South networks such as Solidar, and poor people's movements such as Poor People's Economic Human Rights Campaign.

The WSF sought to accomplish two fundamental tasks.[17] The first was ideological, reflected in concerted efforts to undermine the premises of the reigning market-globalist worldview. WSF member organizations constructed and disseminated alternative articulations of the global imaginary based on the anti-neoliberal core principles of the WSF. The second task was political, manifested in the attempt to realize these principles by means of mass mobilizations and nonviolent direct action aimed at transforming the core structures of market globalism. WSF organizations challenged market globalism by formulating a "justice globalism" centered on five central ideological counter claims: (1) neoliberalism produces global crisis; (2) market globalization has increased global disparities in wealth and wellbeing; (3) democratic participation is essential for solving global problems; (4) another world is possible and urgently needed; and (5) people power, not corporate power![18]

Regarding claim 1, the identification of the economic doctrine of neoliberalism as the basic cause of contemporary global crises constitutes the foundation of all four claims of justice globalism. But in what, precisely, lies the alleged failure of neoliberalism? For the AGM, neoliberalism fails ethically because it puts the needs of markets and corporations ahead of the needs of individuals, families, communities, and nation-states. It comes up short economically because the flawed policies of privatization, deregulation, and liberalization neither benefit ordinary people nor lift the poorest populations of developing countries out of poverty. Indeed, the claim that neoliberal measures at the heart of market globalism must be held responsible for global crises emerged as the most common and consistent allegation across WSF-affiliated organizations. Moreover, these organizations contrasted the dominant neoliberal position unfavorably with their preferred justice-globalist vision of more democratic economic approaches that empowered citizens to regulate markets in various ways in their quest for a more equitable generation and distribution of wealth.

Claim 2—"market globalization has increased global disparities in wealth and wellbeing"—extends beyond the statement that neoliberalism has caused global crises. It makes more specific assertions with regard to the social impact of market globalism. Claim 2 reflects the AGM's conviction that existing disparities of wealth and wellbeing are fundamentally unjust because they violate universal norms of fairness. It is also noteworthy that this claim's emphasis on fundamental disparities implied the importance of solidarity with the disadvantaged. Indeed, Claim 2 carries an important emotional charge designed to confront the reader with the real-life devastation caused by the vigorous application of neoliberal doctrine during the last three decades. Like all ideologies, justice globalism generates claims designed to connect the rational and emotional aspects of human perception based on concrete examples and illustrations that can be readily grasped by everyone.

Claim 3—"democratic participation is essential for solving global problems"—implies that the rectification of the substantial disparities created by market globalism can only be achieved through bottom-up decision-making processes that consciously address the multiple global crises of our time. Justice globalists expect social disparities and ecological imbalances to worsen in the future and thus call for collective action against the major institutions of market globalism. Participatory democracy assumes a central position as a core concept of justice globalism and seeks to move the AGM from mere rhetoric—the diagnosis of shortcomings and the blaming of market globalism—to concrete political action tackling such recalcitrant global problems as poverty, irregular migration, poor health care, and environmental degradation. Finally, the call for multiple models of participatory democracy on a local-global scale represents a crucial conceptual bridge that connects social activists residing in the richer countries of the northern hemisphere to the principal victims of distributive injustice in the global south. WSF-connected organizations recognize that democratic resistance was not guaranteed to weaken but would facilitate the articulation of alternatives to the dominant market globalist discourse.

A variation of the official WSF slogan, claim 4—"another world is possible and urgently needed"—represents perhaps the most well-known and widely recognized demand of the AGM. At its heart lies what the German critical theorist Ernst Bloch called a "concrete utopia" of an alternative social order.[19] In particular, this assertion combines the AGM's commitment to transformative change with a visceral sense of urgency given that the world has reached a crisis moment in the history of humanity. If people fail to bring about a paradigmatic shift in the basic values that drive global politics and economics within the next few decades, our species might have crossed the point of no return—especially with regard to the deteriorating natural environment. It is this sense of urgency that weaves together justice globalism's core concepts of transformative change, social justice, sustainability, and equality. Claim 4 also builds on and extends the three previous claims: since neoliberalism has failed both economically and ethically, humanity faces the vital task of finding alternatives as soon as possible through common action in the spirit of solidarity.

Claim 5—"people power, not corporate power!"—expresses a strong confidence in ordinary people's ability to globalize the world of the twenty-first century in fundamentally different ways than neoliberal forces have in mind. The justice-globalist demand for a fundamental revision of existing power relations relies heavily on the binary of "people" versus "corporations." It is couched in terminology that seeks to expose the undemocratic concentrations of power that dominate the supposedly "democratic" societies in the global north. However, most WSF-affiliated organizations direct their critique of power elites not only toward the corporate world, but also condemn democratically elected representatives for bending all too easily to the will of moneyed interests. For many justice globalists, politics and business have formed a permanent symbiotic relationship designed to monopolize power in the name of democracy. They understand people power as extending beyond existing national borders.

The high levels of frequency, consistency, and clarity with which these five central claims were deployed by WSF-affiliated organizations provide ample evidence that justice globalism grew to ideational coherence and maturity during the 2000s. It not only provided an effective conceptual decontestation of its core concepts but also showed a remarkable degree of responsiveness to a broad range of pressing political issues. The programmatic core of the ideological claims of justice globalism was a "global Marshall Plan" that would create more political space for people around the world to determine what kind of social arrangements they want. To this day, millions of justice globalists believe that "another world" has to begin with a new, worldwide Keynesian-type program of taxation and redistribution, exactly as it was introduced at the national level in Western countries a century ago. The necessary funds for this global regulatory framework would come from the profits of TNCs and financial markets—hence the justice-globalist campaign for the introduction of the global tax on speculative investments.

Other proposals include the cancellation of poor countries' debts; the closing of offshore financial centers offering tax havens for wealthy individuals and corporations; the ratification and implementation of stringent global environmental agreements; the implementation of a more equitable global development agenda; the establishment of a new world development institution financed largely by the global north and administered largely by the global south; the establishment of international labor protection standards; greater transparency and accountability provided to citizens by national governments and global economic institutions; making all governance of globalization explicitly gender sensitive; and the transformation of "free trade" into "fair trade."

Overall, then, justice globalism shows a remarkable ability to bring together a large number of left-wing concerns around a more pronounced orientation toward the globe as a single, interconnected arena for political action. Its unique ideological morphology is no longer bound to a largely national framework but offers an alternative translation of the rising global imaginary critical of market-globalism.

Religious Globalism

The first decade of the new century also saw the rise of another challenger of market globalism from the political Right in the form of religious globalism. While this fledgling thought-system is not tied to one specific religion, the Islamist *salafi* variant of religious globalism—a strict orthodox doctrine advocating a return to the early Islam of the Koran propagated by al Qaeda that gained tremendous publicity in the wake of the 9/11 attacks—emerged as perhaps the most significant manifestation of religious globalism. However, my focus on jihadist globalism is neither meant to downplay the diversity of ideational currents within Islamism nor to present this particular strain as its most representative or authentic manifestation. Rather, my selection of jihadist globalism as articulated by groups such as al Qaeda, ISIS, Al-Shabab, Boko Haram, the Taliban, Jemaah Islamiyah, and others simply reflects the enduring influence of their doctrine around the world.

After the al Qaeda attacks of 9/11, scores of commentators around the world pointed to radical Islamism as one of the most potent ideological challengers to market globalism. Nevertheless, except for al Qaeda's worldwide network, most of these voices saw nothing "global" in Osama bin Laden's worldview. Rather, they castigated his brand of Islamism as "backward" and "parochial"—typical of a religious fanatic who represented one of the reactionary forces undermining globalization. However, al Qaeda's potent political belief system powered by religious symbols and metaphors not only represents a powerful camp of market globalism's challengers from the political Right, but also reflects the complex dynamics of globalization. Just as the ideology of justice globalists clearly transcends the national framework, the same is true for jihadist globalists who incorporate into their militant version of a religiously inspired style of globalist rhetoric to create a comprehensive ideology capable of translating the rising global imaginary into concrete political terms and programs. For this reason, this ideology can best be described as jihadist globalism—an ideological constellation falling under the umbrella category of religious globalism.

Let us focus in this section on al Qaeda. Its origins can be traced back to the *Maktab al-Khidamat* (MAK; "Office of Services"), a Pakistan-based support organization for Arab mujahideen fighting invading Soviet troops in Afghanistan. Set up in 1980 by Osama bin Laden and his Palestinian teacher and mentor Abdullah Azzam, MAK received sizable contributions from the government of Saudi Arabia as well as private donors from other Islamic countries. A decade later, Saddam Hussein's occupation of Kuwait was threatening the balance of power in the Middle East. To counter the threat, the House of Saud invited half a million "infidels"—American and other foreign troops—into their country, ostensibly for a short period of time and solely for protective purposes. Stung by the royal family's rejection of his proposal to organize thousands of Arab-Afghan veterans and outraged by their enlistment of foreign infidels in defense of the kingdom against a possible Iraqi attack, bin Laden severed all ties with the Saudi regime. Like tens of thousands of angry religious dissenters, bin Laden, too, denounced these acts of "religious heresy" and "moral corruption" and openly accused the rulers of selling out to the West. He would later identify as the worst feature of the present age of *jahiliyya* (ignorance; pagan idolatry) the degree of degradation and corruption to which the Saudi religious and political establishments had sunk.[20] The Saudi government immediately responded to bin Laden's criticism with political repression, arresting several opposition leaders and shutting down their organizations.

Bin Laden and his closest associates fled to Sudan but were forced to leave the country in 1996 because of mounting US pressure on the authoritarian African regime. Bin Laden and his entourage returned to Afghanistan, where they entered into an uneasy relationship with the Taliban, whose forces managed to capture Kabul in the same year. Imposing a strict version of *shari'a* (God-given, Islamic law) on the Afghan population, the Taliban based its rule on the "true tenets of Islam" alleged to have been realized in the world only once before by the seventh-century *salaf* (pious predecessors) who led the umma for three generations following the death of the Prophet. By the late 1990s, bin Laden had created al Qaeda ("the base") and openly pledged his allegiance to the Taliban, in exchange for the regime's willingness to shelter his organization from US retaliation following the devastating 1998 al Qaeda bombings of the American embassies in Kenya and Tanzania.

As Bruce Lawrence notes, the bulk of bin Laden's writings and public addresses emerged in the context of a virtual world moving from print to the Internet and from wired to wireless communication. Largely scriptural in mode, the sheikh's "messages to the world" are deliberately designed for the new global media. Bin Laden conveys his ideological claims in carefully crafted language that draws on the five traditional types of Muslim public discourse: the declaration, the juridical decree, the lecture, the written reminder, and the epistle.[21] Bin Laden's writings over the past fifteen years amount to a coherent thought-system that appealed to millions of Muslims. The ideological edifice of his jihadist globalism rests on the claim of an exceptional spiritual and material crisis: the Muslim *umma* (global community of believers) has been subjected to an unprecedented wave of attacks on its territories, values, and economic resources by a global "Judeo-Crusader alliance" led by the United States.[22]

But how, precisely, did bin Laden decontest the core concept *umma*? After all, this idea, together with the other core concepts *jihad* ("struggle") and *tawhid* ("oneness of God"), serves as the ideational anchor of al Qaeda's religious globalism.[23] As social historian Mohammed Bamyeh notes, the concept of the "Islamic community" has functioned historically as an equivalent of the Western idea of "the people," empowered to set limits to the tyrannical tendencies of governing elites.[24] Drawing on this traditional understanding of the *umma*, bin Laden emphasizes that political authority can never rest on popular sovereignty, for political rule is not the exclusive property of the people. Rather, the righteous *umma* exercises political power in the name of God only, thus building its political institutions on the foundation of Islamic sovereignty.[25] Since God's authority transcends all political borders and any humanly designed lines of demarcation, the *umma* supersedes not only ancient tribal solidarities and traditional kinship structures but, most importantly, modern Western conceptions of community rooted in the national imaginary. To be sure, contemporary Muslims carry national passports, but jihadist globalists claim their primary solidarity must lie with the *umma*, a community that encompasses the entire globe. As bin Laden explains, "You know, we are linked to all of the Islamic world, whether that be Yemen, Pakistan, or wherever. We are part of one unified *umma*."[26]

Expressing a yearning for strong leaders who set things right by fighting corrupt elites and returning power back to the "Muslim masses," jihadist globalists seek to restore the *umma* to its imagined past glory.[27] In their view, the process of regeneration has to start with a small but dedicated vanguard willing to sacrifice their lives as martyrs to the holy cause of awakening the people to their religious duties—not just in traditionally Islamic countries but also wherever members of the *umma* yearn for the establishment of God's rule on earth. With a third of the world's Muslims living as minorities in non-Islamic societies, bin Laden regarded the restoration of the *umma* as no longer a local, national, or even regional event. Rather, it required a concerted *global* effort spearheaded by a jihadist vanguard operating in various localities around the world. Hence, al Qaeda's desired Islamization of modernity took place in global space emancipated from the confining territoriality of Egypt or the Middle East that used to constitute the political framework of religious nationalists fighting modern secular regimes in the twentieth century. As French religion scholar Olivier Roy observes, "The Muslim *umma* (or community) no longer has anything to do with a territorial entity. It has to be thought of in abstract and imaginary terms."[28]

It is crucial to point to the global within the apparently anachronistic expressions of a supposedly antiglobalist terrorist. The series of famous post-9/11 "Osama bin Laden videotapes" broadcast worldwide between 2001 and 2008 testified to al Qaeda's immediate access to sophisticated information and telecommunication networks that kept the leadership informed, in real time, of relevant international developments. Bin Laden and his top lieutenants may have denounced the forces of modernity with great conviction, but the smooth operation of their organization was entirely dependent on advanced forms of information and communication technology developed in the context of globalization. Just as bin Laden's romantic salafist idea of a "pure Islam" is itself an articulation of the global imaginary, so has our global age, with its insatiable appetite for technology, mass-market commodities, and celebrities, indelibly shaped the ideological structure of jihadist globalism.

If the restored, purified *umma*—imagined to exist in a global space that transcended particular national or tribal identities—was the final goal of jihadist globalism, then *jihad* surely served as its principal means. For our purposes, it is not necessary to engage in long scholastic debates about the many meanings and "correct" applications of *jihad*. Nor do we need to excavate its long history in the Islamic world. It suffices to note that jihadist globalists endorse both "offensive" and "defensive" versions of *jihad*.[29] Their decontestation of this core concept draws heavily on religious interpretations of *jihad* as a divinely imposed *fard 'ayn* (individual obligation) on a par with the nonnegotiable duties of prayer and fasting: "To kill the Americans and their allies—civilians and military—is an individual duty incumbent upon every Muslim in all countries."[30] As became clear in the 2000s, such tactics include large-scale terrorist attacks, suicide bombings, and the public killing of hostages. Indeed, al Qaeda's jihadist-globalist message to Muslims all over the world was to release their hatred on Americans, Jews, and Christians: "This [hatred] is a part of our belief and our religion."[31]

Thus, bin Laden celebrates *jihad* as the "peak" or "pinnacle" of Islam, emphasizing time and again that armed struggle against global *kufr* is "obligatory today on our entire *umma*, for our *umma* will stand in sin until her sons, her money, and her energies provide what it takes to establish a *jihad* that repels the evil of the infidels from harming all the Muslims in Palestine and elsewhere."[32] This holy war represents the sole path toward the noble goal of returning the *umma* to "her religion and correct beliefs"—not just because the venerable way of *da'wa* (preaching; admonishing) has failed to reform the treacherous Muslim elites or convert the hostile crusaders but, most importantly, because Islam is seen as the religion of *jihad* in the way of God so that God's word and religion reign supreme. In an impassioned post-9/11 letter, bin Laden offers a detailed refutation of the notion that Islam should be a religion of moderation or balance. In his view, "[I]t is, in fact, part of our religion to impose our particular beliefs on others. . . . And the West's notions that

Islam is a religion of *jihad* and enmity toward the religions of the infidels and the infidels themselves is an accurate and true depiction." He also considered UN-sponsored calls for a "dialogue among civilizations" nothing but an "infidel notion" rooted in the "loathsome principles" of a secular West advocating an "un-Islamic" separation of religion and the state.[33] For bin Laden, the core concepts of *jihad* and *umma* were important manifestations of the revealed truth of *tawhid*, the oneness of God and his creation. It demands that Islamic sovereignty be established on earth in the form of a caliphate without national borders or internal divisions. This totalistic vision of a divinely ordained world system of governance whose timeless legal code covers all aspects of social life has prompted many commentators to condemn jihadist Islamism as a particularly aggressive form of "totalitarianism" or "Islamo-fascism" that poses a serious challenge to cultural pluralism and secular democracy.

Its central ideological claims notwithstanding, al Qaeda's religious globalism never lost sight of the fact that jihadists were fighting a steep uphill battle against the forces of market globalism. For example, bin Laden discussed in much detail the ability of "American media imperialism" to "seduce the Muslim world" with its consumerist messages. He also made frequent references to a "continuing and biased campaign" waged against jihadist globalism by the corporate media—"especially Hollywood"—for the purpose of misrepresenting Islam and hiding the "failures of the Western democratic system."[34] The al Qaeda leader left little doubt that what he considered to be the "worst civilization witnessed in the history of mankind" had to be fought for its "debased materialism" and "immoral culture" as much as for its blatant "imperialism." He repeatedly accused the United States of trying to "change the region's ideology" through the imposition of Western-style democracy and the "Americanization of our culture."[35]

A product of the ongoing deterritorialization of Islam, jihadist globalism constituted the most significant ideological attempt in the 2000s to articulate the rising global imaginary around core religious ideas such as *umma*, *jihad*, and *tawhid*. Al Qaeda's central ideological claims—all of which converged in the assertion that the rebuilding of a unified global *umma* involved global *jihad* against global *kufr*—resonated with the dynamics of a globalizing world. In particular, jihadist globalism held a special appeal for Muslim youths between the ages of fifteen and twenty-five who have lived for sustained periods of time in the individualized and often deculturated environments of Westernized Islam or an Islamized West.[36] Thus, far from being a regionally contained last gasp of a backward-looking, militant offshoot of political Islam, al Qaeda jihadism—or violent Christian fundamentalism—represents a potent globalism of worldwide appeal. Unlike national-populist attempts to hold on to a declining national imaginary, radical Islamist globalism contains an ideological alternative to both market globalism and justice globalism, which imagines community in unambiguously global terms.

CONCLUDING REFLECTIONS

During the 1990s, power elites concentrated in the global north stepped up their worldwide efforts to sell their pro-market version of globalization to the public. While not entirely disavowing some coercive measures referred to by Joseph Nye as "hard power"—particularly the application of economic pressure through the IMF, World Bank, and other international lending institutions—this phalanx of neoliberal forces generally sought to enhance the legitimacy of their worldview by means of "soft power," that is, the use of cultural and ideological appeals to effect their desired outcomes without commanding allegiance.[37] Ultimately, these power elites constructed and disseminated their new ideology of market globalism, which extolled the virtues of free trade and globally integrated markets.

For most of the decade, this double-pronged strategy of utilizing the soft power of ideas and ideals in tandem with the "sticky power" of economic pressure seemed to minimize ideological dissent.[38] Many people came to accept market globalism's five core claims, which articulated the rising global imaginary in concrete political terms. By the turn of the twenty-first century, however, the growing divergence between neoliberal truth claims and the everyday experience of growing inequality affecting people in many parts of the world began to undermine market globalism's legitimacy. This, in turn, facilitated the production of ideological counter-discourses powerful enough to seriously challenge the neoliberal worldview. Disseminated by social forces on the political Left, the competing perspective of justice globalism found its political manifestation in the growth of the AGM, which staged successive waves of worldwide alterglobalist protests.

Consistent with their soft-power strategy, influential market globalists like George Soros, Joseph Stiglitz, Jeffrey Sachs, and Paul Krugman responded to the justice-globalist challenge with public admissions that globalization did, indeed, require "some reforms" and "better management." Less reform-minded market globalists, however, began to contemplate hard-power tactics of social control designed to crack down on AGM dissenters. Globalizing markets were increasingly portrayed as requiring protection against the "violent hordes of antiglobalization." Suddenly, the allegedly inevitable and irreversible unfolding of self-regulating markets needed to be helped along by strong law enforcement measures that would "beat back" the enemies of democracy and the free market.

After al Qaeda's devastating 9/11 attacks on the world's most recognized symbols of a US-dominated globalized economy, this market-globalist tendency to tolerate or endorse hard-power tactics grew even stronger. In such a volatile and bellicose environment, many market globalist leaders felt they had little choice but to enter into a shaky ideological compromise with right-wing war hawks. This uneasy and sometimes stormy marriage of convenience marked the reconfiguration of market globalism into what might be called imperial globalism with an American face. Although the neoliberal project did not come to an end in the 2000s, the hard-powering of market globalism led to a modification of its original ideological fingerprint.

For one, the "necessary elimination" of "terrorists" by means of a so-called global war on terror prosecuted by the United States and its allies—as well as the control of the "radical" AGM forces—made untenable claim 3 that nobody is in charge of globalization. Putting the public on notice that their struggle against jihadist globalism would be a long-term commitment, the Bush administration left no doubt that the United States had taken it upon itself to protect the free market against the new barbarian forces bent on destroying Western civilization. Hence, it became necessary for market globalists to add claim 6 to their existing ideological arsenal: "globalization requires a war on terror." The necessary military infrastructure to engage in a massive, open-ended, and global conflict was already in place. As political scientist Chalmers Johnson points out in his sobering analysis of American Empire, the United States operated at least 725 military bases worldwide and maintains some form of military presence in 153 of the nearly 200 member countries of the United Nations.[39]

One of the most original versions of the new imperial-globalist claim that globalization requires a global war on terror flowed from the pen of Thomas P. M. Barnett, managing director of a global security firm and former professor of military strategy at the US Naval War College. *The Pentagon's New Map*, Barnett's best-selling reexamination of American national security, linked the author's military expertise to his long-standing interests in economic globalization.[40] The book presented a straightforward thesis: in the global age, America's national security was inextricably bound up with the continued global integration of markets and free flows of trade, capital, ideas, and people across national borders.

For Barnett, 9/11 marked a critical juncture in human history where America—the home of globalization's "source code"—was called upon to guide the rest of the world toward the noble goals of "universal inclusiveness" and "global peace." The main task was to "make globalization truly global"—by any means necessary.[41] In order to defeat the enemies of global interdependence, Barnett called upon the Pentagon to devise a new strategy that, once and for all, would abandon "antiquated international thinking." In his view, national security in the twenty-first century had to be reimagined in *global* terms as the ruthless destruction of all forces of disconnectedness and the nurturing of networks of political and security connectivity linked to the growing global economy. In short, the Pentagon's new global strategy required a new map—both in a cognitive and in a geographical sense—that divided the globe into three distinct regions.

Barnett called the first region on the Pentagon's new map the Functioning Core, defined as "globalization thick with network connectivity, financial transactions, liberal media flows, and collective security." Featuring stable democratic governments, transparency, rising standards of living, and more deaths by suicide than by murder, the Core was made up of North America, most of Europe, Australia, New Zealand, a small part of Latin America, and, with significant reservations, possible new core countries like India and China. Conversely, he referred to areas where "globalization was thinning or just plain absent" as the Non-Integrating Gap. This region was plagued by repressive political regimes, handcuffed markets, mass murder, and widespread poverty and disease. For Barnett, the Gap provided a dangerous breeding ground for "global terrorists" and other "forces of disconnected-ness" opposed to the "economic and security rule sets we call globalization." This region included the Caribbean Rim, virtually all of Africa, the Balkans, the Caucasus, parts of Central Asia, the Middle East, and parts of Southeast Asia. Along the Gap's "bloody boundaries," the military strategist located Seam States such as Mexico, Brazil, South Africa, Morocco, Algeria, Greece, Turkey, Pakistan, Thailand, Malaysia, the Philippines, and Indonesia. Lacking the Core's high levels of connectivity and security, these seam countries were the logical entry point for terrorists plotting their attacks.[42]

Despite its horrific toll, Barnett considered 9/11 a necessary wake-up call that forced the United States to make a long-term military commitment to "export security" to the Gap. The Core had no choice but to treat the entire Gap region as a "strategic threat environment." Hence, Barnett proposed a "global transaction strategy" built on the central imperative of "shrinking the Gap." To do so meant that the United States and its allies had to increase the Core's "immune system capabilities." In short, globalization's enemies had to be eliminated, and the Gap region had to be forcibly integrated into the Core. And this is, of course, where the new claim 6 comes in. As Barnett emphasized, "I believe it is absolutely essential that this country [the United States] lead the global war on terrorism, because I fear what will happen to our world if the forces of disconnectedness are allowed to prevail—to perturb the system at will."[43]

Throughout the remainder of its two terms, the Bush administration appeared to be committed to Barnett's vision of imperial globalism. But just when it seemed that a turn toward reformed market globalism was on the horizon in the shape of charismatic Democratic presidential candidate Barack Obama, a Global Financial Crisis (GFC) approaching the magnitude of the Great Depression hit. The unexpected 2008 economic meltdown of global proportions shattered both the market fundamentalists' unfaltering confidence in the inexorable global integration of finance, trade, and political structures. As the GFC broadened, morphing into the Great Recession and the Eurozone Debt Crisis, it effected a profound shift in the public mood away from market globalism. To add insult to injury, mainstream governments around the world put together under the auspices of the G-20 gigantic bailout packages for the corporate sector at the expense of ordinary taxpayers. Even reformist market globalists with a pronounced social conscience, like the incoming US president Obama, bowed to the dictates of global capitalism and signed off on hundreds of billions of dollars to rescue Wall Street.

While such efforts to prop up financial markets may have saved the global financial infrastructure, they also strengthened the progressive vision of justice globalism and, most importantly, the reactionary rhetoric of nationalists. New transnational social justice movements on the Left like *Los Indignados* and Occupy Wall Street emerged together with right-wing populist groups and antiglobalist forces such as the American Tea Party or France's refurbished *Front National* under the charismatic leadership of Marine Le Pen. Hence, the next chapter turns to a discussion of the growing stature of post-GFC national populism as the main challenger of both market globalism and justice globalism.

5

The Challenge of
Antiglobalist Populism

The 2008 Global Financial Crisis and the ensuing Great Recession intensified the global climate of social instability that had emerged some years earlier with worldwide anti-free trade protests, global waves of jihadist terrorism, and growing transnational migration flows. Proclaiming the "end of the globalization," influential journalists and academics speculated that these unsettling developments might ultimately turn into a chronic condition, ushering in a long period of economic stagnation, political polarization, cultural backlash, and social fragmentation. Even prominent neoliberals no longer disparaged the threatening prospects of retreating into more regulated forms of capitalism and fortified borders as a knee-jerk reaction of "globalization losers." Harvard economist Dani Rodrik went even further by seeking to impress upon his readers a return to a national regulation of economic activities. He argued forcefully that when the social arrangements of representative democracy clashed with unaccountable demands of market globalism, there was only one rational and practical solution: national problems should take precedence over global concerns.[1]

The GFC-induced prospect of greater national control appealed not only to respected mainstream economists like Dani Rodrik, but also to the leaders of radical national-populist forces on the Right around the world. What former Federal Reserve Chair Alan Greenspan characterized with hindsight as the "irrational exuberance" of market fundamentalists like himself was giving way to widespread fears that their globalist experiment of transcending the nation-state had spiralled out of control and needed to be curbed. The growing public perception that the worldwide integration of markets and societies had failed to deliver on its promises was reflected in popular culture in numerous ways such as the record online sales enjoyed by Stop Being a Globalist and Not a Globalist T-shirts. The emotional promises of right-wing populists to "the forgotten people" were finding more resonance than the rational assurances of market globalists that the liberalization of trade was bound to benefit everyone.

This chapter opens with a brief consideration of the pivotal role of both global financial and migration crises in strengthening nationalist tendencies around the world. Arguing that the surge of right-wing populism starting in the 2010s was intricately connected to negative perceptions of "globalization" in the world, the bulk of the chapter is taken up with a careful conceptual mapping of "antiglobalist populism." This variant of national-populism is reflected most prominently in "Trumpism" and other ideational permutations around the world. The chapter ends with a brief speculation on possible future trajectories of the ideological confrontation over the direction and meaning of twenty-first-century globalization.

THE SIGNIFICANCE OF GLOBAL CRISES

The 2008 GFC marked a watershed not only in the development of disintegrative tendencies in the global system but also in the globalized ideological landscape of the new century.[2] But the potential consequences of a deregulated global financial infrastructure advocated by market globalists had already been visible in the 1997–1998 Southeast Asia Crisis. In the early 1990s, the governments of Thailand, Indonesia, Malaysia, South Korea, and the Philippines had gradually abandoned control over the domestic movement of capital in order to attract foreign direct investment. The ensuing influx of short-term global investment translated into soaring stock and real estate markets all over Southeast Asia. But when those investors realized prices had become inflated beyond their actual value, they withdrew a total of $105 billion from these countries. As a result, economic output fell, unemployment increased, and wages plummeted. By late 1997, the entire region found itself in the throes of a financial crisis that threatened to push the global economy into recession. This disaster was only narrowly averted by a combination of international bailout packages and the immediate sale of Southeast Asian commercial assets to foreign corporate investors at rock-bottom prices.[3]

A decade later, the world was not as lucky. The 2008 GFC was the logical outcome of two decades of neoliberal financial deregulation, unrestrained competition, and marketization of large corporations, which invited the increasingly speculative, high-risk activities of the financial sector during the early 2000s.[4] Derivatives, financial futures, credit default swaps, and other esoteric financial instruments became extremely popular when new computer-based algorithmic models suggested more sophisticated ways of managing the risk involved in buying an asset in the future at a price agreed to in the present. Relying far less on conventional savings deposits, financial institutions borrowed from each other and sold these loans as securities, thus passing the risk on to investors in these securities. Other "innovative" financial instruments such as hedge funds leveraged with borrowed funds fueled a variety of speculative activities. Billions of investment dollars flowed into complex residential mortgage-backed securities that promised investors up to a 25 percent return on equity.[5]

Assured by monetarist policies aimed at keeping interest rates low and credit flowing, investment banks eventually expanded their search for capital by buying risky "subprime" loans from mortgage brokers who, lured by the promise of big commissions, were accepting applications for housing mortgages with little or no down payment and without credit checks. Increasingly popular in the United States, most of these loans were adjustable-rate mortgages tied to fluctuations of short-term interest rates. Investment banks snapped up these high-risk loans knowing that they could resell these assets—and thus the risk involved—by bundling them into composite securities no longer subject to government regulation. Indeed, one of the most complex of these instruments of securitization—so-called collateralized debt obligations (CDOs)—often hid the problematic loans by bundling them together with lower-risk assets and reselling them to unsuspecting investors. Trusting the positive credit ratings reports issued by Standard and Poor's or Moody's, global investors failed to see how these profit-maximizing firms were themselves implicated in the expanding speculative bubble.[6]

The high yields flowing from these new securities funds attracted more and more investors around the world, thus rapidly globalizing more than a trillion US dollars' worth of what came to be known as "toxic assets." In mid-2007, the financial steamroller finally ran out of fuel when seriously overvalued American real estate began to drop, and foreclosures shot up dramatically. Investors finally realized the serious risks attached to the new securities markets and lost confidence. Consequently, the value of securitized mortgage funds fell, and banks desperately tried in vain to somehow eliminate the debts showing on their balance sheets.

Some of the largest and most venerable financial institutions, insurance companies, and government-sponsored underwriters of mortgages such as Lehman Brothers, Bear Stearns, Merrill Lynch, Goldman Sachs, AIG, Citicorp, J P Morgan Chase, IndyMac Bank, Morgan Stanley, Fannie Mae, and Freddie Mac—to name but a few—either declared bankruptcy or had to be bailed out by the US taxpayer. Both the conservative Bush and the liberal Obama administrations championed spending hundreds of billions of dollars on a rescue package for distressed mortgage securities in return for a government share in the businesses involved. The UK and most other industrialized countries followed suit with their own multibillion-dollar bailout packages, hoping that such massive injections of capital into ailing financial markets would help prop up financial institutions deemed "too large to be allowed to fail." But these generous rescue packages allowed large financial conglomerates to lose even more money without having to declare bankruptcy. The cost passed on to the world's taxpayers was truly staggering and committed future generations to repay trillions of dollars used for financing these bailout packages.

One of the major consequences of the failing financial system was that banks trying to rebuild their capital base could hardly afford to keep lending large amounts of money. The flow of global credit froze to a trickle and businesses and individuals who relied on credit found it much more difficult to obtain. This credit shortage, in turn, impacted the profitability of many businesses, forcing them to cut back production and lay off workers. Industrial output declined and unemployment shot up as the world's stock markets dropped dramatically. By 2009, $14.3 trillion, or 33 percent of the value of the world's companies, was wiped out by the GFC. The developing world was especially hard hit with a financial shortfall of $700 billion by the end of 2010.[7]

As the GFC solidified into the Great Recession in the following months, the leaders of the world's twenty largest economies—the G-20—devised a common strategy to combat a global depression. Although these efforts prevented the wholesale collapse of the world's financial infrastructure, economic growth in the early 2010s in many parts of the world remained anemic and unemployment numbers came down only very slowly. Soon, it also became clear that the Great Recession had spawned a second related crisis in the form of a severe sovereign debt crisis and banking problems, especially in the European Union. This rapidly escalating financial turmoil in the Eurozone affected first Greece and then rapidly spilled over into Spain, Portugal, Ireland, and other EU countries. The ensuing economic austerity policies exacerbated people's resentment of neoliberal globalization and sharpened political polarization around the world.

To make matters worse, the new era of global economic volatility that started with the GFC was joined by a migration crisis. The Syrian refugee crisis, for example, was triggered by a protracted civil war. It culminated in 2016, when nearly 6 million Syrians—out of a total population of 23 million—were internally displaced. Close to 5 million people fled the country in search of both personal safety and economic opportunity. While the majority of Syrian refugees ended up in camps in the neighboring countries of Jordan, Lebanon, Iraq, and Turkey, they hoped to find a better future in the prosperous states of the European Union. But some countries like Hungary and Croatia resorted to drastic measures to keep refugees out of their territory by erecting border fences that stretched over many miles. Ultimately, these actions not only proved to be ineffective in stopping such massive population movements, but also heightened anti-immigration sentiments across the continent. Indeed, the Syrian refugee crisis made visible existing cultural biases and strengthened deep-seated us versus them binaries that fueled right-wing populist messages about the impending "replacement" of Western civilization by "foreign invaders." Additional transnational migration streams from the global south in the north throughout the 2010s prompted receiving governments to limit the number of those seeking to cross their borders.

WHAT IS NATIONAL-POPULISM?

Many political commentators likened the dual finance and migration crises to a gathering storm that threatened the dominance of market globalism, which had ruled the world for nearly three decades.[8] But little did these pundits know that the full force of the storm was about to bear down on the global north, reflected most spectacularly in the unexpected 2016 victory of the pro-Brexit forces in the UK and the stunning 2016 election of Donald J. Trump in the United States. The growing political power of national-populism—and the crucial role played by a meteoric rise of the new digital media—prompted influential commentators to coin popular catchphrases such as the "new populist wave" and the "populist explosion."[9]

The French philosopher Jean-Pierre Taguieff coined the term "national-populism" in 1984 in reference to the political discourse of Jean-Marie Le Pen and his newly founded French political party, Front National (FN), renamed in 2018 under the leadership of his daughter Marine Le Pen as Rassemblement National.[10] Soon after the FN party's founding, some of its key politicians openly embraced Taguieff's critical term with much pride.[11] National-populists imagine a mythical national unity based on an essentialized identity through permutations of the ethnic and the cultural. They claim to defend and protect the pure "common people" against the treachery of "corrupt elites" and "parasitical" social institutions. Privileging a direct relationship between the leader and the people, national-populists sometimes combine social values of the left with the political values of the right.[12] Indeed, it is important to note that more pluralistic and culturally inclusive forms of left-wing populism were also on the march in the 2010s. This development was accompanied by new academic publications recommending populism as an effective strategy to revitalize a Left enervated by the apparent petering out of the Occupy Movement.[13]

As some observers were quick to point out, the post-GFC surge of right-wing national-populism was intricately connected to shifting perceptions of the role of globalization in the world.[14] Neoliberal policies had shifted the balance of power between big business and labor decisively in favor of the former. Middle-class and working-class people in the global north paid the price as their wages stagnated and stable jobs—especially in manufacturing—disappeared or turned into precarious and casual work arrangements. Moreover, wealthy liberal democracies failed to implement adequate social protections, like new labor-market programs and redistributive tax policies. The resulting polarization of class structure into globalization winners at the top 10 percent of income earners and the rest of globalization losers prompted social thinkers like Guy Standing to suggest that the entire social stratification structure was changing. Crucially, he pointed to the birth of a new class of insecure workers: the *Precariat*.[15]

The souring of the public perception of neoliberal globalization was demonstrated by the increasingly negative tone of news stories containing the buzzword.[16] As Pippa Norris and Ronald Inglehart point out, the globalization backlash was a relatively short-term reaction rooted in long-term social structural changes in the living conditions and security of citizens in liberal democracies, and the profound transformation of cultural values that was part of these developments. In short, the antiglobalist populist explosion of the 2010s was rooted in a latent "authoritarian reflex."[17] Right-wing populism shifted into hyper-drive in the aftermath of the Great Recession when increasing levels of economic inequality and the shift of income and wealth toward the richest stratum became palpable for large segments of the middle- and working classes in the global north.

At the beginning of the 2010s, it appeared that justice globalists affiliated with Occupy Wall Street—a transnational movement whose founders had coined the immensely popular slogan "The 99% versus the 1%"—would succeed in attracting to their worldview millions of people passed over by the promise of market globalism. Ultimately, however, it was media-savvy antiglobalist national-populists like Donald Trump, Nigel Farage, and Marine Le Pen who managed to capitalize on people's growing globalization fatigue. They supplied right-wing scapegoating narratives that resonated with people's anger and resentment directed against neoliberal practices of "outsourcing of good jobs" and "opening borders" to transnational flows of capital, commodities, ideas, and people. Deliberately exacerbating existing cultural and economic cleavages, national-populists presented globalism as a vicious ideology hatched by unpatriotic liberals and cosmopolitan elites.

By the closing of the 2010s, antiglobalist right-wing populism seemed to be everywhere and anywhere, demonstrating its tremendous adaptability to cultural and geographic contexts as different as Victor Órban's Hungary, Marine Le Pen's France, Matteo Salvini's Italy, Jarosław Kaczyński's Poland, Nigel Farage's United Kingdom, Rodrigo Duterte's Philippines, Jair Bolsonaro's Brazil, and, of course, Donald Trump's America.

MAPPING TRUMP'S ANTIGLOBALIST POPULISM

It would go far beyond the scope of this chapter to examine the ideological makeup of multiple permutations of antiglobalist populism in various geographical and cultural contexts. Instead, my investigation focuses on Trumpism in the United States reflected in a number of key speeches delivered by Trump during his 2016 presidential campaign as well as during his four years in office.

For starters, these documents reveal the prominence of two familiar populist concepts at the heart of his discourse: "the people" versus "the elites."[18] Trump decontests "the people," first and foremost, in national terms by linking the noun to the adjective "American."[19] Accordingly, the American people are imagined as a homogenous community "united in common purposes and dreams" and enjoying the privilege of living in the "greatest nation on earth."[20] This asserted likeness also manifests in racial and gender terms. As Benjamin Moffitt's visual content analysis has shown, Trump's images of "the people" are significantly whiter and more masculine than the political images associated with left populists like Bernie Sanders.[21]

Secondly, Trump narrows the meaning of "the people" to the "common people" understood as "workers," "working people," and "middle-class people." Indeed, these key terms are embedded in an overarching nationalist narrative: "The legacy of Pennsylvania steelworkers lives in the bridges, railways, and skyscrapers that make up our great American landscape."[22]

Thirdly, Trumpism links "the people" to "sovereignty" and "independence."[23] These concepts, too, are consistently infused with nationalistic themes such as the celebration of America's "superior" political system manifested in "a government of the people, by the people, and for the people."[24] Trump's political speeches are rife with essentialist depictions of the "pure" character of the "American people" in such moralistic superlatives as "great," "patriotic," "loyal," "hard-working," "daring," "brave," "strong," "energetic," "decent," "selfless," "devoted," and "honest." Consider, for example, this striking, yet factually incorrect, passage highlighting some of the allegedly superior qualities of the American people: "Americans are the people that tamed the West, that dug out the Panama Canal, that sent satellites across the solar system, that build great dams, and so much more."[25]

Trump continues his decontestation of the core concept "American people" by contrasting it with its Other: the elites. He asserts that the American people's proven loyalty to, and hard work for, the nation has been repaid by the establishment with "total betrayal."[26] Slandered as "deplorables" and demeaned by the liberal political discourse of political correctness, "American patriots who love our country and want a better future for all of our people" are portrayed as having been robbed of their dignity and respect. However, Trump asserts that thanks to their "common sense"—expressed in their "clear understanding of how democracy really works"—the American people will debunk this elitist deception and refuse to sit idly by as they are "being ripped off by everybody in the world."[27]

Trump charges that these elites, "the establishment," "politicians," and "leadership class" have undermined the "true will" of the people with the help of the "corporate media."[28] These cultural insiders are accused of "rigging" the system of representative democracy—most clearly manifested in the "Washington swamp"—to the end of advancing their morally corrupt practices of "selling out the wealth of our nation generated by working people" and filling their own pockets.[29] Most important, Trump links the meaning of "the establishment" to the notion of "globalist enemies" working against the true interests of America. Some of them are explicitly identified as domestic actors such as "Wall Street bankers" or "Washington politicians." Others are characterized as "foreign agents," which includes both individual members of the "international financial elite" such as George Soros or even entire countries like China, Mexico, and Japan, which are denounced for the alleged misdeeds of "subsidizing their goods," "devaluing their currencies," "violating their agreements," and "sending rapists, drug dealers, and other criminals into America."[30]

During his 2016 presidential campaign, Trump consistently stereotyped his political opponent, Hillary Clinton, as the "un-American" epitome of the "corrupt globalist elites"—a politically effective move that allowed him to collapse the distinction between domestic and global foes by creating a unified enemy image under the sign of "globalization." An abbreviated list of Hillary Clinton's alleged "crimes against the American people" includes: proposing mass amnesty for illegal immigrants; advocating for open borders; spreading terrorism; pursuing an aggressive, interventionist foreign policy; making America less secure; robbing workers of their future by sending their jobs abroad; ending American sovereignty by handing power over to the UN and other "globalist" institutions; abandoning Israel in its national struggle for survival; supporting free trade agreements inimical to American interests; titling the economic playing field toward other countries at America's expense; and advancing global special interests.

Trump persistently employs the terms "global" or "globalist" to flesh out the precise meaning of the elites' betrayal as reflected in the crimes of "crooked Hillary" and the global establishment she represents. This semantic link allows us to identify claim 1 of Trump's antiglobalist populism: "Corrupt elites betray the hardworking American people by shoring up a global order that makes them rich and powerful while compromising America's sovereignty and security and squandering its wealth." This claim helps Trump to present his electoral campaign against Hillary Clinton, the treacherous "globalist" *par excellence*, as something much bigger than just a familiar political contest that repeats itself every four years. Rather, he frames the 2016 presidential election as a Manichean struggle that pits America against two globalist enemies: a hostile world order and a domestic leadership class that "worships globalism over Americanism."[31]

During Trump's many stump appearances of the 2016 campaigning season, this assertion of an irreconcilable opposition between Americanism and globalism grew into claim 2—his credo appearing in almost every speech: "Americanism, not globalism, will be our credo." "Credo" carries religious connotations that signify the very essence of a sacred belief system. The constant repetition of this Americanist credo—and its numerous permutations such as "Hillary defends globalism, not Americanism" or "Hillary wants America to surrender to globalism"—indicates the enormous significance of globalization-related concepts in Trump's political discourse.[32] For this reason, it makes sense to refer to this particular strain of national-populism as antiglobalist populism.

Warning his audience not to surrender to "the false song of globalism," Trump emphasizes that "The nation-state remains the true foundation for happiness and harmony."[33] Thus, he decontests globalism as both a set of misguided public policies and a "hateful foreign ideology" devised by members of "the global power structure" who plot "in secret to destroy America."[34] Thus, globalists serve the larger material process of globalization, defined by Trump as an elite-engineered project of "abolishing the nation-state" and creating an international system that functions "to the detriment of the American worker and the American economy."[35] In short, Trumpism denounces both the economic and political dimensions of globalization by arranging associated concepts such as "jobs," "free trade," "financial elites," "open borders," and "immigration" into potent truth-claims.

With respect to its economic dimension, Trump portrays globalization as "wiping out the American middle class and jobs" while making the "financial elites who donate to politicians, very, very, wealthy. I used to be one of them."[36] Almost all of the speeches analyzed in this chapter contain substantial discussions of the dire economic impacts of globalization as reflected in disadvantageous international trade deals, outsourced American jobs, stagnant wages and salaries, the crumbling of America's manufacturing base, hostile foreign corporate takeovers, and unfair, corrupt economic practices devised by the likes of China and Mexico aided by treacherous domestic politicians who have "sold America to the highest bidder."[37] But such lengthy tirades against the nation's "globalist enemies" are always followed by passionate assurances that America's dire situation could be reversed by a strong antiglobalist leader. This confirms populism's affinity for authoritarianism and patriarchy. The latter is reflected in Trump's direct appeals to the women's vote: "Women also value security. They want a Commander-in-Chief that will defeat Islamic terrorism, stop the massive inflow of refugees, protect our borders, and who will reduce the rising crime and violence in our cities."[38]

With regard to politics and culture, Trump links globalization to what he calls the "complete and total disasters" of immigration, crime, and terrorism that are "destroying our nation."[39] Immigration, in particular, receives ample treatment in the form of vigorous denunciations of the establishment's "globalist policies of open borders" that endanger the safety and security of the American people. Once again, "Hillary" becomes the central metaphor of Trump's decontestation of globalization as a nefarious process of national border erasure: "National security is also immigration security—and Hillary wants neither. Hillary Clinton has put forward the most radical immigration platform in the history of the United States. She has pledged to grant mass amnesty and, in her first 100 days, end virtually all immigration enforcement, and thus create totally open borders in the United States."[40]

For Trump, the realization of his campaign slogan, Make America Great Again, requires the systematic separation of the national from the global in all aspects of social life in the United States. Politically, this severance requires the American people to support a nationalistic leader who is "'not running to be President of the World,' but 'to be President of the United States': 'I am for America—and America first.'"[41] In other words, he demands that the inherent greatness and goodness of the American people must be reactivated in the patriotic struggle against the essential evil of globalization. As Trump puts it, "The central base of world power is here in America, and it is our corrupt political establishment that is the greatest power behind the efforts at radical globalization and the disenfranchisement of working people."[42]

Yet, as is the case with Trump's economic narrative, the negative political consequences of globalization are always combined with assurances of the impending glorious rebirth of the nation. Trump's antiglobalist optimism is articulated in a third central ideological claim: "The defeat of globalism and its treacherous ideologues will usher in a bright national future."

It is important to note that Donald Trump did not abandon his antiglobalist populist oratory after his 2016 electoral victory. Quite to the contrary, his nationalist attacks on globalism became enshrined in almost all his major public speeches. For example, in 2018, Trump delivered a high-profile address at the seventy-third session of the UN General Assembly that contained the following ideological centerpiece:

> We will never surrender America's sovereignty to an unelected, unaccountable, global bureaucracy. America is governed by Americans. We reject the ideology of globalism, and we embrace the doctrine of patriotism. . . . To unleash this

incredible potential in our people, we must defend the foundations that make it all possible. Sovereign and independent nations are the only vehicle where freedom has ever survived, democracy has ever endured, or peace has ever prospered. And so, we must protect our sovereignty and our cherished independence above all.[43]

At a midterm election rally in Texas one month later, Trump unabashedly referred to himself as a "nationalist" and urged his audience not to be ashamed to use the word. As he explained, the term "nationalist" signified the opposite of "globalist": "You know what a globalist is, right? You know what a globalist is? A globalist is a person that wants the globe to do well, frankly, not caring about our country so much. And you know what? We can't have that."[44] Indeed, there is little evidence that the American president embraces antiglobalist populism for purely instrumental reasons. Rather than representing a mere instrumental strategy or rhetorical style, Trumpism reveals not only its deep commitment to specific antiglobalist ideas and values but also the richness of the ideational environment in which it is rooted.[45]

THE POPULIST PARADOX

Like all national populisms, Trumpism contains what I call a populist paradox. It manifests as the disconnect between the ideological denunciation of globalization while utilizing globalist symbols and discourses in its transnational outreach. Hence, antiglobalist populists around the world actually serve as the potent catalysts for the globalization of national-populism. Their fiery political messages may sound antiglobalist, but their social practices are globalizing as they communicate with and learn from each other in a global context.

Let us consider three major features of this populist paradox. First, antiglobalist populists like Trump are experts in using the echo chamber of the global social media for their ideological purposes. Whether they accuse footloose cosmopolitans of cheating the toiling masses or reproach the "liberal media" for spreading "fake news," their preferred means of combat are Twitter/X, Meta/Facebook, and YouTube. Fattening the digital platforms of our "post-truth" age with "alternative facts," they greatly benefit from growing and increasingly compartmentalized electronic global flows. Contrary to their powerful siren song of anti-globalization, national populists have emerged as the new priests of digital globalization.

Second, antiglobalist populists often engage in transnational economic activities for personal gain. Donald Trump is the epitome of this practice since his brand name stands for a global network of hotels and luxury golf resorts. Although his slogan Make America Great Again seems to advocate a shift from corporate globalism and free trade to economic nationalism and protectionism, he does not practice what he preaches. Similarly, his desire to build a "beautiful wall" along the 1,989-mile US border with Mexico to keep migrants and refugees out stands in stark contrast to his lucrative business practices of employing them in his corporate empire.[46]

The third aspect of the populist paradox manifests as the disconnect between the professed populist commitment to economic nationalism and its simultaneous embrace of market-globalist tenets such as the deregulation of the economy, the privatization of state-owned enterprises, and massive tax cuts disproportionally benefiting globalist elites. On one hand, Trumpism's rhetorical rejection of neoliberal trade policies resulted in policy reversals of long-standing trade practices between the United States—the world's most voracious consumer—and China—the world's leading manufacturer. In 2018, Trump referred to the growing trade imbalance between these two nations as the "greatest theft in the history of the world—committed by China." Subsequently, he fired the opening shot in what threatened to become a full-blown trade war by announcing a 10 percent tariff on $200 billion worth of Chinese goods. In 2019, the Trump administration slapped additional tariffs of up to 25 percent on $250 billion worth of Chinese products, and threatened to levy further tariffs worth $325 billion. Of course, it did not take long for China to impose retaliatory tariffs on US goods, in the process, doubling duties on American agricultural and fish products.

On the other hand, Trump openly embraced neoliberal principles that defied his economic nationalism at a joint 2018 press conference with Japan's Prime Minister Shinzō Abe:

> There's never been a better time to invest in the United States. Thanks to our massive tax cuts, historic deregulation, a strong trade policy, which has just really begun—because I will tell you over the years it has been an extraordinarily weak trade policy—the opening of American energy, and a return to the rule of law, our economy is absolutely booming. Best it's ever been.[47]

Its vehement rejection of "globalism" notwithstanding, the Trump administration achieved impressive legislative outcomes that contained a significant portion of the neoliberal globalist agenda. Perhaps two of its most relevant neoliberal globalist policy successes were the 2017 Tax Cuts and Jobs Act (TCJA) and the 2018 Economic Growth, Regulatory Relief, and Consumer Protection Act (ERCA). TCJA lowered the rate of most individual income tax rates, including the top marginal rate from 39.6 percent to 38 percent. Most importantly, the new law lowered corporate tax rates from 35 percent to 21 percent, a significant reduction that led to record-levels of corporate profits and a short-term growth of business investments while increasing social inequality and wealth differentials among the general population.

ERCA opened the gate to the biggest rollback of bank regulations since the 2008 Global Financial Crisis. Dismantling the safety and regulatory measures put in place by the Obama administration's 2010 Dodd-Frank bill aimed at Wall Street reform and consumer protection, the new neoliberal measure eased restrictions by raising the threshold to $250 billion from $50 billion under which banks are deemed too important to the financial system to fail. Those institutions also would not have to undergo so-called stress tests or submit "living wills"—safety valves designed to forestall financial disaster. Finally, ERCA eased mortgage loan data reporting requirements for the over-whelming majority of commercial banks.

In addition, Trump's neoliberal globalist agenda was delivered by a flood of Executive Orders (EOs). American heads of government can issue EOs to direct officers and agencies of the executive branch in the management of the operations within the federal government itself. At the end of his first six months in office, Trump announced the elimination of hundreds of existing regulations on industry and business—most of those measures were imple-mented via EOs. Of the nearly 130 EOs signed by the president at the end of his third year in office in 2019, more than half advanced neoliberal agendas.

In short, Trumpism is built on the populist paradox of advancing some core principles of economic nationalism while also furthering significant items of the market globalist agenda. Some astute political observers, like Adriano Cozzolino, have gone so far as to suggest that Trumpism represents an unex-pected evolution of neoliberalism. Its combination of fiercer free-market poli-cies with elements of economic nationalism have yielded a peculiar hybrid of "nationalist neoliberalism."[48]

CONCLUDING REFLECTIONS OF THE
FUTURE OF ANTIGLOBALIST POPULISM

Let us conclude this chapter with a brief speculation on three possible future trajectories of the ideological confrontation involving the three globalisms and its antiglobalist populist challenger discussed in part II of this book. The first framework, the backlash scenario, suggests the continuation of the severe social backlash experienced in the new century as a result of the unbridled economic and cultural dynamics of neoliberal globalization. This explosive reaction against market globalism unleashed ultra-nationalist political forces not dissimilar to those of European fascism between the 1920s and 1940s.

In his celebrated history of early capitalism, the political economist Karl Polanyi chronicled how commercial interests came to dominate European

Table 5.1. Examples of Donald Trump's Neoliberal Executive Orders (2017–2019)

EO Number, Year of Issue, and Title	Affected Policy Area(s)	Mandated Changes	Involved Neoliberal Norms
13771 (2017), Reducing Regulation and Controlling Regulatory Costs	all domestic and foreign policies	for every new regulation issued by a government agency, at least two prior regulations must be eliminated	deregulation, reduction of public spending, downsizing government
13783 (2017), Promoting Energy Independence and Economic Growth	energy, environment, security	suspend, revise, or rescind existing regulations that burden the development or use of domestically produced energy resources	deregulation, privatization, enticement of foreign investment, enforcement of property and private landownership
13812 (2017), Revocation of EO Creating Labor Management Forums	labor	revoke Obama-era EO13522 to create labor-management forums to improve delivery of government services	restriction of labor/union organization; secure labor "flexibility"
13828 (2018), Reducing Poverty in America by Promoting Opportunity and Economic Mobility	social (welfare), housing, family	clear paths to self-sufficiency by cutting public assistance programs and moving poor people into the workforce	reduction of public spending through reduction of social services and welfare programs, replace welfare with "workfare," privatization of public services, downsizing government
13836 (2018), Developing Efficient, Effective, and Cost-Reducing Approaches to Federal Sector Collective Bargaining	labor	encourage highest levels of employee performance on the job, cut taxpayer-funded union negotiation time, and preserve management rights to ensure more efficient outcomes in collective bargaining processes	restriction of labor/union organization, secure labor "flexibility," reduction of public spending
13872 (2019), Economic Empowerment of Asian Americans and Pacific Islanders (AAPI)	all economic policies	establish Presidential Commission on AAPI to develop strategies for encouraging innovation and entrepreneurship in AAPI communities	promotion of entrepreneurship and market-oriented enterprises; expansion of neoliberal logic to "disadvantaged" groups
13878 (2019), Establish a White House Council on Eliminating Regulatory Barriers to Affordable Housing	housing, transportation, environment, labor, tax	eliminate regulatory "barriers" on housing industry such as "burdensome" zoning and growth management controls and rent controls; "excessive" wetland and environment regulations; and tax policies that discourage investment	deregulation, privatization of public services, reduction of taxes, downsizing government

Source: US Federal Register (2019), https://www.federalregister.gov/presidential-documents/executive-orders/donald-trump/2019

societies. The increasingly unbridled principles of free-marketization destroyed complex social relations of mutual obligation and undermined communal values such as civic engagement, reciprocity, mutual aid, and redistribution. As large segments of the population found themselves without an adequate system of social security and communal support, they rallied behind hyper-nationalist political leaders who promised to curb the excesses of capitalism. Polanyi suggested that the stronger the free-market impulse became, the more it would be able to dominate society by means of a ruthless capitalist logic that effectively disconnected people's economic activities from their embedded social relations.[49]

Like nineteenth-century classical liberalism, 1990s market globalism represented an extreme experiment in unleashing the utopia of "self-regulating markets" on society. In fact, the acolytes of neoliberalism were prepared to turn the entire world into their laboratory. As we noted in the previous chapter, left-wing justice globalists challenged market globalism vigorously in the streets of the world's major cities. From the political Right, the religious-globalist forces of radical Islamism launched a series of terrorist attacks against what they considered to be a morally corrupt ideology of western secular materialism that threatened to engulf the entire world. By the mid-2010s, however, it was neither of these two familiar challengers of market globalism that won out. Rather, what triumphed was the antiglobalist populist message of providing nationalist protection against the extraordinary speed and severity of social change brought on by globalization.

What might be the ideological consequences of a further strengthening of antiglobalist populism over the next decade? The backlash scenario suggests that all three forms of globalisms would suffer from antiglobalist policies of increasing restrictions on major forms of mobility; weakening representative democracy and rejecting institutional forms of international coordination that might be capable of tackling our mounting global problems. However, as will be discussed in detail in chapters 7 and 8, even if the backlash scenario were to materialize in the 2020s and beyond, it would be premature to speak of a coming era of deglobalization. After all, the dominant form of contemporary globalization is disembodied globalization—the movement of abstracted capital and culture, including words, images, electronic texts, or encoded capital, including crypto-currencies, through processes of disembodied exchange. And the latest available empirical data on digital global flows show that disembodied globalization has neither stalled nor declined, but significantly increased during the years of national-populism and the COVID-19 pandemic.

The second future trajectory is built on the possibility of massive and persistent losses of antiglobalist populists at the ballot box as a result of a more globally oriented outlook. Such a rebound scenario might have already started with the electoral defeats of prominent antiglobalist populist leaders such as Donald Trump and Jair Bolsonaro. If this electoral trend continues, the question is what sort of political ideology would take the place of anti-globalist populism?

There seem to be two possibilities. The first is propagated by leading left-wing populists like Bernie Sanders in the United States who strongly oppose the xenophobic and anti-pluralist message of national-populists yet embrace the twentieth-century Keynesian ideal of a strong nation-state committed to regulating capitalism for the benefit of working people. The second possibility would be the return of centrist political leaders committed to the restoration of a reformed version of market globalism. The first option would indicate the staying power of the national imaginary, whereas the second would demonstrate the strength of the global imaginary. Given that this rebound scenario is built upon the sagging fortunes of right-wing *nationalists*—and thus the waning appeal of the national imaginary—it appears unlikely that left-wing *nationalists* would be returned to power. For this reason, let us briefly play out the more likely second option, which could be called "market globalism with a human face."

Having been confronted with the populist backlash to the negative consequences of unbridled global market integration, newly empowered market globalists in the late 2020s might exert more caution and make some moderate adjustments to their ultimate goal: the creation of a single global free market. Most likely, they would pledge to restore the liberal postwar international order of the past and propose more "socially responsible" forms of neoliberal globalization to the public. There is ample evidence for such a course of action. For example, market globalists like Nobel–prize winning economist Joseph Stiglitz have long conceded that globalization has been badly "mismanaged" and requires a serious overhaul.[50] Still, these reformist market globalists nonetheless insist that their original project of liberalizing trade and integrating markets is still valid. As James Mittelman has pointed out, Stiglitz and his like-minded colleagues tend to reduce structural problems in the world's economic architecture to mere management issues: A vociferous critic of market fundamentalism, Stiglitz nonetheless routinely expresses his unshaken faith in the redeeming value of a competitive system. At the end of the day, then, his agenda is to stabilize global capitalism by modifying neo-liberal globalization without tugging at the roots of its underlying structures.[51]

The programmatic outline of such reformed market globalism for the 2020s and beyond is already in the making at important ideological sites of global capitalism such as the World Economic Forum. Built on the alleged benefits of digital globalization, the new vision, Globalization 4.0, has been heavily promoted by Klaus Schwab, the German founder and executive chairman of the WEF. In fact, the official theme of the 2019 WEF Annual Meeting in

Davos, Switzerland, was Globalization 4.0: Shaping the Global Architecture in the Age of the Fourth Industrial Revolution.

This reformist vision is based on the construction of a new global architecture of capitalism that would be more attuned to the needs of ordinary people around the world. Schwab asserts that the world finds itself today in the throes of the "fourth industrial revolution"—the "complete digitization of the social, political, and economic." This revolution is said to transform existing social structures in profound ways that would blur the lines between physical, digital, and biological spheres. Admitting that the free-market consensus of the 1990s and 2000s had been smashed by the populist challenge and was beyond repair, Schwab further concedes that, although neoliberal globalization has "lifted millions out of poverty" in the global south, it has also produced "eroding incomes" and "precarious working conditions" for many people in the global north. National populists and protectionists have fed on these ills, but their solutions were misguided attempts to return to a less globalized world that has vanished for good. The only "realistic" objective is to reform globalization by means of the new leading technologies of the twenty-first century such as AI, quantum computing, 3D printing, and the Internet of Things. As Schwab puts it, "The real issue . . . is that the production and exchange of physical goods matters less and less each year. From here on out, decisive competitive advantages in the global economy will stem less from low-cost production and more from the ability to innovate, robotize, and digitalize."[52]

However, the WEF boss insists that such digital turbo-charged resuscitations of the market-globalist paradigm can only succeed if three crucial principles are put in place. It is worth quoting these in full:

> First, the dialogues that take place to shape Globalization 4.0 must involve all the relevant global players. Governments, of course, have a key leadership role to play, but business is the driver of innovation and civil society serves a critical role in making sure this innovation is applied with the public's interest in mind. Second, the preservation of social and national cohesion should be placed front and center. Safeguarding and strengthening the pillars of social justice and equity will be necessary to sustain national social contracts and preserve an open world. This cannot happen without bottom-up decision-making, which enables the substantive engagement of citizens around the world. Third, coordination—achieving shared objectives—will yield more successes than cooperation—acting out common strategy. The Paris Agreement on climate change and the United Nations Sustainable Development Goals are examples of a coordinated approach that leaves room for actors to devise their own strategies.[53]

Note how Schwab's reformed Globalization 4.0 shrewdly incorporates political effective buzzwords associated with justice globalism such as "social justice," "sustainability," and "equity." It also offers an olive branch to national populism in its explicit acknowledgment of the importance of "national cohesion" and "national social contracts."[54] Most importantly, the reformed market rhetoric of Globalization 4.0 seeks to strike a pronounced pragmatic tone in emphasizing the crucial role of innovative digital technology to solve pressing global problems—especially the deteriorating environmental conditions of our planet.

The rebound of a reformist version of market globalism would, most likely, help to address some of the looming global problems that are likely to worsen in the coming decade. However, if implemented at all, Globalization 4.0 would leave the underlying socio-economic structure of global capitalism largely intact. Without the implementation of far-reaching systemic reforms on a global level offered primarily by justice globalists, national and transnational disparities in wealth and well-being would further widen while top earners around the world would continue to benefit from neoliberal measures. Still, in this rebound scenario, neither justice globalism nor religious globalism would make much headway. The latter would simply tread water as an ideology fiercely opposing the secularism that tends to accompany digital globalization, while the former would continue to suffer from neoliberal attempts to steal and reinterpret some of its best ideas to make the resulting ideological stew more palatable to skeptical global audiences. This means that the prospect for a "global new deal" through the building of global networks of solidarity would be rather dim, to say the least.

For both justice globalism and religious globalism to gain in popularity in this scenario would entail the rather unpleasant prospect of another major global crisis emerging in the 2020s—perhaps even bigger than the COVID-19 pandemic—that would unsettle the technology-heavy agenda of Globalization 4.0. Such a crisis might usher in a third stalemate scenario. Perhaps the most likely of the three future trajectories, it would manifest as a prolonged standoff between the somewhat weakened national-populist forces and slightly waxing phalanx of reformist market globalists. However, if such an ideological stalemate between national populists and market globalists were to last throughout the 2020s, it would mean that little meaningful progress could be made toward addressing the current crisis, not to speak of solving the other global problems. It is difficult to predict what would happen if another global calamity of the magnitude of the GFC or the coronavirus pandemic would hit the world in the next few years. Modern political history suggests that the reactionary forces of the Right might find themselves at an advantage, because they have proven to be more adroit than the Left in utilizing people's fears for their purposes. The resulting shift to right-wing authoritarianism—or even worse, open dictatorship—would spell the end of liberal democracy as we know it.

And yet, in the face of such a hypothetical crisis, it is obvious that the world would need, more than ever, a fundamentally different vision of what a better planet could look like. Perhaps the ultimate outcome of a prolonged stalemate scenario would be the narrowing of the contest between the national and global imaginary to a struggle between two opposing ideologies: antiglobalist populism and justice globalism. Ultimately, the three future scenarios remain inextricably intertwined with matters of political ideology and social movements: the ideas, values, and beliefs about globalization and forms of social engagement that shape our communities. It would be foolish to expect that the antiglobalist populist challenge will fade without ideational resistance and social movement contestation. Ideas matter because they provide the motivation for social action. Thus, it seems certain that the great ideological struggle of the twenty-first century will not end anytime soon.

PART III

Issues and Problems

6

The Rise of Global Studies
in Higher Education

During the 1990s, the phenomenon of globalization began to attract attention in social science and humanities departments of major universities around the world. But since the new keyword fell outside the conventional disciplinary framework, it was not of primary concern in established disciplines organized around established core concepts: "society" in sociology; "scarcity" in economics; "culture" in anthropology; "space" in geography; "the past" in history; "power" and "governance" in political science, and so on. A decade later, however, Global Studies (GS) had taken root as a transdisciplinary area of inquiry in its own right. As it became established in the global infrastructure of higher education, the new field placed the study of globalization in all its dimensions at the core of its intellectual enterprise. Hence, the rise of GS in this century represents a clear sign of the academic recognition of the significance of proliferating social interrelations and enhanced forms of mobility.[1]

But GS was not conceived as just another cog in the disciplinary machine of contemporary higher education. From the outset, it welcomed a great variety of approaches and methods that contribute to a transnational analysis of the world as a single interactive system. Taking seriously the trendy talk about globalizing knowledge as activities creating new spaces of epistemological diversity, GS confronted the western academic framework of knowledge specialization that has survived largely intact into the early twenty-first century. It challenged the dominant European disciplinary architecture by rejecting the division of knowledge guarded by privileged insiders against real and suspected threats from outsiders.

In more than the two decades of its existence, GS has thrived on the growing academic disaffection with the status quo of silo thinking. Although it seeks to blaze new trails of social inquiry, the newcomer is not afraid of presenting itself as a porous intellectual terrain. To use Fredric Jameson's apt characterization, GS constitutes a fluid academic "space of tension" framed by both disagreements and agreements in which the very problematic of globalization itself is being continuously produced and contested.[2] From the beginning, the fledgling field attracted scores of unorthodox faculty and unconventional students who shared its commitment to studying transnational processes, interactions, and flows from a variety of disciplinary angles. Hence, GS thrives on a holistic *mentalité* that recognizes our age as one shaped by multiple processes of globalization.[3]

To acknowledge the significance of the global imaginary, however, does not translate into support for premature proclamations of the death of the nation-state. As we discussed in chapter 4, national and local governments have retained significant powers while at the same time being forced to readjust many of their central functions to meet new global demands. GS scholars consider the nation-state as but one major actor in today's fluid web of proliferating non-state entities. Its multi-agency understanding of our globalizing world makes GS a field with strong applied interests in practical politics and public policy connected to citizenship, gender, poverty, global media, public health, migration, technology, and ecology. Consequently, GS scholars encourage the forging of problem-centered links that connect the worlds of the academy, political parties, nongovernmental organizations, and social movements.

This chapter presents the rise of GS in the twenty-first century as an instructive example of the globalizing framework of higher education. Starting with a brief examination of the historical and institutional origins of GS, the opening section also provides a concrete case study of how the new field was established and evolved at a leading US university. The bulk of the chapter presents the intellectual substance of GS in the form of four central pillars or framings: globalization, transdisciplinarity, space and time, and critical thinking. The discussion concludes with a presentation of some influential critiques of GS and a brief reflection on the future of the expanding field.

THE INSTITUTIONAL EVOLUTION
OF GLOBAL STUDIES

In the aftermath of World War II, nation-state-centered approaches to world affairs dominated the relatively new academic disciplines of international studies (IS) and international relations (IR). Originating as a subfield within American political science, IR rose to prominence through the activities of early proponents such as Hans Morgenthau and Henry Kissinger, who assumed dual roles as academics and government advisors. Similarly, IS grew up in an academic environment impacted by intensifying national security concerns. IS also interacted with what came to be known as "area studies" (AS) and "development studies."

As IS and AS gained popularity and institutional support within the US academy during the Cold War era, they mushroomed into largely autonomous fields. Their growth occurred in response to the perceived threat of communism and the establishment of new nation-states—and potential clients of the Soviet Union—in the wake of decolonization. Seeking to thwart the Soviet Union's involvement in Europe and what was then called the "Third World," IR and IS pursued overlapping academic and political agendas that benefited from the generous support of US funding agencies linked to the powerful national security establishment headed by the Pentagon, the FBI, and the CIA as well as philanthropic organizations like the Carnegie, Ford, and Rockefeller Foundations. The same is true for AS. As John Lie notes, the US government and many of the leading private foundations promoted an area studies perspective that was linked to Eurocentric notions of industrial modernization and capitalist economic development. As a result of these powerful funding streams, AS was considered "big business" and became institutionalized in large research centers and academic departments at most major US universities.[4]

Toward the end of the 1950s, the US-based International Studies Association (ISA) arose as a national organization committed to the promotion of "research and education in international affairs."[5] Founded largely by disaffected American political scientists, the ISA embraced a methodological nationalism that served the geopolitical strategies and priorities of the First World in general, and US hegemony in particular.[6] As we noted in chapter 3, mainstream IR scholars treated the state as *the* main actor—and thus the central unit of analysis and the principal mover—of world politics. Traditional IR scholarship focused primarily on the self-interested actions of nation-states in an anarchic international environment—especially with regard to security issues—and often at the expense of other crucial dimensions such as culture, ecology, and ideology. Attached to dominant behaviorist designs and rationalist modeling schemes, IR researchers sought to find generalizable analytical frameworks capable of explaining and predicting power dynamics in international affairs with the hope that such theories might contribute to the prevention of large-scale wars, especially a looming nuclear exchange between the west and the Soviet bloc.

Although the analytic framework of GS owes much to innovative approaches such as world-systems analysis, postcolonial studies, cultural studies, environmental and sustainability studies, and women's studies, its origins can be traced back to the efforts of innovative IR scholars committed to deconstructing the unitary actor model of the state in favor of a more complex conception that emphasizes a multiplicity of interests, identities, and contingencies. Some of these revisionist tendencies in IR appeared under the label "institutionalism." The most serious challenges to the canonical academic status of the "inter-national" in the 1980s came from a number of IR insiders like Robert Keohane who coined the phrase "complex interdependence" to emphasize the changing dynamics of the international system and the part played in it by states *and* a growing variety of non-state actors. Recognizing the rapid transformation of the power and authority of national governments under globalizing conditions, Keohane argued for a revision of IR's key concept of sovereignty from a territorially defined barrier to a bargaining resource for politics characterized by porous transnational networks.[7] This new transnational orientation in IR partly corresponded with the more fluid approaches of "international political economists" who examined cooperation among social institutions in global issue areas such as economic development, climate change, surveillance, and digital technology.[8]

Thus, as globalization scholar James Mittelman has emphasized, the rise of GS in the 1990s occurred in the context of this extended quarrel within the fields of IR and IS where innovative "para-makers" challenged the dominant "para-keepers."[9] But the success of GS depended to a significant extent on the redirection of funding by US government and philanthropic organizations from IS and AS to the academic newcomer. As we discussed in previous chapters, this reorientation of AS and IS toward GS occurred in the ideological context of rising neoliberalism and market globalism. Some commentators coined the term "academic capitalism" as an overarching framework for understanding the profound ways in which neoliberal globalization and its associated knowledge economy were transforming higher education around the world.[10] Part and parcel of this changing academic environment, GS was nurtured by a solidifying neoliberal landscape. The recipient of new market-oriented initiatives, GS benefited from the shift toward the global.

As Isaac Kamola's pioneering work on the subject has demonstrated, starting in the mid-1990s, a number of important funders announced plans to replace area structures with a global framework.[11] For example, the Social Science Research Council (SSRC) recommended defunding "discrete and separated area committees" that were reluctant to support scholars interested in global developments and policy-relevant "global issues." Major universities, too, reduced the level of support for area studies teaching and research programs while developing new investment schemes and strategic plans that provided for the creation of new GS or global affairs programs and centers. Kamola points out that major professional organizations like the National Association of State Universities and Land Grant Colleges and the American Association of Colleges and Universities eagerly joined these instrumental efforts to synchronize the initiatives of "globalizing the curriculum" and "recalibrating college learning" to the neoliberal landscape of the "new global century."

When conventional AS and IS experts realized that traditional sources of funding were quickly drying up, many joined the newly emerging GS cohort of scholars centered on the study of globalization. Initially, they used the related terms "global studies" and "globalization studies" loosely and without much system-building ambition. Some might have used "global studies" in the pursuit of their transdisciplinary research projects or to name new programs and centers at their respective universities. Others experimented with the designations like "critical globalization studies," "transnational studies," and "globalism research." Indeed, some of these titles are still in use today. Looking back, Paul James noted perceptively that "Studies of globalization and, more generally, studies in the broad and loosely defined field of 'global studies' did not become conscious of themselves as such until the 1990s."[12]

By the turn of the twenty-first century, it became possible to present GS as a reasonably holistic transdisciplinary academic project keen to engage the complex global issues and problems. The new funding sources allowed for the development of GS, which included upgrading previous international or

Figure 6.1. International Relations, International Studies, Area Studies, or Global Studies?

comparative study programs, as well as creating entirely new academic infra-structures.[13] In the 2000s, GS programs, departments, research institutes, and professional organizations sprang up in major universities around the world, including in the global south. Many existing IR or IS programs were renamed "global studies" to meet the demand for courses and undergraduate and post-graduate degrees in this dramatically rising new field. The terms "global" or "globalization" proliferated in course titles, textbooks, and academic job postings. By the 2010s, there were three hundred GS undergraduate and grad-uate programs in the United States alone.[14] The creation of these successful degree-granting programs occurred simultaneously with the creation of new GS journals, book series, academic conferences, and professional associa-tions like the Global Studies Consortium and the Global Studies Association.

THE GLOBAL STUDIES STORY AT THE UNIVERSITY OF CALIFORNIA SANTA BARBARA (UCSB)

To illustrate the difficult process of establishing GS at a major US university, let us consider the formation and evolution of a trailblazing program at UCSB. In most cases, the translation of a new intellectual vision into viable academic courses, programs, and institutions requires both a dedicated team effort and good luck in the sense of connecting to an existing constellation of engaged people who share the vision. The successful founding of GS at UCSB was no exception to this rule. While it is impossible for the ensuing summary to do justice to the contributions of all the faculty and staff involved in the initial formative years of what would eventually grow into the Department of Global Studies, it is crucial to note that it was a collective endeavor.

In late 1994, Richard Appelbaum accepted an appointment to chair his pro-vost's ad hoc planning committee to study the feasibility of creating a com-mon administrative home to several international programs located in various colleges and research units at UCSB. A noted sociologist and long-term faculty member at UCSB, Appelbaum was a firm believer in the virtues of inter- and multidisciplinarity as reflected in his own broad academic training, which included formal coursework and degrees in such diverse fields as pub-lic law, political science, economics, philosophy, communications, sociology, anthropology, urban studies, labor studies, international studies, and foreign languages. Committed to an "international perspective" in higher education, he had been attentive to the growing impact of globalization dynamics in the rapidly changing post–Cold War environment. His recognition of globalizing dynamics was further enhanced after encountering the work of globalization pioneers such as Roland Robertson and Anthony Giddens, both of whom confirmed his own understanding of the global dimensions of social change.[15]

Opportunities for the successful establishment of an overarching "global studies" unit at UCSB dramatically increased with expanding faculty support, especially from comparative literature scholar Giles Gunn and religion expert Mark Juergensmeyer. Like Appelbaum, Juergensmeyer was a skilled academic entrepreneur with significant institution-building experience and committed to designing new academic programs anchored in transdisciplinary approaches to a rapidly globalizing world. Advocating a more explicitly "global orientation" toward the study of international affairs, Juergensmeyer had previously served as the head of School of Hawaiian, Asian, and Pacific Studies at the University of Hawai'i at Mānoa (UHM). However, when he continued to encounter what appeared to be intractable bureaucratic resistance to his vision of developing a new graduate program in international studies especially designed to engage "global issues," Juergensmeyer decided to leave UHM and take his ideas to UCSB.

Serving together on Appelbaum's committee, Juergensmeyer and Gunn agreed that UCSB's new international unit should primarily address the globalization dynamics that were shaping the world now and into the future. Emphasizing the contemporary transition into a transnational era in which global issues were the signature elements, they embraced the label "global studies," by which they meant paying primary attention to transnational events, processes, and flows rather than maintaining the conventional IR focus on relations between nation-states. At the same time, however, they agreed that such a GS framework ought to acknowledge in explicit ways the continued relevance of nationalisms and nationhood and, therefore, should be assembled around the dialectic tensions between the global and the international. They offered two additional pragmatic reasons for why they thought it would be prudent not to dispose of the conventional "international" label altogether. First, as their extensive research on the subject had revealed, no other academic institution in the United States was using the designation "global studies." In short, GS programs simply didn't exist in the country. Second, they pointed out that some influential colleagues at UCSB had reacted negatively to "global studies," complaining that it sounded like a rather hazy concept and thus seemed a poor substitute for the familiar term international.[16]

In early 1995, the provost's ad hoc committee completed its work and recommended the establishment of a separate administrative locale bearing the compromise name Global and International Studies (G&IS). Located directly under the provost's office rather than the offices of the divisional deans, it was to serve as the institutional umbrella for a variety of new undergraduate programs, including a Global, Peace and Security undergraduate minor and an Islamic and Near Eastern Studies major. Impressed with the work of the committee, the provost approved its recommendations and appointed Mark Juergensmeyer as the first director of the incipient G&IS program. In the

1996–1997 academic year, the new unit was elevated to a department-size program with independent status and its own budget and faculty positions.

No sooner had Juergensmeyer, Gunn, and Appelbaum secured much needed office and meeting spaces than they were joined by a number of internal and external faculty recruits such as Sucheng Chan, a tenured Asian studies expert who transferred half of her position to G&IS. Over the next decade of the 2000s, Gunn continued his mission to integrate a strong humanities perspective into a program dominated by social scientists. A noted scholar of unusual intellectual breadth as well as a seasoned academic administrator, Gunn was also willing to step into central administrative positions and eventually served as the chair of the G&IS program, guiding it through a decade of phenomenal growth. Within the first year of the establishment of the G&IS Program, more than a dozen UCSB tenured faculty applied for affiliate studies and committed themselves to cross-listing some of their courses with the new program. Aided by a 1997 system-wide call to internationalize the University of California as well as to develop new interdisciplinary programs, the GS Bachelor of Arts program at UCSB was approved in spring 1998, thus allowing the first undergraduate students to be admitted into it. Only a year later, Sajeed Ashgar became the first student to graduate with a BA from G&IS and later decided to pursue a graduate degree in International Service at American University. Within three years, student enrollment in GS skyrocketed to eight hundred majors, making it the most popular undergraduate major on the entire UCSB campus.

Like Ashgar, many of these students were keen to pursue graduate work on the subject. Consequently, the growing global studies faculty embarked on the lengthy process of establishing new graduate programs in GS, which included a transdisciplinary PhD with emphasis in GS and a terminal master's degree program, which focused on global civil society and was designed to prepare students to work for international NGOs. This process was greatly aided by the generosity of philanthropist, Kinko's founder, and serial entrepreneur, Paul Orfalea, who began teaching an immensely popular seminar in global business and leadership at UCSB in spring 2002. Sharing the global vision of Juergensmeyer and Appelbaum, the Orfalea Family Foundation provided a $10 million endowment at UCSB that permitted not only the successful inauguration of the proposed terminal MA program under Director Appelbaum, but also the establishment of the Orfalea Center for Global and International Studies. Providing the intellectual and programmatic focus for UCSB's activities in global studies, international studies, and area studies, the Orfalea Center under the directorship of Mark Juergensmeyer began to work closely with G&IS and other international units on campus. It also pursued projects with academic collaborators around the world, thus engaging in research and policy questions of global scope, implications, and relevance.

In 2015, precisely a decade after the inauguration of the Orfalea Center, the G&IS program dropped "international" from its name and became the Department of Global Studies. In the same year, it launched the first doctoral program in GS at a Tier-1 research university in the United States. But it is worth remembering that this auspicious moment was preceded by eight years of hard collective labor dedicated to designing the PhD program and shepherding it through various faculty committees and administrative levels. Gunn had pushed for it from the moment he took over as chair in 2005 and then worked with his colleagues to triple the faculty's size at the same time that the University of California system was dealing with a $1 billion deficit. With the support of his college dean Melvin Oliver and his GS team, Gunn conceived and wrote the proposal for the doctoral program, and then, with the new chair, Eve Darian-Smith's assistance, at the end of the long process, worked for its acceptance by the university in the face of considerable institutional skepticism and opposition. Reflecting areas of centrality in the field of GS at large, UCSB's doctoral curriculum was configured around three areas of specialization: (1) global political economy, sustainable development, and the environment; (2) global culture, ideology, and religion; and (3) global governance, human rights, and civil society.

To be sure, the many processes that led to the establishment and development of GS at UCSB were not always smooth and uncontroversial. The troubling flipside of relative departmental autonomy in American higher education has been the impact of a silo mentality that breeds resistance to the development of new programs perceived as threatening the disciplinary terrain of existing departments. Other obstacles included procuring the necessary faculty lines for the very quickly growing program; motivating core GS faculty to put countless unpaid overtime hours into serving on planning committees, developing new gateway courses, and teaching sometimes unremunerated course overloads to keep up with the exploding enrollments; engaging in long discussions with faculty senators from other colleges suspicious of the value of GS while wielding the power to delay or block time-sensitive curricular or administrative proposals; and getting bogged down in seemingly endless negotiations with deans and other high-level administrators reluctant to allocate scarce resources to untested ideas and initiatives. In the end, however, the GS faculty at UCSB succeeded in taking a giant step toward the realization of a dream that Appelbaum, Juergensmeyer, and Gunn had shared since the beginning of their auspicious collaboration in 1990s: the ultimate establishment of a Global Studies School at UCSB that would be at the vanguard of pertinent twenty-first-century developments.

Throughout the 2000s, a growing number of universities and colleges in the United States and around the world followed suit by creating their own GS units on campus. However, as Jan Nederveen Pieterse pointed out, in many cases these activities did not involve the generation of brand-new programs *ex nihilo*, but the upgrading and reconfiguring of existing offerings in IR, comparative studies, regional studies programs, or development studies.[17] Other universities, like the University of Hawai'i, chose the route of interdisciplinary undergraduate major and minor programs in GS. Still other universities, like the University of Illinois Urbana-Champaign or the London School of Economics, opted for integrating global studies as a subfield within conventional departments that increased their program menus by offering global studies degrees.

Perhaps the most "global" novelty in the twenty-first-century evolution of GS involves the creation of inter-university consortia that offer degrees in the new field. In such cases, a group of universities entered into binding collaboration agreements for the purpose of sponsoring a common course of study. The GS degree is given by the consortium itself, and the course of study is taught by professors from the sponsoring universities. Perhaps the best known such consortium is the EU's Erasmus Mundus program, which sponsors a GS master's program supported by faculty from European universities such as Leipzig University, the University of Vienna, Wroclaw University in Poland, the London School of Economics, and Roskilde University in Denmark. This European GS consortium is also supported by Stellenbosch University in South Africa, Macquarie University in Australia, Dalhousie University in Canada, Jawaharlal Nehru University in India, and Fudan University in China. The increasing variety of GS programs and GS research centers, together with the rapidly growing number of students at both the undergraduate and graduate levels, presents the most convincing evidence for the rising popularity of the new field.

Having provided the necessary background on the origins and evolution of GS, we are now in a position to make our case for the gradual coalescence of the new field into a reasonably coherent academic area of inquiry that employs shared analytical frameworks in order to explore the main issues and problems of the integrating world of the twenty-first century and its problems. To this purpose, the next section of this chapter offers a general overview of the four major conceptual pillars that give intellectual consistency to the new field.

THE FIRST PILLAR OF GLOBAL
STUDIES: GLOBALIZATION

Globalization is the key concept and primary subject of GS and thus constitutes the foundational pillar of the new field. Since we discussed the meaning, evolution, definitions, and major dimensions of globalization in previous chapters, we can keep this section short.

In spite of enduring disagreements over how to define globalization, GS scholars have put forward various definitions and collected them in comprehensive classification tables.[18] One major obstacle in the way of producing useful definitions of globalization is that the term has been variously used in both academic literature and the popular press to describe a process, a condition, a system, a force, and an age. Given that these concepts have very different meanings, their indiscriminate usage is often obscure and invites confusion. For example, a sloppy conflation of process and condition encourages circular definitions that explain little. The familiar truism that globalization—the process—leads to more globalization—the condition—does not allow us to draw meaningful analytical distinctions between causes and effects. Hence, we ought to adopt the term "globality" to signify a social condition characterized by extremely tight global economic, political, cultural, and environmental interconnections across national borders and civilizational boundaries.

The term "globalization," by contrast, applies not to a condition but a multidimensional and complex set of social processes enveloped by the rising global imaginary that propel us toward the condition of globality. Thus, we arrive at the definition offered at the end of chapter 1: *globalization refers to the multidimensional expansion and intensification of social relations and consciousness across world-time and in world-space.*

GS scholars exploring the dynamics of globalization have been pursuing research questions that engage themes related to social change. How does globalization proceed? What is driving it? Is it one cause or a combination of factors? Is globalization a major cause of worldwide social change or merely a descriptor for the consequence of more primary drivers such as capitalism, the international political system, or technology? Is globalization a continuation of modernity or a radical break? Does it create new forms of inequality and hierarchy, or is it lifting millions of people out of poverty? Is it producing cultural homogeneity, diversity, or hybridity? What is the role of new digital technologies in accelerating and intensifying global processes? What is the relationship between globalization and the deteriorating natural environment of our planet? To be sure, GS researchers will continue to wrestle with these and other related questions for many years to come.

THE SECOND PILLAR OF GLOBAL
STUDIES: TRANSDISCIPLINARITY

The profound changes affecting social life in the global age require examinations of the growing forms of complexity and reflexivity. This means the global dynamics of interconnectivity can no longer be approached from a single academic discipline or area of knowledge. Exploring global complexity commits GS scholars to the development of more comprehensive models of globalization, which highlight the intersection between a multiplicity of driving forces, embracing economic, technological, cultural, and political change. As we noted in chapter 3, the exploration of complex forms of global interdependence in GS not only combats knowledge fragmentation and scientific reductionism, but also facilitates an understanding of the big picture, which is indispensable for tackling the pressing global problems of our time. Thus, GS scholars consciously embrace transdisciplinarity in their efforts to understand the shifting dynamics of interconnectedness and their associated global challenges such as climate change, pandemics, terrorism, digital technologies, marketization, migration, urbanization, and human rights.

Let us start with an etymological clarification of the concept "discipline." Its Latin roots are the verb *discere* ("to learn"), and the nouns *disciplina* and *discipulus*, which translate into "education" and "student," respectively. However, the meanings associated with these nouns are far broader. *Disciplina*, for example, took her place in the ancient Roman pantheon as a minor female deity, worshipped fervently by soldiers for her martial virtues of physical training, self-control, and mental determination rather than her equally strong affinities for education and knowledge. These potentially violent and confining aspects of *disciplina* were brilliantly deconstructed in Michel Foucault's postmodern interpretation of "discipline" as involving modern micro-practices of power capable of producing and normalizing new scientific institutional arrangements responsible for the creation of docile bodies and minds.[19] The French philosopher also pointed to the formation of academic disciplines as part and parcel of this all-pervasive link between power and knowledge—a crucial insight worth remembering for those exploring the role of *trans*disciplinarity in GS.

The concept of "transdisciplinarity" is configured around the Latin prefix "trans," meaning "across" or "beyond." It signifies the systemic and holistic integration of diverse forms of knowledge by cutting across and through existing disciplinary boundaries and paradigms in ways that reach beyond each individual discipline. If "interdisciplinarity" can be characterized by the mixing of disciplinary perspectives and "multidisciplinarity" connotes the bringing together of different fields—both of these practices involving little or moderate integration—then transdisciplinarity should be thought of as a deep fusion of knowledge that produces new understandings capable of transforming or restructuring existing disciplinary paradigms.[20] While the transdisciplinary imperative to challenge, go beyond, transgress, and integrate separate academic orientations favors generalists, it does not ignore the importance of attracting specialists with specific disciplinary groundings. Moreover, transdisciplinarians often put complex real-world issues at the heart of their intellectual efforts. The formulation of possible solutions of these practical problems requires the deep integration of a broad range of perspectives from multiple disciplinary backgrounds.[21]

Yet, full transdisciplinarity remains an elusive goal for most academics. This includes GS scholars associated with currently existing academic programs in the field. Some achieve a high degree of transdisciplinary integration, whereas others rely more on limited multi- and interdisciplinary activities that benefit students and faculty alike. For GS, the task is to expand its foothold in the dominant academic landscape while at the same time continuing its work against the prevailing disciplinary order. To satisfy these seemingly contradictory imperatives, GS has retained its ambition to project globalization across the conventional disciplinary matrix while, at the same time, accepting with equal determination the pragmatic task of finding some accommodation within the very disciplinary structure it seeks to transform. Such necessary attempts to reconcile these diverging impulses forces scholars to play at least one, and preferably more, of three distinct roles—depending on the concrete institutional opportunities and constraints they encounter in their academic home environment.

First, GS scholars often assume the role of *intrepid mavericks* willing to establish their new field as a separate discipline—as a first but necessary step toward the more holistic goal of comprehensive integration. To be sure, mavericks possess a certain spirit of adventure that makes it easier for them to leave their original disciplinary setting behind to cover new ground. But being a maverick also carries the considerable risk of failure.

Second, a number of GS scholars have embraced the role of *radical insurgents* seeking to globalize established disciplines from *within*. This means working toward the goal of carving out a GS dimension or status for specific disciplines such as political science or sociology.

Finally, some GS faculty have slipped into the role of *tireless nomads* traveling perpetually across and beyond disciplines in order to reconfigure existing and new knowledge around concrete globalization research questions and projects. The nomadic role, in particular, demands that academics familiarize themselves with vast literatures on pertinent subjects that are usually studied in isolation from each other. Indeed, one of the most formidable intellectual challenges lies in the integration and synthesis of multiple strands of knowledge in a way that does justice to the complexity and fluidity of our globalizing world.

THE THIRD PILLAR OF GLOBAL
STUDIES: SPACE AND TIME

The "global village" is one of the earliest yet most enduring phrases marking the rise of the global imaginary. Coined in the early 1960s by Marshall McLuhan, the slogan reflected the growing public awareness of a rapidly shrinking world. However, what the Canadian literature and media scholar had in mind was a far more nuanced process than the one suggested by this popular slogan. Emphasizing the expanding reach of electricity-based communication technology, McLuhan sought to capture in a memorable phrase the complex and often uneven dynamics of spatial stretching that made geographic distance much less of an obstacle in human interaction. Observing that the "mechanical age" of the industrial revolution was rapidly receding, he predicted that the contemporary "electric contraction" of space and time would eventually make the entire globe as open to instant and direct communication as small village communities in previous centuries had been. McLuhan opened his magisterial study on the globalization of the media by driving home his thesis in dramatic fashion: "Today, after more than a century of electric technology, we have extended our central nervous system in a global embrace, abolishing both space and time as far as our planet is concerned."[22]

The development of GS has been crucially framed by new conceptions of space and time. After all, globalization manifests in volatile dynamics of both spatial integration and differentiation. These give rise to new temporal frameworks dominated by notions of instantaneity and simultaneity, which assume ever-greater significance in academic investigations into globalization. As French philosopher and sociologist Henri Lefebvre noted, space and time are interrelated dimensions of social existence: "When we evoke 'space,' we must immediately indicate what occupies that space and how it does so: the deployment of energy in relation to 'points' and within a timeframe. When we evoke 'time,' we must immediately say what it is that moves and changes therein. Space considered in isolation is an empty abstraction; likewise, energy and time."[23]

Globalization processes create continuously new geographies and complex spatial arrangements. As we discuss in more detail in the next chapter, this is especially true for the latest spatial frontier in human history: cyberspace. The dynamics of digital connectivity and mobility have shown themselves to be quite capable of pushing human interaction deep into the virtual reality of a world in which physical geography is becoming redundant. Several GS pioneers have developed approaches to globalization that put matters of time and space at the very core of their research projects.

Consider, for example, Roland Robertson's snappy definition of globalization as "the compression of the world into a single place." It underpinned his efforts to develop a spatially sophisticated concept of "glocalization" capable of counteracting the relative inattention paid to spatiality in the social sciences. Commenting on the remarkable fluidity of spatial scales in a globalizing world, Robertson focused on those complex and uneven processes in which "the constraints of geography on social and cultural arrangements recede and in which people become increasingly aware that they are receding."[24] Similarly, Arjun Appadurai developed subtle insights into what he called the "global production of locality"—a new spatial dynamic that was occurring more frequently in "a world that has become deterritorialized, diasporic, and transnational."[25] David Harvey's influential inquiry into the spatial origins of contemporary cultural change centered on the uneven geographic development of capitalism. His innovative account generated new concepts such as "time-space compression" or "the implosion of space and time," which affirmed the centrality of spatio-temporal changes at the heart of neoliberal globalization and its associated postmodern cultural sensibilities.[26]

Finally, Anthony Giddens argued that modern forms of "time-space distanciation" worked hand in hand with "disembedding mechanisms" like the modern state, media networks, or transnational corporations that lifted social relations out of their purely local interactions and then restructured them across large time-space distances. Thus, by extending the scope of time-space distanciation these disembedding institutions were able to connect the global and the local in ways, which would have been unthinkable in more traditional societies and in so doing affect the lives of many millions of people. Focusing his attention on the latest phase in this centuries-old expansionist dynamic, Giddens linked modernization to globalization by arguing that "modernity is inherently globalizing." Hence, he saw globalization as the latest phase of a modernization process that had become so intensified and extended that it required new terminology: "We can interpret this process as one of *globalisation*, a term which must have a key position in the lexicon of the social sciences."[27]

Other GS scholars, like Martin Albrow, rejected Giddens's thesis of globalizing modernity in the strongest terms possible and instead argued for an "epochal shift" from the "Modern Age" to the dawning "Global Age." For Albrow, modernity was actually running out of steam at the end of the twentieth century as a result of "globalization." For this reason, he reproached his colleague for misreading what is actually a manifestation of rupture and discontinuity as the continuation of modernity's logic of expansion and intensification. Thus, Albrow's provocative inversion of Giddens's thesis: rather than embracing the idea that modernity is inherently globalizing, we should recognize that globality is inherently "demodernizing."[28]

In addition to this ongoing debate on whether globalization represents the consequence of modernity or a postmodern break, GS scholars have explored a number of crucial spatio-temporal themes such as the changing relationship between territory and sovereignty; the increasing fluidity of spatial scales; and new ways of periodizing global history. As we noted at the outset of this chapter, of particular interest has been the impact of globalization on conventional forms of territoriality such as the nation-state and the related changing nature of the international system. This spatial agenda involves not only the growth of supraterritoriality—comprised of global governance structures or transworld regimes that operate with significant autonomy from the state—but also crucial processes and practices of down-scaling that occur deep inside the local, national, and regional. As GS scholar Saskia Sassen emphasizes, "An interpretation of the impact of globalization as creating a space economy that extends beyond the regulatory capacity of a single state is only half the story; the other half is that these central functions are disproportionately concentrated in the national territories of the highly developed countries."[29] Perhaps the most critical of these spatial restructuring processes facilitated by states involves the localization of the control and command centers of global capitalism in "global cities" that assume great significance as pivotal places of spatial dispersal and global integration located at the intersection of multiple global circuits and flows involving migrants, ideas, commodities, and money.

Finally, as our discussion of the third pillar of GS has shown, the transdisciplinary field owes much to the efforts of innovative human geographers and urban studies experts to develop new theoretical approaches that help us understand the changing spatial dynamics of our time. But GS is equally indebted to the intellectual initiatives of sociologists and historians willing to rethink the conceptual frameworks governing the temporal record of human activity. As discussed in chapter 2, the related field of global history has advanced the central premise that processes of globalization require more systemic historical treatments, and, therefore, that the study of global interconnectivities and flows deserves a more prominent place on the agenda of historical research.

THE FOURTH PILLAR OF GLOBAL
STUDIES: CRITICAL THINKING

Few GS scholars would object to the proposition that their field is significantly framed by "critical thinking." After all, their field constitutes an academic space of tension that generates critical investigations into our age as one shaped by the intensifying forces of globalization. Going beyond the purely cognitive understanding of critical thinking as "balanced reasoning" propagated by leading Anglo-American educators during the second half of the twentieth century, this fourth pillar reflects the new field's receptivity to the activity of social criticism, which problematizes unequal power relations and engages in ongoing social struggles to bring about a more just global society.

This emphasis on the crucial link between theory and practice has served as common ground for various socially engaged currents of critical thinking that have openly associated themselves with "critical theory." Originally used in the singular and upper case, "Critical Theory" has been closely associated with mid-twentieth-century articulations of "Western Marxism" as developed by Max Horkheimer, Theodore Adorno, Herbert Marcuse, Walter Benjamin, and other prominent members of the Institute for Social Research in Frankfurt, Germany. More recently, however, thinkers from around the world have drawn on a variety of currents and methods of social criticism, thus making "critical theory" an umbrella term for multiple modes of thought committed to the reduction of exploitation, commodification, violence, and injustice.

By the early 2000s, a growing number of globalization scholars were willing to adopt a socially engaged approach to their subject that became variously known as "critical globalization studies," "critical global studies" (CGS), and "critical theories of globalization."[30] Such a CGS puts forward a number of principles: methodological skepticism regarding positivistic dogmas; the recognition that "facts" are socially constructed and serve particular power interests; the public contestation of uncritical mainstream stories spun by corporate media; and the decolonization of western epistemological frameworks.[31] Taking sides with the interests of social justice, CGS thinkers exercise what William Robinson calls a "preferential option for the subordinate majority of global society."[32] In particular, Robinson emphasized that CGS must provide a cogent critique of the social dynamics and impacts of global capitalism. In his view, asymmetrical power relations based on the centrality of the capital-labor relation are responsible for the systemic reproduction of unjust social structures worldwide. At the same time, however, Robinson argues that capitalism was undergoing tremendous change. The current phase of globalization presented an epochal shift from the "nation-state phase of world capitalism" to the "transnational phase of global capitalism" characterized by the globalization of the production of goods and services and the forging of so-called flexible capital-labor relations. Moreover, global capitalism generated novel organizational forms such as decentralized management techniques, subcontracting and outsourcing, and transnational business alliances. Hence, a proper understanding of emergent global society required sophisticated forms of political economy analyses capable of explaining the emergence of new transnational structures—most importantly the social formation of a "transnational capitalist class" and its political expression, the "transnational state."[33]

There is, indeed, much empirical evidence to suggest that dominant neoliberal modes of globalization have produced growing disparities in wealth and wellbeing within and among twenty-first-century societies.[34] The negative consequences of such a corporate-led globalization-from-above served not only as the catalyst for the alterglobalization movements discussed in chapter 4, but also for the proliferation of new critical theories developing within the novel academic framework of GS. Such critical intellectuals have advanced their critiques of market globalism in tandem with constructive visions for alternative global futures. They have pursued research that has been useful both to global social movement activists and academics. Most of these critical thinkers could be characterized as "rooted cosmopolitans" embedded in local environments while at the same time cultivating a global consciousness because of their vastly enhanced contacts to global academic networks and social organizations across national borders. Stimulated by the vitality of emergent global civil society, CGS scholar-activists have thought of new ways of making their intellectual activities in the ivory tower relevant to the global public sphere.

These novel forms of global activist thinking also manifest themselves in the educational project of cultivating what has been referred to as "global citizenship." In the twenty-first century, the global citizenship framework has been embraced by educational institutions, transnational corporations, advocacy groups, community service organizations, and the UN. Although the phrase means different things to different social groups, it has increasingly been associated with educational initiatives seeking to inspire young people to grow into morally responsible, intellectually competent, and culturally perceptive global citizens. The promotion of the global imaginary in the educational arena involves a number of elements: the cultivation of thinking beyond one's imagined physical boundaries toward a global consciousness of planetary interdependence; a sense of one's global responsibility and shared moral obligations across humankind; and the strengthening of democratic ideals of democratic empowerment and participation.[35] Mark Juergensmeyer has added another element by linking global citizenship to specific educational efforts to create "global literacy"—the ability of students to see themselves as active "citizens of the world" capable of critical examinations of specific aspects of diverse cultures and economic practices as well as influential global trends and patterns.[36] In fact, the entire field of GS itself has forged multiple educational paths to global citizenship that promotes critical ways of thinking and living within transnational geographical, intellectual, and moral parameters.

Since the struggles over the meanings and manifestations of globalization have occurred in interlinked local settings around the world, these dynamics signify a significant alteration in the geography of critical thinking and knowing. As the French sociologist Razmig Keucheyan emphasizes, the academic center of gravity of these new forms of critical thinking was shifting from the traditional centers of learning located in "old Europe" to the top universities of the "new world." The United States, in particular, served as a powerful economic magnet for job-seeking academics from around the globe while also posing as the obvious hegemonic target of their criticisms.[37] American institutions of higher education have managed to attract a large number of talented postcolonial critical theorists to its highly reputed and well-paying universities and colleges. A significant number of these politically progressive recruits, in turn, have promptly put their newly acquired positions of academic privilege into the service of their socially engaged ideologies, which have resulted in a vastly more effective production and worldwide dissemination of their critical publications. The global struggle against neoliberalism has also contributed to the heightened international exposure of cutting-edge critical theorists located in Asia, Latin America, and Africa. Moreover, the permanent digital communication revolution and the rise of the social media has made it easier for voices of the global south to be heard in the dominant north. Although this growing academic community of critical thinkers is far from homogenous in its perspectives and approaches, its formation has had a profound influence on the evolution of GS.[38]

At the same time, one must be careful not to exaggerate the hold of such critical global studies perspectives on the field. Our discussion of the developing links between the global justice movement and CGS scholars should not lead us to assume that all academics affiliated with GS programs support radical, or even moderate, socially engaged perspectives on what constitutes their field and what it should accomplish. Still, my informal perusal of influential globalization literature produced during the last twenty-five years suggests that about two-thirds of well-published GS academics expressly take their understanding of "critical" beyond the positivistic ideal of detached objectivity and value-free research, thus challenging the dominant social arrangements of our time by promoting emancipatory social change.

CONCLUDING REMARKS: CRITIQUES
OF GLOBAL STUDIES

After presenting the conceptual and thematic framework of GS, it might be appropriate to close this chapter by considering the emerging field's capacity for self-criticism. Obviously, the critical thinking framing creates a special obligation for all GS scholars working in the field to listen to and take seriously internal and external criticisms with the intention of correcting existing shortcomings, illuminating blind spots, and avoiding theoretical pitfalls and dead-ends. As is the case for any newcomer bold enough to enter today's crowded and competitive arena of higher education, GS, too, has been subjected to a wide range of criticisms ranging from constructive interventions to ferocious attacks.

One influential criticism relates to what Jan Nederveen Pieterse calls the limited scope and status of "actual global studies as it is researched and taught at universities around the world." For sympathetic critics like Pieterse, the crux of the problem lies with the field's alleged intellectual immaturity and lack of focus. He argues that currently existing GS programs and conferences are still put together haphazardly and thus resemble a "scaffolding without a roof." He also bemoans the supposed dearth of intellectual GS innovators willing and able to provide necessary "programmatic perspectives on global studies" framed by forms of "multicentered and multilevel thinking" that are capable of "adding value" to the field.[39]

Such assessments resonate with the often-shocking discrepancy between the rich conceptual and thematic promise of the field and the poor design and execution of "actual global studies as it is researched and taught at universities around the world." There is some truth to Pieterse's complaints that because a good number of GS programs lack focus and specificity, it makes the field appear to be a rather nebulous study of everything global. Like most of the transdisciplinary disciplinary efforts originating in the 1990s, GS programs sometimes invite the impression of a rather confusing combination of wildly different approaches pushing the global level of analysis.

Another troubling development in recent years has been the use of "global studies" as a convenient catch phrase by academic entrepreneurs eager to cash in on its popularity with students. Consequently, this desirable label has become attached to a growing number of conventional area studies curricula, international studies offerings, and diplomacy and foreign affairs programs—primarily for the purpose of boosting their market appeal without having to make substantive changes to the traditional teaching and research agenda attached to such programs. Unfortunately, these instrumental appropriations have not only caused much damage to the new GS "brand" but also cast an ominous shadow on the innovative evolution of the field.

In spite of their valuable insights, however, some critiques of GS appear to be unbalanced and somewhat exaggerated. Much of the available empirical data shows that there are, in fact, promising pedagogical and research efforts underway in the field. These initiatives suggest that the instructive pessimism of the critics must be matched by cautious optimism. To be sure, an empirically based examination of the field shows GS as a project that is still very much in the making. Yet, its tender age and relative inexperience should not deter affiliated scholars from acknowledging their field's considerable intellectual achievements and growing institutional infrastructure. GS as it actually exists in the twenty-first century has come a long way from its rather modest and eclectic origins in the 1990s. For example, the regular meetings of the Global Studies Associations (UK and North America) and the annual convention of the Global Studies Consortium provide ample networking opportunities for globalization scholars from around the world. Moreover, GS scholars are developing serious initiatives to recenter the social sciences toward global systemic dynamics and incorporate multilevel analyses. They are rethinking conventional analytical frameworks that expand critical methodologies and mix various research strategies.[40]

Another important criticism of GS comes from postcolonial thinkers. While most have expressed both their appreciation and affinity for much of what GS stands for, they have also offered incisive critiques of what they see as the field's troubling geographic, ethnic, and epistemic location within, and fixation on, the hegemonic western framework. The noted ethnic studies scholar Ramón Grosfoguel offers a clear summary of such postcolonial concerns: "Globalization studies, with a few exceptions, have not derived the epistemological and theoretical implications of the epistemic critique coming from subaltern locations in the colonial divide and expressed in academia through ethnic studies and women studies. We still continue to produce a knowledge from the Western man 'point zero' god's-eye view."[41]

As we noted in chapter 3, postcolonial critiques of globalization research provide a useful service by highlighting remaining conceptual parochialisms behind its allegedly "global" theoretical and practical concerns. Indeed, their intervention correctly points out that GS thinkers have not paid enough attention to the postcolonial imperative of contesting the dominant western ways of seeing and knowing. Global south perspectives force GS scholars into confronting crucial questions that are often relegated to the margins of intellectual inquiry. These questions also relate to the central role of the English language in their field. With English expanding its status as the academic lingua franca, thinkers embedded in Western universities still hold the monopoly on the production of critical theories.[42] Important contributions from the global south released in languages other than English often fall through the cracks or only register in translated form on the radar of the supposedly "global" academic publishing network some years after their original publication. While GS has made some progress in recent years to expand its space of tension in the postcolonial direction, there is still plenty of room for improvement on heeding and integrating voices from the global south.

Let me end this chapter with the tiniest of speculations about the future of GS. Perhaps its most pressing task for the coming decade is to keep chipping away at the disciplinary walls that still divide the academic landscape today. Animated by an ethical imperative to globalize knowledge, such transdisciplinary efforts have the potential to reconfigure our discipline-oriented academic infrastructure around overlapping research questions and issues of global public responsibility.[43] While this integrative endeavor must be undertaken steadily and tirelessly, it must tread carefully and with the proper understanding that diverse and multiple forms of knowledge are sorely needed to educate a global public.

The necessary appreciation for the interplay between academic specialists and generalists must contain a proper respect for the crucial contributions of the conventional disciplines to our growing understanding of globalization. But the time has come for the new field to take the next step. The rising global imaginary demands nothing less from GS students and faculty hailing from all disciplines and fields of inquiry. Their core activities of learning, teaching, and research should be approached with the spirit of critical openness and embedded cosmopolitanism befitting the interconnected world of the twenty-first century.

7

Digital Globalization in the COVID-19 Era

The twenty-first century has been a time of extremely rapid social change, brought on by a combination of escalating global problems and the exponential growth of digital technology. The series of worldwide crises discussed in chapter 5 culminated in 2020 when a once-in-a-century pandemic raced across the planet. First observed in Wuhan, China, COVID-19, a disease caused by SARS-CoV2, presented with a wide spectrum of severe symptoms affecting multiple parts of the human body. Trade and travel, two essential components of globalization, contributed significantly to the fast spread of the disease. In response, most national governments severely curtailed social interrelations and transnational mobilities by means of full-scale lockdowns, stringent travel restrictions, prolonged quarantines, unprecedented social distancing rules, and systemic shifts to work from home.

Although these preventive measures saved many lives, they also contributed to a decrease in production, consumption, employment, and supply-chain disruptions that dragged down the global economy. Healthcare systems and frontline hospital workers across the world exhausted themselves in their treatment of patients while scientists raced to develop effective vaccines in the record time of less than eighteen months. Still, the drastic isolation mandates adversely affected the mental health of millions of people, especially children and young adults. When COVID-19 finally showed signs of abating in early 2023, the World Health Organization (WHO) reported that a total of 800 million people had contracted the disease, resulting in more than 7 million confirmed deaths. But many health experts put the actual global fatality rate about three times higher than these official numbers.

The social turmoil and disruptions caused by the global spread of the novel coronavirus underlined in dramatic fashion that the story of twenty-first-century globalization should be told in the larger context of the Great Unsettling. We remember from our previous discussion that this term is shorthand for intensifying levels of risk, volatility, insecurity, dislocation, anxiety, and political polarization that have been threatening familiar life-worlds and cultural identities around the world.[1] This COVID-19 heightened phase of global instability has further amplified geopolitical tensions and large-scale conflicts such as the ongoing military tensions in the South China Sea and the protracted Russia-Ukraine war. Indeed, the Great Unsettling appears to be at least as serious as the socioeconomic and political upheavals brought on by the Great Transformation of the Industrial Revolution.[2]

Assessing the globalization dynamics in the COVID-19 era has proved to be an enormous research challenge, even when tackled with big data sets and innovative multidisciplinary collaborations. Academic attempts to analyze our present moment of global crisis typically involve approaches that have split globalization experts into two antagonistic camps. On one side, pessimistic deglobalizers have posited a retreat of globalization measured by its allegedly diminishing economic and political dimensions such as trade, FDI, and stagnant global governance structures.[3] In the other corner, optimistic reglobalizers have read the current phase as an advance of globalization, especially as related to the purported expansion of its technological and cultural aspects such as thickening digital interconnectivities and swelling symbolic flows.[4] Ironically, these clashing assessments have been advanced on both sides with a degree of confidence that belies our contemporary condition of uncertainty.

Drawing on previous discussions in this book, this chapter continues the appraisal of the state of globalization in the twenty-first century by placing it in the troubling context of the Great Unsettling without resorting to blanket statements that globalization-in-general is either waning or waxing.[5] A more nuanced assessment must start with a fundamental rethinking of the dominant dimension-based framework that lends itself to a reduction of globalization to economics. We must not approach globalization as a phenomenon primarily based on transnational trade exchanges and financial flows, but as a multi-braided assemblage of social formations involving global interconnectivities and mobilities of people, things, institutions, and ideas.

To this end, the chapter extends our brief discussion of a new classification scheme introduced in chapter 1 to highlight the crucial role of structural disjunctures and fissures that have been developing among the four major globalization configurations. The rapid advancement of digital technology in the twenty-first century—captured by the trendy term "digitization"—has played the lead role in the intensification of these disjointed dynamics first noticed by global studies scholar Arjun Appadurai more than three decades ago.[6]

Digitization refers to a set of processes that originally started with micro- and network-computing in the second half of the twentieth century, but it hardly stopped there. As discussed below, proliferating electronic technologies based on a series of electronic binary digits known as "bits" have been operating in the everyday lives of billions of people, in the process transforming nearly all aspects of social relations. In fact, we now live in a world where digital technologies, systems, and platforms of global reach have become so commonplace that they have become largely invisible.[7] The thickening "global network society" of the twenty-first century shows high levels of interdependence, but it also nurtures widening rifts that threaten its systemic integrity.

This chapter examines the increasingly disjointed globalization formations not merely on the macro-level of material-objective processes but also gauges their impact on the micro-plane of individual consciousness. While the ease of multiplying virtual connections to others can provide much-needed social support, it can also lead to social alienation and isolation—not to speak of the serious occupational health hazards linked to spending long hours daily in front of screens. One of these micro-dynamics of disjuncture involves the production of an "unhappy consciousness" in the form of a self divided between the enjoyment of the flexibility of global digital mobility and the visceral attachment to the fixity of familiar local arrangements. The discussion ends with the proposition that although the COVID-19 pandemic appeared to foster a distinctly low-tech response as lockdowns and quarantines slowed certain forms of global interconnectivity and mobility, it also significantly boosted disembodied dynamics such as video calls and social media encounters, thus accelerating and intensifying the disjunctive globalization dynamics that had been building since the turn of the twenty-first century.

FOUR SOCIAL FORMATIONS OF GLOBALIZATION

Let us start the assessment of globalization in the COVID-19 era by recalling competing conceptual globalization models presented in previous chapters. We noted that most GS scholars prefer domain frameworks that distinguish between economic, political, and cultural dimensions of transnational interconnectivities and mobilities. These basic analytic distinctions serve two important functional objectives. First, they make it easier to break down the enormity of globalization dynamics into more easily digestible dimensions and parts. Second, they facilitate important multidisciplinary research projects aimed at a holistic understanding of globalization built on the disciplinary expertise of contributing scholars.

While such practices of analytical demarcation are indispensable in any scientific endeavor, it is questionable whether the domain approach to globalization still constitutes the most effective framework for understanding current dynamics. My doubts derive primarily from an observation made by virtually all global studies scholars, regardless of their conflicting assessments: the dimensions of politics, culture, and economics have become enmeshed and interrelated in social life in much tighter and more complex ways than ever before.[8] Consider, for example, the role of Cambridge Analytica and WikiLeaks in the 2016 US presidential election. Or the development of the Chinese "One Belt, One Road" initiative reaching across dozens of countries. Or the construction of the International Space Station requiring the cooperation and resources of all five participating regional space agencies. Or the American football quarterback Colin Kaepernick taking the knee at the playing of the national anthem, in the process triggering a global controversy that went viral on social media. Or, most recently, the rapid spread of a novel coronavirus—as well as the lightning-fast development of effective vaccines—that changed the world as we knew it.

Are these examples of economic, political, or cultural globalization? The complex convergences and multiple overlaps among these domains suggest that the correct choice should be "all of the above." Since the continued reliance on the dimensional framework seems to obscure more than it illuminates, this chapter relies on the new conceptual framework of "four social formations of globalization" that also guided our historical discussion in chapter 2.

To refresh our memory, *embodied globalization* refers to the worldwide interconnectivities and mobilities of people, including tourists, refugees, business travelers, and so on. *Disembodied globalization* relates to worldwide interconnectivities and mobilities of increasingly digitized ideas, information, images, and data. *Objectified globalization* involves worldwide interconnectivities and mobilities of things, ranging from tradable commodities transported by gigantic container ships to the molecular components of greenhouse gases. *Institutional globalization* refers to worldwide interconnectivities and mobilities of organizations, including TNCs, economic institutions like the IMF and the WTO, legal institutions like the International Court of Justice, and sports clubs such as Real Madrid and the New York Yankees.

These macro-configurations of globalization resemble perpetually moving tectonic plates whose complex dynamics shape the geology of our planet in profound ways. Possessing both an underlying structure—a "formation"—and a visible morphology or shape—a "form"—both geological and global formations are both bonded by substantial synergies and driven apart by potent antagonisms. In the contemporary context of the Great Unsettling, the movements of the four globalization formations have become increasingly disjointed. Disjunctures have developed both exogenously between the four globalization formations and endogenously within each configuration. For example, within the objectified configuration, large objects like tradeable commodities have been outpaced by small objects like greenhouse gas molecules and viruses.

DIGITIZATION AND DISJUNCTIVE GLOBALIZATION

The most consequential disjuncture destabilizing the current globalization system has been occurring between its increasingly digitalized, disembodied formation—which might be called digital globalization—and the other three configurations. As measured in terms of extensity, intensity, velocity, and impact, digital globalization has been charging ahead while the other formations have been lagging behind. Global flows of data primarily consist of information, searches, communications, transactions of all kinds, video, streaming, gaming, and so on. Indeed, the datasphere is currently growing by about 18 million gigabytes per minute, aided by digital technologies capable of capturing and processing human behavioral information at an unprecedented speed and volume.[9] Commercial enterprises from large corporations like Amazon and Alibaba to small and medium-sized enterprises increasingly turn to digital platforms to connect to customers and suppliers across national borders. In addition, small start-up companies can become global in a heartbeat by exploiting digital platforms.[10]

The digital disjuncture driving apart the four major globalization formations is likely to intensify with the ongoing inventions of new digital technologies that are being scaled at an ever-faster pace while decreasing rapidly in price. Indeed, digital technologies are so-called exponential technologies, which means that they do not develop in linear fashion, but at an accelerating pace of more than 10 percent per year for several decades. Consider, for example, TikTok, the Chinese-owned social network for sharing videos. In a matter of months, it went from a virtually unknown digital service to the most downloaded app in the world.[11] The compounding effect of such exponential innovations translates into the speeding up of digitization processes across the globe while institutional and embodied interrelations are struggling to keep up. The result is disjunctive globalization reflected in what economist Azeem Azhar calls the "exponential gap": a widening chasm between the world created by turbocharged digital globalization and the lagging human understanding of these dynamics.[12]

This digital leap pertains to everything some globalization analysts associate with the current Fourth Industrial Revolution. Major technological innovations include: Big Data and augmented analytics that enable the integration of digital information through automated mining, harvesting, tagging, linking and archiving of data; the expansion of bandwidth that allows for the emergence of 5G networks; quantum computing that operates far more quickly than the fastest processors available only a few years ago; digital platforms that infuse day-to-day disembodied social practices and engagements; the Internet of Things (IoT) and advanced smart devices that provide world-wide online connections among billions of everyday devices and objects; blockchain technologies like Bitcoin and other cryptocurrencies that allow multiple parties to engage in secure digital transactions without intermediaries; digitally extended realities; AI and digital machine learning capable of making decisions, carrying out tasks, and even predicting future outcomes based on what they process from data; robotics and drones that respond to their environment and perform routine or complex tasks autonomously; and nanotechnology that manipulates and controls matter at the atomic and molecular levels. These digital systems and practices run on algorithms, which are programmable series of logical steps that organize and act upon data to achieve specific outcomes.[13] The infusion of algorithms throughout all areas of everyday life and the associated transformative impact of digital technologies is particularly visible in the massive changes affecting the conventional professions, which provide employment for hundreds of millions of people around the world.

For example, in the medical sector, patients are enjoying ever great access to digital health information through specialized search engines like BetterDoctor and expanding online platforms like WebMD. More powerful computerized diagnostic systems run by complex algorithms assume important health tasks such as scanning mammograms and running insulin-delivery pumps. Autonomous robots are poised to complete mass prescription orders and deliver medications to hundreds of hospitalized patients without human assistance. The practice of telemedicine has progressed to the point where doctors use video links across the Internet to carry out medical diagnoses and procedures at a distance, including telesurgery supported by advanced robotics. There is now a growing mobile health market of tens of thousands of devices, systems, and apps built on existing communication technology such as mobile phones and tablets. Self-monitoring health devices like Fitbit trackers and Apple watches have become commonplace electronic "wearables." Advancing digital technology in health and biology sectors has allowed for a sequencing of a full human genome for a cost of less than $100. Previously unimaginable feats of biotechnical engineering such as gene splicing and repair are in advanced stages of development and testing.[14]

In the architectural professions, desktop design software like AutoCAD, Revit, and CATIA have replaced hand-drawn sketches and assist professionals to click, drag, and drop their design components into place on screen. Increasingly, 3D simulations supply creators and consumers with endless architectural shapes and structures that can be turned, deconstructed, and reconfigured at will. Computational curve and bubble designs have been realized in vanguard buildings such as the Beijing National Stadium ("The Nest") or the London City Hall ("The Egg"). The largest of the three new concert halls housing Hamburg's classical orchestra, the Elbphilharmonie, is the product of parametric design, which relied entirely on AI-generated algorithms to develop the building's final form. The combination of digitized architecture, computer-aided engineering, and additive manufacturing has resulted in the digital fabrication of houses made entirely from 3D-printed parts that are put together by robots equipped with versatile "arms" capable of utilizing almost every conceivable tool. The potential of 3D printing technology was also demonstrated during the COVID-19 pandemic when global production facilities in China and Turkey were under lockdown and hundreds of decentralized supply chains run by ordinary citizens turned their 3D printers to work producing equipment.[15]

In the field of journalism, the traditional print-based industry has long given way to a digital environment dominated by online news platforms. In 2021, 86 percent of US adults indicated that they received their news "often" from a smartphone, computer, or tablet. Only 10 percent of customers relied on print publications. Among digital platforms, news websites or apps were preferred by 26 percent of US adults. Twelve percent opted for online searches, 11 percent relied on social media, and 3 percent preferred podcasts.[16] Digital-only news organizations like the *Huffington Post* allow any reader to submit an article, along with contributions from paid writers. *Vox Media* is one of the more successful US-based, for-profit online news platforms financed by digital advertising and venture capital. In recent years, online news consumers have increasingly turned to social media platforms like Meta/Facebook, Twitter/X, or YouTube. Of the nearly 5 billion global users of social media in 2023, 3 billion have made Facebook their leading news source. Caught in this growing trend, professional journalists now routinely rely on computerized search systems like Storyful to sift through proliferating social media platforms in their search for breaking news or popular stories.[17]

Finally, in the education sector, tools and methods of instruction have been digitized at a brisk pace. Charter schools, in particular, are at the forefront of using online learning platforms. Specially designed "learning labs" draw on individual performance data to deliver contents tailored to the specific needs and abilities of each student. Such "adaptive digital learning systems" are developed and delivered by a growing number of companies such as Knewton, Reasoning Mind, and DreamBox. These are capable of replicating in cyberspace the one-to-one embodied tutorial systems that have worked so effectively at top UK universities such as Cambridge and Oxford. At the same time, teachers have experienced a standardization of their activities by using online "teacher-proof" pre-scripted lessons. They also work increasingly alongside digital content "recommender systems" and automated grading systems. Online platforms like Khan Academy and YouTube EDU provide massive educational contents, mostly in the form of free online instructional videos that attract millions of visitors each month.

In higher education, online courses have proliferated and diversified. Even those like Massive Open Online Courses (MOOCs) that launched with much fanfare but experienced little demand only a few years ago are now enjoying record enrollments. For example, more people signed up for Harvard's MOOCs in a single year than have attended the actual university in its 377 years of existence. The growing academic "open-access" movement has made available free of charge digital big-data academic bases. For example, the arXiv database contains more than 25 million downloaded papers across the disciplines, which allow for a much more effective global sharing of scholarly thinking.[18]

Most recently, AI-driven language and image generators with voice interfaces have invaded the ivory tower in the form of online chatbots, which anyone with an Internet connection can access. Provider start-up companies like OpenAI have drawn on billion-dollar investments from tech giants such as Microsoft to bring to the market their celebrated tool, ChatGPT, which utilizes huge amounts of data to generate humanlike language and thought. Capable of answering questions, writing poetry, composing essays, generating computer codes, and carrying on conversations, chatbots have quickly emerged as the digital saviors of students who are either unwilling or incapable of writing essays or answering multiple choice exams. Global academic publishers like Elsevier are at the forefront of developing new author policies on AI and AI-assisted tools in scientific writing, which mandate that "authorship implies responsibilities and tasks that can only be attributed to or performed by humans."[19] But the global impact of chatbots goes far beyond the educational professions as it threatens dozens of human jobs performed by audio-to-text transcribers, paralegals, accountants, journalists, writers, and many others. Indeed, the impact of automation and digitization on traditional work in general has been the subject of an increasing number of critical commentaries.[20]

Some pundits have hailed this digital invasion of embodied and objectified social relations as the beginning of a new era of artificial general intelligence that will accelerate the material and moral progress of humanity by, for example, developing of a cure for cancer and inventing permanent solutions for our climate and energy crises. Others, including big tech entrepreneurs such as Tesla and Twitter/X CEO Elon Musk, have urged AI labs to pause the development of the most advanced systems, warning that AI tools present profound risks to society and humanity.[21] The prominent historian Yuval Hariri recently spelled out some of these dire consequences in his argument that AI's new mastery of language means that "it can now hack and manipulate the operating system of civilization. . . . By gaining mastery of language, AI would have all it needs to contain us in a Matrix-like world of illusions, without shooting anyone or implanting any chips in our brains."[22] Regardless of their differences, experts on both sides of the AI issue consider the latest innovations in machine learning like the ChatGPT as significant a shift in the evolution of digitization as the creation of the web browser and the iPhone.

To sum up, then, disembodied globalization has accelerated and intensified in the twenty-first century through the growth of the digital platform economy. Production has become increasingly automated and trans-spatial through the introduction of robotics and AI. Infused by digital technology, the banking and the finance sector have remained drivers of a global capitalist framework where derivatives markets continue to thrive, despite the recent shocks administered by the 2008 Global Financial Crisis and the COVID-19 pandemic. The proliferation of intangible assets and the expansion of blockchain technology beyond its controversial manifestation of cryptocurrency have created what some economists call a "capitalism without capital," which thrives on growing global investments in intangible assets like design, branding, and software.[23] The rise of intangible capital has been spectacular. In 1975, tangible capital—including financial assets such as stocks and bonds—accounted for more than 80 percent of corporate value. By 2020, this historic pattern had been completely reversed as intangible capital reached 85 percent and thus constitutes the core of a global economy based on rapid and comprehensive digitization.[24]

This explosion of immaterial production benefits not only from neoliberal intellectual property regimes, but also from cognitive labor performed by "knowledge workers." As the mobility of people, things, and institutions fails to keep up with the broadening and thickening of digital networks, disembodied globalization begins to scrape off pieces of its adjacent tectonic plates. Global studies scholar Richard Baldwin refers to this ongoing digital transformation of previously objectified and embodied forms of interconnectivity as a "globotics upheaval" that affects both manufacturing and the service sector by devouring millions of embodied jobs. Threatening to overwhelm the human capacity to adapt, accelerating digital globalization could result in rapid social disintegration: "Any new upheaval—the globotics upheaval, if you will—could spread very quickly since globots are really a worldwide challenge."[25]

As noted, the rise of additive manufacturing through the application of 3D printing has been transforming the global merchandise trade built on global value chains—an aspect of objectified globalization—into regionalized and localized networks of exchange based on digitally enabled production-on-demand as close to the end market as possible. Familiar neoliberal practices of outsourcing and offshoring—hallmarks of objectified

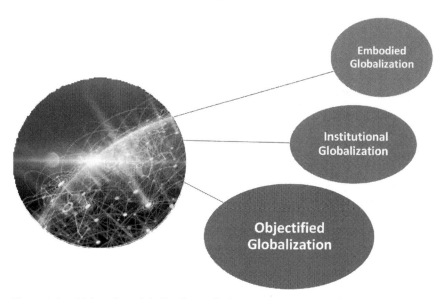

Figure 7.1.   Disjunctive Globalization: Velocity

globalization dynamics in the 1990s—have slowed down and even been reversed as intensifying digital globalization makes "reshoring" an attractive option for many companies. Similarly, the service sector is being cannibalized by disembodied globalization's growing ability to transform embodied workers thousands of miles away into digital tele-migrants by means of collaborative software packages like Slack or Office 365 and electronic project-management platforms like Trello or Basecamp.[26]

Political economist Finbarr Livesey refers to the tendency of disembodied globalization to devour its lagging cousins as "physical deglobalization."[27] While this term captures some of the dynamics described above, it is more accurate to see digitization as a form of disjunctive globalization, that is, a profound rearrangement of its constituent formations that move at different speeds and at different levels of intensity. To be sure, the current globalization system still entails significant embodied and objectified interconnectivities and mobilities. Although embodiment and place remain a grounding basis of the human condition, the main story of twenty-first-century globalization has nonetheless been the emergent power and dynamism of its disembodied formation. And, as I argue in the final section of this chapter, the COVID-19 pandemic has further accelerated and intensified disjunctive globalization.

Thus, the assessment of current globalization processes on the basis of the globalization formations framework enables global studies scholars to push back on the popular claim of deglobalization. Typically, such assertions focus

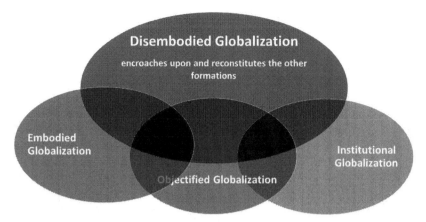

Figure 7.2.   Disjunctive Globalization: Extensity

on plateauing embodied and objectified globalization flows such as trade and foreign-direct investment flows as though these were still the dominant globalization dynamics in our digital age. Yet, post-COVID data show that even global trade flows have rebounded and stabilized at high levels with the introduction of effective vaccines and the resulting uptick of conventional forms of mobility.[28] Hence, "reglobalization" is a more appropriate term by which to characterize the contemporary dynamics of disjunctive globalization.

Finally, the recognition that today's dominant social formation of globalization is digitally disembodied also opens new perspectives on the dynamics of power in our global network society. After all, digital technologies are not neutral tools applied by human users, but artifacts built by people under specific social-economic conditions that reflect inherent asymmetrical power relations. Such a critical analysis of intensifying disembodied globalization brings into sharper focus novel forms of intangible power that seek to control and exploit human behavior across national borders by encoding digital technology into global infrastructures that are more increasingly opaque and unaccountable to ordinary citizens. This power dimension linked to digital globalization has been the subject of landmark studies authored by Nick Srnicek, Shoshana Zuboff, Timothy Ström, and others.[29] These scholars describe and analyze the exploitative practices of TNCs like Google, Meta/ Facebook, and Amazon rooted in what they call "surveillance capitalism" or "platform capitalism." For years, these tech giants have been unilaterally claiming everyday human experience as free material for translation into behavioral data designed to fuel and shape human beings towards profitable outcomes and ever more encompassing surveillance infrastructures.

Critical observers fear the coming of totalitarian surveillance, perhaps in the form of governments forcing citizens to wear biometric bracelets.

Ostensible mandated for public health reasons, these devices can harvest biological data that can be hoarded and analyzed by government algorithms. Major pandemics like COVID-19 might be stopped quickly, but the necessary digital surveillance system might outlast periods of emergency and turn into a permanent tool of government oppression. Thus, the necessary pandemic lockdowns could serve as dry runs for how runaway digitalization might open the door for government and dominant groups to restructure space an exercise greater political and economic control over other citizens.

Such digital exploitation practices strip away the illusion that the networked form has some kind of indigenous moral content, that being "connected" is somehow intrinsically pro-social, innately inclusive, or naturally tending toward the democratization of knowledge. Rather, digital connectivity can easily degenerate into an algorithmic authoritarianism that serves both unaccountable power and commercial profit.[30] As globalization theorist Barrie Axford notes, the prospect of a datafied lifeworld dominated by corporate giants draws attention to the posthuman features of a new global cultural economy, wherein communication technologies constitute an indifferent globality of machines and the hidden agency of algorithms.[31] Thus, global capitalism retains its central features—alienation and exploitation—but does so in increasingly disembodied and abstracted ways, even as they impact heavily the bodies of workers and consumers.

However, it is crucial to recognize that the dominance of disembodied global relations cuts across the conventionally drawn social domains. While surveillance capitalism deserves to be recognized as a new phase in the history of capitalism, digitization involves all four globalization formations, not just the material dimension of economic production and exchange. As Zuboff notes, "Industrial capitalism transformed nature's raw materials into commodities, and surveillance capitalism lays its claims to the stuff of human nature for a new commodity invention. Now it is human nature that is scraped, torn, and taken for another century's market project."[32] Hence, we need to link our discussion of the macro-dynamics of digitization and disjunctive globalization to the micro-level of everyday human consciousness.

THE PRODUCTION OF THE
UNHAPPY CONSCIOUSNESS

The acceleration and intensification of digital globalization at the expense of the other formations means that people around the world increasingly struggle to cope with the rapid changes impacting their everyday lives linked to digitally extended layers of space and time. As a result of the advancing processes of cyberspatiation and digital instantaneity, people experience a sense of dislocation and alienation from the local as manifested in conventional embodied, objectified, and institutionalized places. As our discussion of antiglobalist populism in chapter 5 has shown, these dynamics often lead to the romanticization of visceral localities and reference points—in terms of nation, language, ethnicity, food, dress, sports, music, buildings, and so on. At the same time, people also become alienated from the newly perceived sluggishness of the local and its imperviousness to the thrills of digital mobility and plasticity. Thus, they develop the contradictory tendencies of glorifying the shrinking sphere of the local and national, while spending more time in the expanding realm of global cyberspace.

Even before the outbreak of the pandemic, the average American spent more than six hours a day online, which equates to more than one hundred days a year.[33] To be sure, Internet use and information flows on social media are primarily domestic. Still, one should bear in mind that the medium itself is irreducibly global and hence appropriately named the "worldwide web." Indeed, proliferating digital tools and software programs are highly globalized phenomena that bear a plethora of meanings and symbols that circulate freely in the global datasphere.[34] Facebook/Meta, for example, is the most widely used social network in most countries—with its 290 million users in India easily outnumbering its 190 million American subscribers.[35] Similarly, Google has a 95 percent share of mobile search traffic worldwide, and more clicks for American business ads on Google come from outside the United States.

The growing disjuncture between people's experiences of intensifying global interconnectivity in virtual reality and their existence in the more slowly moving spheres of embodied, objectified, and institutional globalization has unsettled the ontological foundations of personhood.[36] The chasm produces what German philosopher Georg W. F. Hegel called an unhappy consciousness that experiences itself as divided within and against itself.[37] Characterized as "the consciousness of self as a dual natured, merely contradictory being," Hegel's "unhappy consciousness" appeared first in the "master-slave" section of his philosophical masterpiece, *The Phenomenology of Spirit*, penned in 1807.

This chapter famously describes a crucial phase in the struggle of dualistic consciousness to move to a higher stage of rational unity. For the German idealist philosopher, the unhappy consciousness is the synthesis of the master's "stoicism"—an attitude of mental superiority based on edifying universalistic ideas that are nonetheless barren of substance because they are cut off from the real world—and the slave's "skepticism"—a this-worldly particularistic perspective of radical doubt linked to the bondsman's unstable and insecure conditions of existence. Although the unhappy consciousness represents the fusion of the dualism of master and slave into one single consciousness and

thus advances beyond its historical stage of master-slave relations in antiquity, the opposing elements of stoicism and skepticism are not fully unified.
As Hegel puts it, "The Unhappy Consciousness itself is the gazing of one's
self-consciousness into another and itself *is* both, and the unity of both is also
its essential nature. But it is not as yet explicitly aware that this is its essential
nature, or that it is the unity of both."[38] At this stage of their spiritual development, humans experience themselves as divided, alienated, and inwardly
disrupted. As social philosopher Peter Singer explains, "The unhappy consciousness aspires to be independent of the material world, to resemble God
and be eternal and purely spiritual; yet at the same time it recognizes that
it is a part of the material world, that its physical desires and its pains and
pleasures are real and inescapable. As a result, the unhappy consciousness is
divided against itself."[39]

Although Hegel associates the unhappy consciousness primarily with
experiences of religious life, specifically medieval Catholicism, the concept has subsequently been applied to more secular contexts. For example,
the nineteenth-century Danish philosopher Søren Kierkegaard interpreted
Hegel's concept as a situation in which the essence of a self-conscious individual is no longer present to them, but in some manner outside themselves,
such that the individual manifests a dichotomy of temporal alienation. Such
a situation develops when a person lives in the past, or in the future, without
being reconciled to their present self, their present essence.[40]

Critical theorists of the Frankfurt School of Social Research, like Herbert
Marcuse, popularized Hegel's concept by linking it to their critique of consumerism and the culture industry in the context of advanced twentieth-century
capitalism.[41] Reversing the original meaning, they referred to it ironically
as the "happy consciousness" because it was considered to be a vapid state
of the acquisitive mind. Hostile to ethical reflection, the happy consciousness was seen as focused on hollow pleasures that drained the liberating and
critical potential of autonomous individuals. Thus, they associated the happy
consciousness with consumerist conformism and loss of individuality. Only
true nonconformists, with an understanding of the constraints of freedom,
and therefore endowed with an unhappy consciousness, could affect rational
progress. For this reason, critical theorists called for resistance against the
alienating power of the happy consciousness—not as an occasional act but as
an ethical imperative that applied especially under the modern conditions of
"one-dimensionality."[42]

The unhappy consciousness in its original Hegelian sense is an extremely
useful concept in its application to the production of everyday consciousness
in the context of the disjunctive movements of globalization that characterize
our current moment of the Great Unsettling. To be sure, dislocating experiences brought on by the rapidity of late twentieth-century global social change

have been documented before. For example, Zygmunt Bauman argued that many people living under postmodern conditions of "liquid modernity" lose a sense of familiarity with their local environment, spawning intense feelings of alienation, marginalization, and disembeddedness.[43] Similarly, Anthony Giddens wrote of the disembedding of ontological security that occurs within what he calls "the wasteland of everyday life."[44]

Most importantly, the social psychologist Kenneth Gergen pointed to a powerful dialectical dynamic involving our digital social presence that can now exist in places far away from our physical presence. He characterized persons deeply enmeshed in the global cyberspace as "absent-present" to explain how they may be physically present in one specific locality but psychologically lodged in virtual global space.[45] As applied to digital globalization, the absent-present signifies an unhappy consciousness stuck in the uneasy coexistence of its absence from the local (although physically present in the local) and its presence in the virtual global (although physically absent in the global).

This powerful absence-presence dialectic drives the current global production of individual selves torn between their desire for the pleasures of digital mobility and plasticity and their visceral affection for the political and cultural fixity of familiar local and national life worlds. For this reason, our analysis of disjunctive globalization pays as much attention to the micro-level of personhood as to the macro-level of the digital economy to explain people's heightened sentiments of dislocation, anxiety, alienation, anomie, and anger in the era of the Great Unsettling.[46] Recognizing the impact of accelerated digital globalization makes for a better understanding of how, precisely, objective dynamics interact with the subjective sphere of individual consciousness to produce new forms of unhappiness.

Consider, for example, the experiences of knowledge workers such as English language teachers located in the United States, Australia, Canada, New Zealand, or the UK who instruct Chinese students on Chinese-owned digital education platforms. Their work in this new digital mode is framed by an internally divided unhappy consciousness that values flexibility of working hours, greater job satisfaction, and higher income, while at the same time detesting new online surveillance measures as well as feeling detached from tangible embeddedness in the local social world. A recent empirical study involving dozens of English language teachers tethered to digital platforms shows that the benefits of cyberspace work—including the possible combination of regular work and easy travel as "digital nomads"—are experienced on the micro-level of subjective consciousness in ambivalent ways. Many contractors realized that they were exploited in new digital ways as well as losing touch with the physical world.[47]

Since Chinese digital platform managers do not dictate western teachers' working hours, the latter decide individually when to open their instructional windows and how many slots they prefer. Thus, the contractors enjoy the freedom to design their schedule to fit their needs. On the other hand, the digital transnational work and schedule flexibility make some teachers more detached from local time and more likely to impose demanding working hours on themselves. Their work schedule can look especially demanding because of the time zone differences. To fit Chinese students' preferred learning hours during the early evenings, many contractors living in North America have to teach in the morning hours of 4 to 7. Some teachers even work through the whole night during summer and winter vacations, when Chinese students spend more learning time at their homes. Indeed, some contractors became more used to their digital work time zones than the physical zones they lived in. Thus, the acceleration of digital globalization that makes for disjuncture with the other three globalization formations on the macro-level, also reveals itself on the micro-level in the form of digital workers' detachment from local time and space. Such a growing disengagement from local contexts applies to not only issues of time and space, but also to cultural matters such as differing interpretations of health issues as causes for course cancellation. Increasingly embedded in a Chinese cultural environment as a result of their digital work, teachers became increasingly willing to accept Chinese health policies that would be considered far too harsh by most western workers.[48]

Other examples of specific manifestations of the unhappy consciousness include the digital American shopper surfing the web for inexpensive Chinese-made tools needed for the purposes of home renovation in her small Midwestern town while taking a hardline attitude against cheap Chinese steel exports flooding the domestic market and thus hurting the "American economy." Or take the Canadian anti-immigration activists making online bookings for their vacation at the Mexican Riviera Maya. Or the Austrian industrial workers proud of the Formula 1 successes of their country's Red Bull Racing Team rushing to buy a new Korea-assembled SUV. Or German neo-Nazis mourning the loss of *Heimat* who spend hours in the social media hate sphere rather than their local pub to beef up their worldwide digital presence.

As noted in chapter 5, national populist leaders like Donald Trump, Jair Bolsonaro, or Victor Órban have benefited from the disjunctive production of the unhappy consciousness in the current moment of the Great Unsettling. They are experts in utilizing the ideological echo chamber of the global social media and accuse footloose "cosmopolitans" of cheating the toiling masses while laughing at their parochial lifestyles. Fattening their Twitter/X, Facebook, and YouTube platforms with transnationally produced "alternative facts," the populist captains of our "fake news" era successfully globalize their antiglobalist slogans, each communicating with and learning from each other in a global context. For example, Trump's anti-impeachment mantra of "witch hunt" was seamlessly turned into indicted Benjamin Netanyahu's national election campaign rallying cry of "witch hunt." Hence, as we noted in chapter 5, national populism is not just a backlash against globalization, but also an expression of it. The global appeal of the new nationalism attests to the role of the unhappy consciousness as a significant factor in the political power dynamics of the Great Unsettling.

CONCLUDING REFLECTIONS ON
THE IMPACT OF COVID-19

COVID-19 further accelerated and intensified the systemic dynamics of disjunctive globalization that were already underway prior to the outbreak. The pandemic represented a fundamental inflection point that slowed embodied and objectified globalization while extending the reach of digital technology into people's everyday lives. For many months, most national borders were closed to migrants and travelers other than citizens returning home. Physical mobility was curtailed, even within the nation-state. For example, Australian states closed their internal borders, which made it impossible for a Victorian grandfather to visit his granddaughter in Western Australia. The various member states in the European Union implemented similar mobility restrictions that reduced internal business and leisure travel in the summer of 2020 by almost 80 percent. Even those few countries that allowed embodied in- and outflows during the height of the crisis required visitors to self-quarantine for up to two weeks in isolated facilities.

"Social distancing" became a ubiquitous global term referring to a government-mandated practice of physical dispersion while instances of distant socializing via digital platforms exploded. Zoom video communications, for example, accommodated in June 2020 over 300 million daily meeting participants. The number of corporate users surged to about 300,000, which represents an increase of over 350 percent since December 2019. In that month alone, Zoom reported 71 million app installs and tens of thousands of schools around the world as users of their services.[49] COVID-related social distancing mandates and stay-at-home measures enticed people to spend record time in cyberspace. Social media platforms like Facebook, Twitter/X, LinkedIn, and Snapchat, in particular, experienced double digit increases in the first two quarters of 2020. In April 2020, UK adults spent longer than four hours online each day—more than a quarter of their waking life.[50] Economist Azeem Azhar aptly summarizes the social manifestations of this accelerated digital leap at the height of the pandemic:

During lockdowns, billions of us were compulsory billeted in our homes. For those with internet access and a computer, tablet, or phone, creature comforts—from Netflix to online games—were not in short supply. We filled our fridges with groceries bought online, with Door Dash or Deliveroo providing a wide variety of choice if we wanted a treat. Companies and students flipped to remote work and learning, relying on videoconferencing. The Californian company Zoom became the standard bearer, its mosaic of just-too-small faces and exaggerated waves a familiar backdrop for many a working day.[51]

Scores of colleges and universities across the globe—like the massive California State University system that enrolls nearly five hundred thousand students—decided to offer all or more than 90 percent of their fall 2020 course offerings in online mode only. Under such conditions of enhanced cyberspatiation, the concept of "international students" ceased to carry a special meaning since the borderless landscapes of virtual reality served as the shared gathering places for disembodied learners and teachers scattered across the local-global nexus. As instruction massively migrated to online modes, many students balked at the price of their e-education, clamoring for significant tuition cuts. Universities were trying to find ways to accommodate these demands by slashing their labor costs and rethinking the costly tenure system along even stronger neoliberal parameters. As a result, up to 50 percent of colleges and universities could go out of business in the United States alone.[52] Institutions of higher learning facing this existential threat are primarily small liberal arts colleges that rely on the human touch of embodied campus experiences to attract both domestic and international students. In the wake of the pandemic, many students might choose to pursue their education in virtual space only. Slowing transnational student flows would further decelerate the embodied globalization process while accelerating what was initially seen as a temporary stop-gap measure related to COVID-19: the full-scale digitization of content delivery across world-space and world-time.

A new cohort of adapted distance learners might no longer be too eager to return to the physicality of on-campus instruction. Still, given that Zoom-mediated online learning often receive low satisfaction student ratings, universities contemplate new post-COVID measures of putting their faculty through a series of mandatory training programs that teach them how to use evolving e-tools, how to restructure their classes, and how to enhance their online lectures. It is likely that the intensification of digitization will facilitate the entry of giant tech firms like Google and Amazon into the college market. Plans are already underway to partner with universities to offer traditional four-year undergraduate degrees in online mode for less than half the conventional price. Higher education pundits like NYU business school professor Scott Galloway expect the rapid emergence of such partnerships, which he imagines as MIT/Google, University of Washington/Microsoft, Carnegie Mellon/Amazon, and so on.[53] Moreover, in a learning landscape where the significance of physical geography and embodied relations is rapidly dwindling, it will become easier to market specific university brands globally. As of the time of this writing, in 2023, Galloway's projection still sounds quite utopian. But recent articles in academic journals and magazines like the *Chronicle of Higher Education* concur with such future scenarios. Challenging their readers to prepare for a digital restructuring of campus spaces, these essays reinforce the disjunctive globalization dynamics described in this chapter.[54] The related transformation of physical learning spaces into cyberspace will make many campus spaces redundant, thus opening up new, and badly needed, revenue sources for cash-strapped universities ready to sell or rent their physical accommodations to the highest bidder.

As we noted, the same disjunctive globalization dynamics that apply to education also pertain to a host of other industries and practices such as healthcare, travel and tourism, service, entertainment, real estate, and banking and insurance, labor markets, remote work arrangements, geopolitics, the environment, behavioral patterns, and moral choices. Even conventional religious practices have been changing dramatically through new digital ways of online narration, interpretation, service diffusion, and parish networking—a phenomenon social theorist Roland Benedikter calls "digitized religion."[55]

Global capitalism, in particular, has been eager to accelerate and multiply its digital flows. After catastrophic losses of nearly 35 percent in the early phase of the pandemic, most stock markets around the world recovered surprisingly quickly. Even as main street was struggling with multiple small business closures and record unemployment caused by multiple mandatory lockdowns, Wall Street was flourishing while the official number of virus cases continued to rise across the world. For example, the S&P 500, which is the benchmark index for stock funds at the heart of many retirement accounts, managed to top its closing record in mid-August 2020—only six months after its pre-COVID-19 record set on February 19. Reflecting the massive shift of social relations of all kinds from embodied face-to-face mode to screen events conducted in cyberspace, the technology-heavy Nasdaq index did even better. Aided by gigantic government aid packages and central banks infusing the markets with cheap money at nearly zero interest rates, the profits of Big Tech soared at a time when the global number of people infected with coronavirus cases passed the 20 million mark. Indeed, the combined net worth of the five big-tech oriented giants—Apple, Microsoft, Amazon, Facebook/Meta, and Alphabet, Google's parent company—skyrocketed to an astonishing record of $7.6 trillion by August 2020.[56]

By the time the WHO announced that COVID-19 no longer qualified as a global health emergency in May 2023, neither the pace of disjunctive globalization had slowed down nor had the pandemic-intensified social dynamics faded away. People around the world continued to look to digital media sites of all kinds to cultivate disembodied connections to supplement the waning physical experiences. Scientific research confirmed that extended time spent online produces new patterns of everyday consciousness, many of which are detrimental to mental health. Recent medical studies have established a link between COVID-19-intensified social media use and an increased risk of mental health issues such as internalizing problems—social withdrawal, difficulty coping with anxiety or depression, or directing feelings inward—and externalizing issues—aggression, acting out, and violence, especially among young adults.[57]

However, it is important to acknowledge that intensifying digital globalization does not *only* have negative impacts. People with particular disabilities, for example, rely on the cybersphere for social contact. Mats Steen, a young Danish man who suffered from muscular dystrophy and was unable to leave the house, developed deep friendships in an online gaming community where his material body's condition was not an obstacle. As he put it not long before his death at the age of twenty-five, "There [in cyberspace] my handicap doesn't matter, my chains are broken, and I can be whoever I want to be. In there, I feel normal."[58]

During the COVID-19 pandemic, the availability of virtual forms of communication might have saved the world from even greater disruption and calamity. Moreover, the unprecedented speed of COVID-19 vaccine development represented a remarkable triumph of disembodied globalization in the form of transnational data-sharing, global investment flows, and the utilization of the much-criticized global supply chains to produce the vaccine. Unfortunately, the ensuing distribution of the vaccines suffered from "vaccine nationalism"—the systematic efforts of wealthy countries in the global north to reserve millions of doses for domestic use. Such practices during the COVID-19 crisis produced not only extremely inequitable vaccine access but also reinforced the long-standing inequalities in public health between higher- and lower-income countries.[59]

What should be done to counteract the negative social and geopolitical impacts of disjunctive globalization? I agree with insightful commentators like Joseph Stiglitz and Klaus Schwab that a principal task at hand is to "manage globalization better."[60] However, it is not enough to reduce this necessary task to the economistic imperative of reforming neoliberalism. The present assessment of twenty-first-century globalization points to the significance of attempting a comprehensive realigning of the widening globalization cleavages. The success of such an endeavor depends, in the first instance, on the enhancement of institutional capabilities to make the increasingly complex and differentiated dynamics of globalization work in a more synchronized and balanced manner that serves socially equitable ends. Even if institutions managed to direct their efforts to moderating the digital hypermovement of disjuncture—by slowing down disembodied globalization and recharging the others—this task would be immensely difficult. After all, the two main mechanisms required to achieve the objective of readjustment—the strengthening of global solidarity and the assemblage of more widely shared and effective global governance architecture—face a steep uphill struggle in our era of the Great Unsettling. As surging antiglobalist populism and escalating geopolitical conflicts like the Russia-Ukraine War have demonstrated, the nation-state might be weakening, but the national imaginary still retains significant power in the dawning geopolitical order of the twenty-first century.

Still, this does not mean that the quest for a more synchronized globalization system is necessarily doomed. There are some encouraging developments, especially on the micro-level. Take, for example, the surprising trend to return to "dumb phones" currently popular with Gen Z populations in North America and Europe. As Joe Hollier, cofounder of the company Light explains, "What we're trying to do with the Light phone isn't to create a dumb phone, but to create a more intentional phone—a premium, minimal phone—which isn't inherently anti-technology, but it's about consciously choosing how and when to use which aspects of technology that add to my quality of life."[61] Such concerted efforts to limit screen time have been taken up by increasing numbers of young people willing to experiment with other measures such as intermittent online fasts—turning off your digital devices for extended periods of time—and physical reattachment exercises— enhanced in-person socializing in multiple settings—to counteract the negative psychosocial effects of the turbocharged digital leap.

Indeed, the end of our period of the Great Unsettling—turbocharged by the global COVID-19 pandemic—must come through the rebalancing of the disjunctive globalization formations. The solution does not lie in the creation of a digital Luddite movement eager to embark on a quixotic quest to smash digital technology, but a collective social process of realignment that nurtures and reenergizes embodied, institutional, and objectified processes of global integration and interchange. Some commentators see the COVID-19 crisis as a golden opportunity to "reflect, reimagine, and reset our world."[62] While I applaud such optimism, it should be clear that the goal of such a Great Reset must be the advancement of a global ethic that guides the transformation of our planetary condition in a more just and sustainable direction.

8

Globalization in 2040

ENVIRONMENT, POPULATION, DEVELOPMENT

Our comprehensive assessment of globalization in the twenty-first century is drawing to a close. Before we end this book with a consideration of some future global trends, let us briefly summarize our six most important findings. First, our critical genealogical mapping of the term "globalization" in its formative period from the 1920s to the 1990s dispels the neoliberal myth of it solely as the liberalization of trade and global integration of markets. As demonstrated, its historical meaning formation of the keyword involved at least four major interpretive branches associated with the fields of education and psychology; sociology and cultural studies; politics and international relations; and economics and business. The neoliberal appropriation of globalization that has shaped the public discourse on the subject for more than three decades was by no means a foreordained outcome. Rather, it required the active promotional efforts of pro-market forces, which took advantage of the decline of regulated capitalism in the 1970s and 1980s and the collapse of Soviet-style communism in the early 1990s. As the world's sole remaining hyperpower, the United States found itself in a hegemonic position to impose its neoliberal Washington Consensus via its subordinated international economic institutions like the IMF and the World Bank on the rest of the world. At the same time, however, the neoliberal conflation of globalization with free-market economics that dominated the public discourse did not spill over into the academic world where lengthy debates on the subject managed to cover new conceptual territory, but failed to produce a single, decontested meaning of the keyword.

The second finding is linked to our new classification scheme of globalization based on four major social formations: embodied, disembodied, objectified, and institutional. These analytically distinct, yet interactive, globalization configurations provide the foundation for a historical periodization framework that avoids the conventional pitfalls of presentism, epochalism, and Eurocentrism. Drawing on pioneering research in the new academic subfield of global history, this alternative model delineates four distinct ages of globalization based on their corresponding configurations that move at different speeds and levels of intensity. For example, we observed that the earliest historical period involved primarily the motion of human bodies across planetary space, whereas the contemporary age is dominated by disembodied flows of digital information in cyberspace. At the same time, the dominance of specific globalization formations during particular historical epochs goes hand in hand with their multiple intersections and overlaps. Hence, a careful mapping of these interplays is fundamental to understanding the long-term historical dynamics that culminated in the rise of digital globalization in the twenty-first century.

Thirdly, we found that, in spite of today's fashionable deglobalization talk, the last few decades have witnessed significant advances in both explanatory and normative globalization theory. Challenging the methodological nationalism associated with the established academic disciplines of International Studies and International Relations, Global Studies scholars developed a methodological glocalism that places the interaction between global and local interconnectivities at the center of analysis. Their theoretical efforts have not only provided new conceptual frameworks for addressing long-standing global problems such as human-induced climate change, economic inequality, and migration, but also facilitated richer intellectual engagements with sudden global disruptions such as nuclear accidents, large-scale oil spills, transnational terrorist attacks, and the spread of novel pandemics like COVID-19 or Ebola.

Innovations in globalization theory have also contributed to the rapid growth of the new transdisciplinary field of GS in this century. Its four major conceptual pillars—globalization, transdisciplinarity, space and time, and critical thinking—have given intellectual consistency to this expanding area of scholarly inquiry. The firm establishment of GS in the higher education infrastructure of the United States and around the world represents a clear sign of the increased academic attention given to proliferating global social interrelations and expanded forms of mobility. In spite of these impressive intellectual advances in both GS and globalization theory, however, there remains much room for improvement, especially with regard to obstinate problems of definitional murkiness, inadequate integration of postcolonial and ecological perspectives, spotty transdisciplinarity, and outdated classification models. Thus, we introduced an alternative conceptual framework that organizes existing globalization theories according to three intersecting modes of thinking. While affirming the uniqueness of each genre, this innovative model also emphasizes dynamic synergies among these intersecting styles that have spawned mutually reinforcing insights as well as sharp disagreements.

The fourth finding emerges from a careful mapping of the shifting ideological landscape of the twenty-first century. Articulated by corporate elites and transnational social movements, newly emerging globalisms compete fiercely for the minds and hearts of global audiences. In spite of its decline in recent years, market globalism still operates as a powerful ideology, which endows globalization with neoliberal meanings. Contesting it from the political Left, justice-globalist movements have constructed alternative visions of globalization based on egalitarian ideals of global solidarity and distributive fairness. From the political Right, religious globalists have reacted against both market globalism and justice globalism as they utilize specific ideas and values to expand their preferred religious paradigm across national borders.

In spite of their considerable differences, however, these three globalisms share an orientation toward the rising *global* imaginary, which then becomes articulated in competing political programs and agendas. Over the last decade or so, these rival ideologies have been confronted by powerful antiglobalist discourses shaped by populists like Donald Trump in the United States, Marine Le Pen in France, Nigel Farage in the United Kingdom, and Victor Órban in Hungary. Seeking to revive national imaginaries of the past, these backward-looking firebrands have made much headway in challenging the ideological dominance of market globalism as they scored impressive electoral victories. Although their vision reflects their fierce opposition to the transnational dynamics at the core of globalization, they exhibit globalist tendencies in their efforts to build alliances with like-minded political forces around the world.

Fifth, we found that, even if the current antiglobalist surge were to strengthen further in the coming decades, it would be premature to pronounce a definitive end of globalization. After all, the latest available empirical data on global flows demonstrate that all four globalization formations have neither disappeared nor declined. In fact, the currently dominant disembodied configuration has significantly intensified, and even global trade volumes are reaching new heights.[1] The national-populist surge and the protracted COVID-19 pandemic notwithstanding, the world remains a deeply interconnected place as more goods, services, institutions, ideas, and people are crossing international borders than ever before. While these thickening interdependencies have fostered economic growth and supported poverty alleviation in some parts of the world, such gains have not been evenly distributed. Moreover, many workers find their jobs have been displaced or lost to automation. Consequently, our appraisal of the state of globalization in the early twenty-first century suggests that our current era of the Great Unsettling should not be equated with deglobalization. Rather, today's mounting uncertainties and insecurities should be analyzed in the context of reglobalization, manifested as a massive reconfiguration of global interconnectivities and mobilities.

Finally, we observed that the movement of the four major globalization formations have become increasingly disjointed as a result of accelerated digitization that include recent advances in AI such as chatbots and voice assistants. Driven by such turbocharged disembodied dynamics, disjunctive globalization occurs not merely on the macro-level of material-objective processes, but also on the micro-plane of individual consciousness. One of these subjective manifestations of disjuncture involves the global production of an unhappy consciousness in the form of a self divided between its enjoyment of disembodied flexibility and its visceral attachment to embodied fixity. Although the COVID-19 crisis has forced governments around the world to impose unprecedented lockdowns and mandate other drastic forms of social distancing, the pandemic has also significantly boosted digital globalization and thus further accelerated disjointed dynamics that have been building up for some decades.

Today's disjoined reglobalization phase faces additional challenges in the form of systemic global problems that contribute to the exacerbation of existing disjunctures. Hence, let us end our appraisal of globalization in the twenty-first century with a consideration of pertinent future trends involving three global issues that have not yet been sufficiently covered in this book: the environment, population, and development.[2] However, we should keep in mind that the ensuing projections are neither predictions nor forecasts but educated guesses based on a wealth of empirical data collected by governments, international institutions, and transnational civil society organizations. What might these three crucial arenas of global interdependence look like in 2040?

ENVIRONMENT

Ecological globalization refers to the expansion and intensification of society-nature relations across planetary space, which have resulted in rapid changes to all life on this planet. Linked to the normative concept of "sustainability," these relations are meant to lead to deeper and more integrated human engagements with the natural world that enhance the ability of future generations to meet their own needs. Eurocentric knowledge systems steeped in classical philosophical dualisms have habitually separated nature from society.[3] This conceptual divide reflects the dominant understanding that the environment is somehow disconnected from people who are supposed to conquer, control, and manage nature. However, if one pays closer attention to the intrinsic links between nature and social practices, discourses, and materialities, then even the human body itself can be seen as a permanently evolving ecological site that both enables and is constrained by the production of cultural meanings while also serving as a medium for the extension of political power and economic management.

As we noted in chapter 2, humans have greatly intensified their impact on the planet since the Industrial Revolution. Their actions have become embedded into something as basic as Earth's geological rock formations. Whether it be in soot particles, radioactivity from nuclear bomb testing and plant spills, or plastic micro-fragments, the materiality of human activity is now being recorded on the skin of our planet. This critical insight prompted a growing number of scientists to recognize the extended scope of human activity by arguing that we now live in the "Anthropocene." Coined by chemistry Nobel laureate Paul Crutzen and biologist Eugene Stoermer, this new keyword refers to the present geological epoch during which our species has become a significant geophysical force acting upon Earth's biosphere.[4] Although the Anthropocene framework can be misused to protect the economic privileges of the global north from legitimate material demands of disadvantaged populations in the global south, it also facilitates our understanding of the planetary totality of current social change. Hence, the multidimensional social processes that go by the name of "globalization" can be more easily linked to shifting planetary dynamics that constantly interact with emerging global problems of human making.[5]

The Anthropocene framework has found generative ground in a world beset by multiple crises that threaten the very survival of humanity. Ecologically unsustainable practices have given rise to what Ulrich Beck has called a world risk society.[6] In his final book, *The Metamorphosis of the World*, the late German sociologist captures a foreboding sense of a planet spinning out of human control. "The world is unhinged," he writes. "As many people see it, this is true in both senses of the word: the world is out of joint, and it has gone mad. We are wandering aimlessly and confused, arguing for this and against that."[7]

Offering an encompassing description of our present socioecological condition, such powerful statements have touched all but the most hardened economic-growth advocates. While the mounting ecological damage to our planet is still being denied by such voices, it can no longer be ignored. Heated environmental debates have resounded through academic ivory towers, parliaments, corporate boardrooms, and the discursive spaces of nongovernmental international organizations. Much attention has been focused on the impact of unsustainable capitalist production on the environment. For the first time in human history, human-made materials such as concrete and asphalt outweigh the Earth's biomass. Microplastics are now everywhere, including in people's lungs and blood. It seems that the planet is rapidly approaching a breaking point, thereby introducing new forms of planetary insecurity for which we have no real guide in human history.[8]

In recognition of these multiplying and deepening manifestations of uncertainty linked to unsustainable socioecological practices, the UN Development Program changed its conventional term of "security" to "human security." The new concept includes not only safety from chronic threats such as hunger, disease, and political repression, but also protection from sudden and harmful environmental disruptions of the patterns of everyday social life. Moreover, the negative effects of ecological globalization have prompted some concerned international organizations to adopt the neologism "ecocide" to characterize large-scale human acts that disrupt or destroy planetary ecosystems. These dynamics include, among others, anthropogenic (human-induced) climate change (ACC); chemical and radioactive transboundary pollution such as acid rain and nuclear plant breaches that occurred in Chernobyl (1986) and Fukushima (2011); the degradation of farmlands and wetlands; and the rapid depletion of biodiversity.[9] Principally caused through the emission of greenhouse gases (CHGs) such as carbon dioxide and methane, ACC represents the most serious ecological threat—not only because of its capacity to alter the entire planet's atmosphere, oceans, cryosphere, and biosphere, but also because of its proven amplifying effect on other environmental problems.

For example, ACC is a major contributing factor to the worldwide reduction of biodiversity. Seven out of ten biologists believe that the world today is in the midst of the fastest mass extinction of living species in the 4.5-billion-year history of the planet. Thousands of irreversible losses of local species have been driven by increases in the magnitude of heat extremes, with mass mortality events recorded on land and in the oceans. As warming levels increase, so do the risks of species extinction in ecosystems including forests, coral reefs, and permafrost regions. More than half the world's wetlands have already been destroyed, and the biodiversity of freshwater ecosystems is under serious threat. Three-quarters of worldwide genetic diversity in agricultural crop and animal breeds have been lost since 1900.

Current measures to safeguard biodiversity include the creation of hundreds of gene banks located in countries around the world. One of the most spectacular of these banks is the Svalbard Global Seed Vault buried in permafrost in a mountain on the Arctic island of Spitzbergen. Officially opened in 2008, this "Doomsday Vault" was funded by the Global Crop Diversity Trust and financed by international donors like the Gates and Rockefeller Foundations. It has been specially designed to store back-up copies of the seeds of the world's major food crops at −18°C. Operating like a safe-deposit box in a bank, the Global Seed Vault is free of charge to public and private depositors and kept safe by the Norwegian government. Still, such laudable back-up measures are insufficient to reverse the escalating loss of biodiversity exacerbated by ACC. Hence, let us focus our discussion on this most threatening of global environmental problems facing humanity today, with eye toward its possible trajectory to 2040.

In December 2015, the representatives of the 195 nations at the UN Framework Convention on Climate Change Summit held in Paris, France, signed off on a legally binding international treaty, which was hailed as a "breakthrough climate deal." It includes many significant commitments such as the limitation of global temperature rises to below 2°C; the enhancement of adaptive capacities; the strengthening of resilience; the reduction of glaring vulnerabilities to climate change; and, perhaps most importantly, the globally coordinated pursuit of domestic legislation to achieve net-zero emissions by mid-century.

Reaching the first goal of keeping temperature rises below 2°C, in particular, is fundamental for the achievement of optimistic future projections. After all, the rapid build-up of GHGs in the atmosphere over the last decades has greatly enhanced our planet's capacity to trap heat. By the early 2020s, the accelerating greenhouse effect was responsible for raising average temperatures worldwide by 1.1°C above the average 1850–1900 level. The past ten years, since 2013, were the hottest on record, and every decade since the 1960s has been steamier that the previous one. In its 2023 Synthesis Report, the UN Intergovernmental Panel on Climate Change states that a planetary warming of more than 2°C would push the world into ecological and social chaos, with the most severe impact felt in the equatorial regions.[10] To give a better sense of what the difference of only 0.5°C of warming means, consider that at 1.5°C around 80 percent of coral reefs would die; at 2°C, they would be 99 percent destroyed.

But loss of coral reef sea level and water temperature rise because of ACC are not the only serious problems threatening the health of our planet's oceans. Overfishing, coastal pollution, acidification, mega-oil spills, and illegal dumping of hazardous wastes have had a devastating impact on Earth's marine environments. Consider, for example, the "Great Pacific Garbage Patch"—a gigantic floating mass of often toxic, non-biodegradable plastics and chemical sludge twice the size of Texas that circulates permanently in the powerful currents of the Northern Pacific Ocean. Moreover, massive glacial melts are threatening significant sea level rises. At sustained global warming levels between 2°C and 3°C, the Greenland and West Antarctic ice sheets will be lost almost completely and irreversibly over many millennia, causing several meters of sea level rise. However, even a much smaller sea level rise would spell doom for many coastal regions around the world. The small Pacific island nations of Tuvalu and Kiribati, for example, would disappear.

Large coastal cities such as Tokyo, New York, London, and Sydney would lose significant chunks of their urban landscapes.

Extreme weather events associated with ACC have already resulted in massive storms and rain events, which have caused epic floods that are often followed by lengthy periods of drought. The resulting threat of unprecedented wildfires became especially visible in the more than eleven thousand Australian bushfires that burned 13 million acres between July 2019 and February 2020; the nearly sixty thousand wildfires affecting more than 7 million acres in the United States in 2021; and the hundreds of wildfires in Canada in 2023 that blanketed the East Coast of North America in a gigantic veil of smoke. Especially worrisome have been the wildfires plaguing the Amazon region of Brazil with great regularity because the Amazonian rainforests serve as the world's lungs by producing 20 percent of our planet's oxygen. Encouraged by the anti-ecological views of national populist leaders like former President Jair Bolsonaro and some regional governors, scores of Brazilian ranchers and farmers have been encouraged to intentionally set fires to clear heavily forested land for agricultural and ranching purposes.

As GS scholar Eve Darian-Smith emphasizes, considering the challenges of ACC through the lens of such catastrophic wildfires allows us to better understand the connection between the global degradation of the environment and the political erosion of liberal democracy. When authoritarian leaders like Bolsonaro and Trump roll back environmental protections and promote extractive industries such as logging, mining, and industrial-scale agriculture, they also chip away at elements of democracy such as a free press, nonpartisan judges, public health programs, public education, and the rights to vote and protest injustice and suppression.[11]

Ironically, the environmental damages associated with this ominous link between anti-ecological views and political authoritarianism have already slowed improvements in global agricultural productivity, with crop yields shrinking annually especially in the middle and low latitudes of Africa and Asia. The resulting food shortages and water insecurity not only endanger millions of people—especially in the poorer countries of the global south—but also cause billions of dollars of damage. Some of the effects of recurrent food crises plaguing vast regions of our planet are already visible in large-scale food riots in Haiti, Indonesia, the Philippines, China, Cameroon, and South Sudan in recent years. These unrests highlight increasing limitations to food access in part as a result of environmental problems such as drought. Another major factor is inflation. In 2023, the International Monetary Fund ascertained that food and energy were the main drivers of inflation, as rising prices continue to squeeze living standards worldwide. Although global inflation is expected to fall from 8.8 percent in 2022 to 6.6 percent in 2023, it still remains far above the pre-COVID-19 levels of 3.5 percent. If such high costs of living levels persist during the 2020s, they will leave poor households and communities struggling to meet basic necessities, let alone save for future emergencies.

As of the early 2020s, little progress has been made to meet the climate targets agreed upon at the 2015 Paris Accords. Even the most recent 2021 UN Climate Change Conference in Glasgow, Scotland—with the new US administration headed by President Joe Biden rejoining the Paris agreement and fully represented at the meeting—achieved only moderate outcomes that were greeted by most environmentalists with great disappointment. Thus, model pathways that explore future emissions and possible mitigation and adaptation strategies project gloomy scenarios. It is now highly likely that warming will exceed the key Paris threshold of 1.5°C before 2040, and perhaps even surpass the 2°C ceiling at the mid-century mark—if no drastic actions to reverse these frightening trends will be taken by the global community. Indeed, the UN estimates that emissions will continue to rise by nearly 15 percent in the 2020s. Moreover, cumulative GHGs already in the atmosphere will drive temperature increases in the next two decades even if emissions were to reach net zero immediately. By 2040, no country in the world will be immune from the physical effects of ACC and environmental degradation. People in the global south will suffer more than those dwelling in the global north due to their lack of adaption and resilience capacities. Within these poorer countries, indigenous peoples and women will bear a disproportionate share of the harmful social consequences of the deteriorating environment.

On the positive side of the ecological ledger, however, governmental efforts to set a global path toward net zero GHGs are likely to intensify in the next fifteen years. A critical factor in the world's ability to mitigate climate change will be the speed of the necessary transition from fossil fuels to renewable energy. While fossil fuels will continue to supply most of the energy needs up to 2040, wind and solar are certain to grow faster than any other energy source because of technological advances and falling costs. While the development of green hydrogen—produced through electrolysis with no by-products—is still at its infancy, it has great potential to help decarbonize the atmosphere. To be sure, advanced energy storage will be needed to enable more renewables in electric grid systems and support the broad development of electric vehicles and solar-powered homes. In spite of the environmental dangers associated with nuclear power, it is likely that small modular nuclear power production will grow over the next two decades, especially if safer designs can be developed quickly and in cost-efficient ways.

In addition to increasing afforestation efforts, much-touted technologies to capture and store carbon—such as carbon sinks, saline aquifers, giant air filters, and ionic liquids—have emerged as potential weapons in the fight against ACC. But the roughly thirty commercialized carbon dioxide removal projects operating in the early 2020s have only managed to offset a negligible amount of annual GHG emissions. The necessary efforts to scale up carbon capture schemes quickly and efficiently will face serious policy constraints, even if more countries introduced a carbon tax or offered businesses tax credits for removing carbon. Moreover, the technological innovations required for large-scale carbon capture and removal are estimated to take decades of development and testing, and thus it is doubtful if they will make a significant contribution by 2040.[12]

Short of reaching the goal of net zero emissions by 2040, or even by 2050, governments and civil society actors will be forced to expand their investment in adaptive infrastructure and resilience measures. Some effective measures like restoring mangrove forests or increasing rainwater storage are relatively simple and inexpensive. Others, like building massive sea walls and schemes for the relocation of the most vulnerable populations, are complex and expensive. Hence, massive public-private partnerships aimed at creating large-scale resilience measures will have to be created within the next two decades. Perhaps the most ambitious resilience project involving state and non-state actors concerns the development and deployment of innovative geoengineering measures. Current research is largely focused on interventions in Earth's nature systems to counteract climate change such as solar radiation management to cool the planet by reflecting the sun's energy back into space, and stratospheric aerosol injection that would spray particles in the stratosphere that cause global dimming.

There are, of course, serious problems with such techno-utopian approaches. First, even experts have no idea whether there would be harmful side effects to such massive interventions in our planet's atmosphere. In fact, there is a chance that the medicine might actually be worse than the disease. Second, the global north's penchant for placing great weight on new technologies as the panacea to all our environmental problems deflects from the need to make profound changes to our dominant political and socioeconomic systems. As Eve Darian-Smith points out, the belief that technology can save us from the environmental consequences of our actions reinforces an instrumental logic that underpins extractive capitalism in the form of exploiting cheap labor and natural resources through mining, fracking, logging, fishing, and drilling industries.[13]

But even if we approached new technologies as the solution to our ecological problems from a purely instrumental perspective, it is almost certain that technological progress on such geoengineering projects will happen too slowly to have much of an impact by 2040. Finally, most observed technological adaptation responses up to date have been fragmented, incremental, and unequally distributed around the world. The dearth of effective global governance structures has made it especially difficult to rectify these adaptation inequalities that exist across political borders and geographic regions. While there is unquestionably sufficient global capital and liquidity to increase ecological investment, it is much less clear whether there exists a serious commitment to spend the money. Although global climate finance flows have increased over the last decade, private and public investments in the early 2020s have fallen well short of the levels needed to keep warming below the critical 2°C ceiling in the near future.

Perhaps the most important factor in bringing ACC under control by mid-century would be a major shift in public perception of ecological threats to our planetary existence. One of the most influential recent efforts to raise people's environmental consciousness came from a rather unexpected quarter: the Vatican in Rome. Drawing on his "green" encyclical letter *Laudato Si*, Pope Francis stood in 2015 before the UN General Assembly and issued a radical call for the world's nations to engage in more effective environmental dialogue that would bring about more rapid action on global climate change and its socioeconomic roots.[14] Praising the worldwide ecological movement for making considerable progress in shaping public opinion, the pontiff condemned obstructionist attitudes on the part of government and business, which included denial, indifference, nonchalant resignation, and blind confidence in technical solutions.

As the late French sociologist Bruno Latour feared, however, the transformation of human consciousness desired by Pope Francis might only come by way of cascading environmental calamities that might finally spark people's recognition of their ecological limits as "terrestrials," who are obliged to share their living space with a myriad of species.[15] Humanity's survival in the unsettled world of the Anthropocene requires, according to Latour, a retreat from the utopian hopes in quick technological fixes as well as from market-globalist pipedreams of unlimited economic growth. Instead, humans must cultivate new ecological sensitivities that would bring them "down to earth" as embodied terrestrials embedded in local lifeworlds and yet still be endowed with a global vision. Note that Latour's emphasis on the reestablishment of embodied social relations closely corresponds to my earlier call for greater balance among the four disjointed globalization formations.

If such attitudinal change were to materialize on a global scale during the next decades, it could result in the worldwide wave of domestic environmental legislation envisioned at the 2015 Paris Summit. Yet, there seems to be little evidence of a pending ecological shift in human consciousness, even though more than 3 billion people live today in highly vulnerable regions. Almost 800 million of these vulnerable people are clustered in twenty-seven hotspot countries that face catastrophic ecological threats. Most of them are located in sub-Saharan Africa and the Middle East–North Africa region.

But as the 2022 Ecological Threat Report issued by the Institute for Economics & Peace shows, the number of people who are currently concerned about the future effects of climate change has decreased by 1.5 percent to 48.7 percent since the onset of the COVID-19 pandemic in 2020. In China, the world's largest GHG emitter, only 20.2 percent of citizens believe that ACC is a major problem. In India, the world's most populous country, only 38.8 percent of respondents expressed major concern. Sub-Saharan countries that will be most affected by ACC in 2040 recorded some of the lowest scores—mostly because they are faced with more immediate problems such as violence, terrorism, and food and water insecurity. Even the wealthy United States, the world's second largest polluter, expressed concerns about ACC barely clearing the 50 percent threshold. European countries, whose citizens recorded the highest global levels of ecological threat recognition, only reached the 56 percent mark.[16]

Ironically, humanity was afforded a rare glimpse of what a more sustainable future might look like when the COVID-19 pandemic forced multiple global lockdowns in 2020 and 2021. Satellite images showed that within weeks, the skies over heavily polluted global cities like Beijing, Delhi, and Cairo began to clear up. Not only did air and water quality increase, but the reduced human impact on the environment also boosted wildlife, including several endangered species. Many public commentators observed that such an unprecedented "anthropo-pause," however tragic and unintended, highlighted the urgency of finding alternative paths of ecological globalization.

Table 8.1. The World's Top Ten Carbon Dioxide Emitters (2020)

Country	*Total Emissions (million tons of CO_2)*	*Per Capita Emissions (tons per capita)*
People's Republic of China	11,680	8.2
United States of America	4,535	13.7
India	2,411	1.7
Russian Federation	1,674	11.6
Japan	1,067	8.3
Islamic Republic of Iran	690	8.3
Germany	636	7.7
South Korea	621	12.1
Saudi Arabia	589	16.7
Indonesia	568	2.1
Global total	36,153	4.7

Source: World Population Review (2022), https://worldpopulationreview.com/country-rankings/carbon-footprint-by-country

Unfortunately, this short glimpse into an alternative ecological future did not sway public opinion, and things started to return to "normal" in 2023.

To summarize, putting our planet on a secure path toward ecological sustainability depends on major attitudinal changes of ordinary people whose political pressure on governments could lead to significant policy changes. Fortunately, a new generation of global activists like Greta Thunberg have begun to exert environmental leadership on the global stage. Given the UN's unequivocal warning that global warming will increase during the next two decades in all its considered scenarios and modeled pathways, the time for action is now. While further ecological damage is unavoidable, it can be limited by deep, rapid, and sustained GHG emissions reductions. Even delayed climate action would significantly enhance environmental risks and hazards, which by 2040 might turn out too complex and costly to be managed by the global community. In short, there is a rapidly narrowing window of opportunity to secure a liveable and sustainable ecological future for all sentient beings on this wondrous blue planet.

POPULATION

The ecological degradation of our planet has amplifying demographic impacts. For example, one major environmental concern relates to still uncontrolled population growth in parts of the global south and the lavish consumption patterns in the global north. Since farming economies first came into existence about 480 generations ago, the world population has exploded a thousand-fold to reach over 8 billion in 2024, and it is projected to reach over 9 billion by 2040. Half of today's increase has occurred in the last thirty years. With the possible exception of rats and mice, humans are now the most numerous mammals on earth. Concerns about the relationship between population growth and environmental degradation are frequently focused rather narrowly on aggregate population levels. Yet the global impact of humans on the environment is as much a function of per capita consumption as it is of overall population size. The United States, for example, comprises only 6 percent of the world's population, yet it consumes 30 to 40 percent of our planet's natural resources.

In addition to rising levels of economic inequality within countries affecting populations worldwide, there are at least three additional challenges: disjoined population growth-and-decline dynamics, runaway urbanization, and swelling migration flows.[17] Starting with the first point, some countries will have to accommodate more citizens whereas others will have to cope with a net population loss and an aging citizenry. For example, the global cohort of over-65-year-olds is likely to approach 25 percent by 2040, up from only

15 percent as recently as 2010. Japan and South Korea will reach a median age of 53, with Europe not far behind at 47. Short of massive immigration inflows of younger people, these countries will see a significant productivity slowdown in the coming decades. Moreover, a growing share of their national incomes will be used to fulfill pension and healthcare obligations to seniors.

Globally, however, the population will continue to increase every year. Most of the increase will occur in the global south, with sub-Saharan Africa absorbing nearly two-thirds of the growth, which will put extensive strains on infrastructure, education, and healthcare. In fact, the median age in sub-Saharan Africa will be around 22 in 2040, and more than one-third of the region's population will be younger than 15. Since this region already struggles today to meet the basic needs of their population, the exploding number of young people with little educational and work prospects will add to the political volatility and security problems of these regions.

The second growing demographic problem is runaway urbanization. The world's urban population is expected to rise from 56 percent in 2020 to 66 percent in 2040, with nearly all the growth accruing in poorer countries. Globally, large cities of more than 1 million residents have been growing at twice the rate of the overall population, and about 35 percent of the world's population will live in such a gigantic city by 2040. There are currently 33 megacities, and their number is likely to increase to 40 to 45 by 2040, with a combined population increase of more than nearly 200 million people. The UN projects that 8 out of the 10 largest megacities will be located in the global south. The top 6 urban centers in 2040—Mumbai, India; Delhi, India; Dhaka, Bangladesh; Kinshasa, Democratic Republic of Congo; Kolkata, India; and Lagos, Nigeria—will have to accommodate more than 32 million inhabitants each. The associated sprawl of urban slums is bound to have not only devastating social and environmental impacts but will also put tremendous strain on the governance relations between city councils, provincial governments, and national political institutions. Many governments in poorer countries will not be able to fund the necessary urban transportation, public services, and education infrastructures—even with the help of projected increasing foreign aid inflows emanating from richer countries and international nongovernmental organizations.

Thirdly, demographic trends will continue to drive large-scale migration during the next two decades. Most experts agree that the familiar push-pull factors responsible for cross-border movements of people will intensify globally, thus continuing the trend since the early twenty-first century, which brought large migration increases in both absolute numbers and as a percentage of the global population. Such intensifying population movements within and across countries present tall challenges to some of the most crucial powers of nation-states: immigration control, population registration, and security protocols. From 2001 to 2020, the proportion of the world's population living outside of their birth country increased from 2.8 percent to 3.6 percent, its highest level on record. The number of international migrants reached 281 million in 2020, which represents an increase of more than 100 million since 2000. In addition to millions of people fleeing disasters and conflict, demographic trends and economic incentives will continue to drive large-scale migration for decades to come. With about 3.6 percent of the world's population living outside their country of origin in the early 2020s, immigration control has become a central issue in most advanced nations. Many governments seek to restrict population flows, particularly those originating in the poor countries of the global south. In the United States, annual inflows of about 1.2 million legal permanent immigrants during the 2010s are surpassed by the estimated 1.6 million undocumented migrants entering the country in the 2020s. The US-based Center for Immigration Studies reports that the total number of illegal immigrants in the country in 2022 surpassed the 11 million mark.[18]

Most migrants leave their homes to pursue better economic prospects, but tens of millions are fleeing conflict, crime, religious and social repression, natural disasters, and environmental hazards. Migration scholar Eliot Dickinson argues that the number of future climate refugees is potentially enormous, with some estimates in the hundreds of millions by 2040.[19] As the 2015–2016 Syrian refugee crisis demonstrates, environmental and political factors often work hand in hand. The wave of political repression initiated by Syrian dictator Bashar al-Assad—and backed by authoritarian Russian President Vladimir Putin—coincided with years of drought that devasted agriculture and made large swaths of lands virtually uninhabitable. Both dynamics contributed to the country's quickly descending into a civil war that would kill more than 250,000 people over the next five years. By 2016, nearly 6 million Syrians—out of a total population of 23 million—had been internally displaced. Five million people had fled the country in search of both personal safety and economic opportunity. The majority of Syrian refugees ended up in camps in the neighbouring countries of Jordan, Lebanon, Iraq, and Turkey. But more than a million people attempted the dangerous trip across the Mediterranean from Turkey to Greece, hoping to find a better future in the prosperous states of the European Union, especially Germany.

But the Syrian refugee crisis represents only the most massive case among similar migration trends around the world. According to 2021 UN figures, a record 84 million refugees have been forced to flee their homes—despite the conditions of reduced mobility because of the COVID-19 pandemic. Examples include the forced expulsion of an estimated 1.1 million Rohingya people—an Islamic minority in Myanmar excluded from citizenship—as well as the millions of Mexican and Central American refugees who have sought political asylum in the United States during the 2010s and 2020s. There is near unanimity among migration experts that global migration will increase during the next decades because major drivers such as economic pressures, changing age structures, population growth, rapid urbanization, and environmental stress are likely to intensify.[20]

DEVELOPMENT

Development is the third major vector intersecting with the growing demographic and ecological problems discussed in this chapter. While it has been a central issue for many years, development will become even more significant in the coming decades. The notion of "development" was originally linked to the modernist Eurocentric vision of steady economic growth unfolding along the trajectory of western, industrial market societies and measured by their gross domestic output of goods and services (GDP). During the 1960s, the concept slowly broadened to include not just institutions and structures, but the concrete lives of people in their socioecological context. A decade later, Mahbub ul Haq, a World Bank economist and Minister of Finance of Pakistan, coined the concept "human development" to highlight the significance of seeing development as a force that enlarges people's freedoms and opportunities while also improving their material and spiritual wellbeing.

Central to ul Haq's human development approach was the concept of "capabilities"—the sorts of things people can do and what they can become—which he saw as the necessary equipment to pursue a life of value. Ul Haq argued that basic capabilities valued by virtually everyone are good health, access to knowledge, and a decent material standard of living. Others central to leading a fulfilling life include the ability to participate in the decisions that affect one's life, to have control over one's living environment, to enjoy freedom from violence, to have societal respect, and to relax and have fun. Collaborating with fellow economist and later Nobel Prize Laureate Amartya Sen, ul Haq was commissioned in 1990 by the United Nations Development Program to draft the first *Human Development Report*, which also included a pioneering Human Development Index as an alternative to reductionistic GDP money metrics. This accessible numerical measure is made up of the very basic ingredients of human wellbeing—health, education, and income—and ranks each country in the world accordingly.[21]

In the twenty-first century, "sustainable development" has emerged as the organizing concept that links the objectives of human development to the protection of ecological systems, which provide the necessary environmental resources on which the economic and social development depend. Hence, we can define sustainable development as the sum of actions needed to advance human wellbeing in all its dimensions while easing planetary pressures and fostering diversity and inclusion. Such a holistic understanding has become the basis of official development strategies adopted not only by the UN Development Program but by countless government agencies, nongovernmental organizations, and academic research institutes around the world.[22]

In 2015, the UN General Assembly formally signed off on the most comprehensive global development initiative up to date, titled *Transforming our World: The 2030 Agenda for Sustainable Development.* The document contains an implementation framework of 17 sustainable development goals (SDGs), 169 targets, and 244 indicators.[23] The SDGs are related to the world's most pressing development issues such as no poverty (SDG 1); Zero Hunger (SDG 2); Good Health and Well-Being (SDG 3); Quality Education (SDG 4); Gender Equality (SDG 5); Clean Water and Sanitation (SDG 6); Affordable and Clean Energy (SDG 7); Decent Work and Economic Growth (SDG 8); Industry, Innovation and Infrastructure (SDG 9); Reduced Inequalities (SDG 10); Sustainable Cities and Communities (SDG 11); Sustainable Consumption and Production (SDG 12); Climate action (SDG 13); Life Below Water (SDG 14); Life on Land (SDG 15); Peace, Justice and Strong Institutions (SDG 16); and Partnerships for the Goals (SDG 17).

During the first years of the 2030 Agenda, there was noticeable progress related to decreasing poverty, improving health, building energy infrastructures based on renewables, protecting marine areas, implementing policies to support sustainable urbanization, and supporting efforts to cut carbon emissions. However, the COVID-19 crisis—compounded by the Ukraine War, deteriorating food systems, climate-related natural disasters, refugee emergencies, and various other global problems—delayed or reversed this positive trajectory towards meeting most targets. In addition, this confluence of crises multiplied existing difficulties in interpreting and understanding the SDGs on the public policy level, while also exposing conflicts between the contents of the goals and their intended outcomes.[24] When the COVID-19 pandemic finally eased up in 2023, it became abundantly clear that the world was unlikely to reach the SDGs by 2030, or even 2040. Even the world's richest country, the United States, was not on track to fully achieve a single SDG by 2030. Its failure mattered not only to the 14 million American households that lacked reliable access to affordable, nutritious foods, but to all poor people around the globe. After all, most development experts agree that the global community needs a US government fully committed to the SDGs to have any possibility of realizing the 2030 Agenda.[25]

Hence, much of the positive future trajectory to 2040 depends on a dramatic increase in sustainable development investment by the global community. Current levels of financial commitment suggest there is much room for improvement. For example, the United States gave $25.5 billion in official development assistance in 2020, representing 22 percent of the total assistance provided by all donor countries. However, relative to its economic power, America's declining generosity during the Trump years translated into a major shortfall of the country's DSG 17 target to equal 0.7 percent of its GDP. To take matters worse, large parts of the global investment intended for sustainable development in the early 2020s had to be redirected to fight COVID-19. These emergency measures caused the financial gap to meet the SDGs to increase considerably from $2.5 trillion before the pandemic to $3.5 trillion thereafter.[26] Hence, the overall objective of moving human development to the next level by 2040—including expanding education, more applied skills training, better opportunities for women and minority groups, and improved urban infrastructure—appears to be in serious trouble.

While stagnant or declining funding in human development has hit the poorest of the poor especially hard, it also has negative consequences for the global middle classes. During the first decades of the twenty-first century, the number of households falling into the broad definition of "middle class"—with annual incomes of $4,000 to $40,000—edged up by 13 percent to about 35 percent of the global population. Stagnant levels of development investment make it almost certain that middle-class growth will come to a stop soon and might even reverse during the decade of the 2030s. Moreover, lower levels of development support will jeopardize the advances in basic healthcare during the past few decades that are linked to middle-class lifestyles. Consequently, the world in 2040 will be challenged by increasing numbers of known and new infectious diseases such as tuberculosis, malaria, and novel coronavirus strains; growing antimicrobial resistance; rising levels of noncommunicable disease like cancer, diabetes, cardiovascular disease, and chronic respiratory diseases like asthma; and increasing strains on people's mental health, especially among youth.[27]

CONCLUDING REFLECTIONS

The future trajectories of the three intersecting global issues covered in this final chapter are far from encouraging. While the world will have become an even more interconnected place in 2040, its socioecological systems will likely deteriorate to the point where existential threats to most sentient beings on this planet have become lived experiences rather than abstract projections. As noted in the preface of this book, the most pressing task at hand is to manage globalization better with the overarching aim of fostering deep socioecological reforms at the global level. Improving globalization processes depends, in the first instance, in the creation of new global governance structures as well as the enhancement of existing institutional capabilities to make the increasingly complex and disconnected globalization formations work in a more coordinated and balanced manner.

This is not to say that we should—or could—stop digital globalization. For better or worse, twenty-first-century innovations in digital technology—especially AI, biogenetics, geoengineering, bioengineering, and green energy—will play a decisive role in this collective effort to reduce the insecurities of the Great Unsettling. But we should keep in mind that various technologies do not just connect people ever faster and across greater distances. They can also operate as catalysts of social isolation when substituting the disembodied pleasures of the virtual world for face-to-face social contact and direct forms of civic and cultural engagement. Indeed, digital addiction has become a growing concern not only for the privileged gaming communities in the global north, but also for people who seek to escape the dire conditions of their crumbling lifeworlds in the global south.

But even if we succeed in advancing more harmonious processes of reglobalization, the task of setting our planet on a more sustainable path will be immensely difficult. After all, the twin mechanisms required to achieve this goal—the strengthening of global solidarity and the assemblage of more widely shared and effective global governance architecture—are still elusive prospects in our era of the Great Unsettling. The powers of the nation-state might be weakening, but people's attachment to narrow national interests remains a major driver in the portentous geopolitical order of the early twenty-first century. Hence, the understandable, yet counterproductive, impulse to deglobalize must be contested by the politically difficult, yet necessary, imperative to reglobalize. The severity and magnitude of today's confluence of global crises calls for sweeping changes on a global scale. The success of a constructive planetary vision for sustainable human development depends on the building of new global institutions and expanding existing cooperative social networks that are especially attuned to the needs of the poor and marginalized around the world.

A few years ago, UN Secretary General António Guterres envisioned the 2020s as a Decade of Action, in which global and local actors would come together to initiate and sustain transformative social change.[28] While the years and decades ahead will bring new global crises and further challenges, we can no longer afford to procrastinate. Humanity has reached yet another critical juncture in the early twenty-first century—the most significant yet in the relatively short history of our species. Unless we are willing to let global problems fester to the point where intolerance, violence, and political authoritarianism appear to be the only realistic ways of coping with our self-created mess of planetary proportions, we must be guided by the polestar of a global ethic of solidarity, reciprocity, truthfulness, and diversity. While the severity of our current global problems should never be downplayed, it would be equally foolish to bank on humanity's inability to make this world a better place. The transition to a more just and sustainable global order is not merely an abstract possibility in the twenty-first century, but constitutes a universal responsibility for present and future generations. The responsibility for the future viability of our wondrous planet lies with all of us.

Notes

CHAPTER 1

1. See, for example, Paul James et al., *Central Currents in Globalization Series*, comprising *Globalization and Violence, Vol. 1–4* (London: Sage Publications, 2006); *Globalization and Economy, Vol. 1–4* (London: Sage Publications, 2007); *Globalization and Culture, Vol. 1–4* (London: Sage Publications, 2010); and *Globalization and Politics, Vol. 1–4* (London: Sage Publications, 2014); and Manfred B. Steger, Paul Battersby, and Joseph Siracusa, eds., *The Sage Handbook of Globalization*, 2 vols. (London: Sage Publications, 2014).

2. Jean-Baptiste Michel, Yuan Kui Shen, Aviva Presser Aiden, Adrian Veres, Matthew K. Gray, The Google Books Team, Joseph P. Pickett, Dale Hoiberg, Dan Clancy, Peter Norvig, Jon Orwant, Steven Pinker, Martin A. Nowak, and Erez Lieberman Aiden, "Quantitative Analysis of Culture Using Millions of Digitized Books," *Science* 331, no. 6014 (2011), 176–82.

3. Pim Martens, Marco Caselli, Philippe De Lombaerde, Lukas Figge, and Jan-Aart Scholte, "New Directions in Globalization Indices," *Globalizations* 12, no. 2 (2015), 217–28.

4. Stephen A. Altman and Caroline R. Bastion, *DHL Global Connectedness Index 2021 Update,* https://www.dhl.com/content/dam/dhl/global/dhl-spotlight/documents/pdf/2021-gci-update-report.pdf, 54–56.

5. Reinhart Koselleck, *Sediments of Time: On Possible Histories* (Stanford: Stanford University Press, 2018).

6. Raymond Williams, *Keywords: A Vocabulary of Culture and Society*, rev. ed. (New York: Oxford University Press), 22.

7. Phillippe Bourbeau, "A Genealogy of Resistance," *International Political Sociology* 12, no. 1 (2018), 21.

8. William Boyd and M. M. MacKenzie, eds., *Towards a New Education* (London: Knopf, 1930), 350.

9. C. W. de Kiewiet, "Let's globalize our universities," *Saturday Review*, September 12, 1953, 13.

10. See Manfred B. Steger and Amentahru Wahlrab, *What Is Global Studies? Theory & Practice* (London and New York: Routledge, 2017).

11. See, for example, James H. Mittelman, *Implausible Dream: The World-Class University and Repurposing Higher Education (Princeton, NJ: Princeton University Press, 2017)*.

12. Lucius C. Harper, "He is rich in the spirit of spreading hatred," *Chicago Defender*, January 15, 1944, 4.

13. Theodore Bilbo quoted in David Runciman, "Destiny vs. Democracy," *London Review of Books* 35, no. 8 (April 25, 2013), 13.

14. Caryl A. Cooper, "The Chicago Defender: Filling in the Gaps for the Office of Civilian Defense, 1941–1945," *The Western Journal of Black Studies* 23, no. 2 (1999), 111–17.

15. Paul Meadows, "Culture and Industrial Analysis," *Annals of the American Academy of Political and Social Science* 274 (1951), 11.

16. Roland Robertson, *Globalization* (London: Sage Publications, 1992); and Saskia Sassen, *The Global City* (Princeton, NJ: Princeton University Press, 1991).

17. Meadows, "Culture and Industrial Analysis," 11.

18. See, for example, Charles S. McCoy, *When Gods Change: Hope for Theology* (Nashville: Abingdon Press, 1980).

19. Sigmund Timberg, "The Corporation as a Technique of International Administration," *University of Chicago Law Review* 19, no. 4 (1952), 747–50.

20. Inis Claude, "Implications and Questions for the Future," *International Organization* 19, no. 3 (1965), 837.

21. Aurelio Peccei, *The Chasm Ahead* (New York: Collier Macmillan, 1969), 148.

22. George Modelski, "Communism and the Globalization of Politics," *International Studies Quarterly* 12, no. 4 (1968), 389.

23. James Rosenau, "International Studies in a Transnational World," *Millennium* 5, no. 1 (1976), 1–20; and Robert Keohane and Joseph Nye, *Power and Interdependence: World Politics in Transition* (Boston: Little, Brown, 1977).

24. Robert Keohane, *After Hegemony* (Princeton: Princeton University Press, 1984).

25. François Perroux, "L'économie planétaire," *Tiers-Monde* 5, no. 20 (1964), 843–53.

26. Michael Haider quoted in "The Long-Term View from the 29th Floor," in *Time* (December 29, 1967).

27. Jan-Aart Scholte, "Whither Global Theory?" *Protosociology* 33 (2016), 213–24.

28. Mark Juergensmeyer, Arjun Appadurai, and Jonathan Friedman, interviewed in Manfred B. Steger and Paul James, eds., *Globalization: The Career of a Concept* (London and New York: Routledge, 2015), 117, 62, and 95.

29. Theodore Levitt, "The Globalization of Markets," *Harvard Business Review* 61, no. 3 (1983), 92–102.

30. Friedman, *The Lexus and the Olive Tree* (New York: Random House, 2000), 9.

31. Friedman, *The Lexus and the Olive Tree*, 8–9.

32. Friedman, *The Lexus and the Olive Tree*, 27.

33. Friedman, *The Lexus and the Olive Tree*, 45–46.

34. Friedman, *The Lexus and the Olive Tree*, 474–75.

35. See, for example, George Ritzer, *The McDonaldization of Society: An Investigation into the Changing Character of Contemporary Social Life* (Thousand Oaks, CA: Pine Forge Press, 1993); and Benjamin Barber, *Jihad vs. McWorld* (New York: Ballantine Books, 1996).

36. Barnaby J. Feder, "Theodore Levitt, 81, who coined the term 'globalization,' is dead." *New York Times* (July 6, 2006); https://www.nytimes.com/2006/07/06/business/06levitt.html.

37. Appended corrections to Feder, "Theodore Levitt, 81, who coined the term 'globalization,' is dead."

38. Stéphane Dufoix, *La Dispersion: Une Histoire des Usages du Mot Diaspora* (Paris: Éditions Amsterdam), 30–31.

39. Michel Foucault, *Aesthetics, Methods, and Epistemology: Essential Works of Foucault, 1954–1984* (New York: New Press, 1998), 263.

40. Pankaj Ghemawat, *The Laws of Globalization* (Cambridge, Cambridge University Press, 2017).

41. Victor Roudometof, *Glocalization: A Critical Introduction* (London and New York: Routledge, 2016); and Jan Nederveen Pieterse, *Globalization and Culture: Global Mélange*, 4th ed. (Lanham, MD: Rowman & Littlefield, 2020).

CHAPTER 2

1. Manuel Castells, "Nothing New Under the Sun?" in Øystein LaBianca and Sandra Arnold Schram, eds., *Continuity in Antiquity: Globalization as a Long-Term Historical Process* (London and New York: Routledge), 158.

2. Recently, Bruno Latour has made the "terrestrial" a key concept in his discussion of the impact of globalization on the global environment. See Bruno Latour, *Down to Earth: Politics in the New Climatic Regime* (Cambridge, Polity Press, 2018). The term "walkabout" has been used to characterize a rite of passage in Australian Aboriginal societies during which adolescent males undergo a solitary journey into the wilderness that can last up to six months.

3. See David Held, *Global Transformations* (Redwood City, CA: Stanford University Press), 26–27.

4. Jan Nederveen Pieterse, "Periodizing Globalization: Histories of Globalization," *New Global Studies 6, no. 2 (2012), 1.*

5. Evgeny Morozov, *To Save Everything, Click Here* (New York: PublicAffairs, 2013).

6. Michael Mandelbaum, *The Ideas that Conquered the World: Peace, Democracy and Free Markets in the Twenty-First Century* (Washington, DC: PublicAffairs, 2002).

7. Roland Robertson, *Globalization: Social Theory and Global Culture* (London: Sage, 1992), 57–60.

8. James Blaut, *The Colonizer's Model of the World: Geographical Diffusionism and Eurocentric History* (New York: The Guilford Press, 2021).

9. Philip D. Curtin, *Cross-Cultural Trade in World History* (Cambridge, UK: Cambridge University Press, 1984); Jerry H. Bentley, *Old World Encounters: Cross-Cultural Contacts and Exchanges in Pre-Modern Times* (Oxford, UK: Oxford University Press, 1993); Kenneth Pomeranz, *The Great Divergence: China, Europe, and the Making of the World Economy* (Princeton, NJ: Princeton University Press, 2001); A. G. Hopkins, ed., *Globalization in World History* (New York: W. W. Norton, 2002), and *Global History: Interactions between the Universal and the Local* (London: Macmillan 2006); Robbie Robertson, *Three Waves of Globalization: A History of a Developing Global Consciousness* (London: Zed Books, 2003); David Northrup, "Globalization and the Great Convergence: Rethinking World History in the Long Term," *Journal of World History* 16, no. 3 (2005), 249–67; Barry K. Gills and William P. Thompson, eds., *Globalization and Global History* (London and New York: 2006); Nayan Chanda, *How Traders, Preachers, Adventurers and Warriors Shaped Globalization* (New Haven, CT: Yale University Press, 2007); Pamela Kyle Crossley, *What Is Global History?* (Cambridge, UK: Polity, 2008); Dominic Sachsenmaier, *Global Perspectives on Global History: Theories and Approaches in a Connected World* (Cambridge, UK: Cambridge University Press, 2011); and Akira Iriye, *Global and Transnational History: The Past, Present, and Future* (New York: Palgrave, 2012); Jeffrey D. Sachs, *The Ages of Globalization: Geography, Technology, and Institutions* (New York: Columbia University Press, 2020).

10. For an accessible introduction to the global history framework, see Sebastian Conrad, *What Is Global History?* (Princeton, NJ: Princeton University Press, 2017). Some global historians have sought to establish a subfield called "new global history." See, for example, Bruce Mazlish, *The New Global History* (New York and London: Routledge, 2006). New global historians like Mazlish insist that the contemporary phase of globalization starting after the end of World War II should be seen as an entirely new and unprecedented historical period. As someone who recognizes the dangers of presentism and epochalism, I remain skeptical of these "new global history" arguments without dismissing their valuable contribution to the study of our immensely intense current phase of globalization.

11. Jeffrey Sachs, too, emphasizes the significance of the interplay among what he considers to be the key forces of human history: geography, technology, and institutions. See Sachs, *The Ages of Globalization* (New York: Columbia University Press), 1.

12. See Northrup, "Globalization and the Great Convergence: Rethinking World History in the Long Term," 249–67; Pomeranz, *The Great Divergence*; and Richard Baldwin, *The Great Convergence: Information Technology and the New Globalization* (Cambridge, UK: Harvard University Press, 2016).

13. Manfred Steger and Paul James, *Globalization Matters* (Cambridge, UK: Cambridge University Press, 2019).

14. David Harvey, *The Condition of Postmodernity: An Enquiry into Origins of Cultural Change*, (London: Basil Blackwell, 1989); and Fredric Jameson, *Postmodernism or, the Cultural Logic of Late Capitalism* (London: Verso, 1991).

15. Peter N. Stearns, *Globalization in World History* (London and New York: Routledge, 2010), 7–8.

16. Sachs, *The Ages of Globalization*, 34 and 40.

17. Franz J. Broswimmer, *Ecocide: A Short History of the Mass Extinction of Species* (London: Pluto, 2022), 22–26.

18. Jürgen Osterhammel and Niels Petersson, *Globalization: A Very Short History* (Princeton: Princeton University Press, 2005), 27–28.

19. Pieterse, "Periodizing Globalization: Histories of Globalization," 12.

20. See, for example, Anthony Giddens, *The Consequences of Modernity* (Redwood City, CA: Stanford University Press, 1990).

21. Dipesh Chakrabarty, *The Climate of History in a Planetary* Age (Chicago, IL: University of Chicago Press, 2021), 41.

22. Sachs, *The Ages of Globalization*, 48–50; and Jared Diamond, *Guns, Germs and Steel* (London, Vintage, 1998).

23. Sachs, *The Ages of Globalization*, 57. Indeed, Sachs considers the domestication of the horse important enough to refer to one of his seven ages of globalization as "The Equestrian Age" (3000–1000 BCE).

24. Karl Moore and David Lewis, *The Origins of Globalization* (London and New York: Routledge, 2009), 26–27; and Robertson, *Three Waves of Globalization*, 50.

25. See Tarak Barkawi, *Globalization and War* (Lanham, MD: Rowman & Littlefield, 2005).

26. Robertson, *Three Waves of Globalization*, 49.

27. Polybius, *The Histories*, trans. W. R. Paton (Cambridge, MA: Harvard University Press, 1979), Book 1, chapter 3.

28. James Scott, *Against the Grain: A Deep History of the Earliest States* (New Haven, CT: Yale University Press, 2017); and Martin Pitts and Miguel John Versluys, eds., *Globalization and the Roman World: World History, Connectivity, and Material Culture* (Cambridge, UK and New York: Cambridge University Press, 2015), 21.

29. Sachs, *The Ages of Globalization*, 94.

30. Jack Goody, *The Logic of Writing and the Organization of Society* (Cambridge, UK: Cambridge University Press, 1986).

31. See, for example, David Grewal Singh, *Network Power: The Social Dynamics of Globalization* (New Haven, CT: Yale University Press, 2008).

32. Aztec witness quoted in Sterns, *Globalization in History*, 60.

33. Alexander Koch, Chris Brierley, Mark M. Maslin, and Simon L. Lewis, "Earth Systems Impacts of the European Arrival and Great Dying in the Americas after 1492," *Quaternary Review* 207 (1 March 2019), 13–36.

34. Alfred W. Crosby Jr., *The Columbian Exchange: Biological and Cultural Consequences of 1492* (New York: Praeger, 2003).

35. Arnold Pacey and Francesca Bray, *Technology in World Civilization: A Thousand-Year History* (Cambridge, MA: MIT Press, 2021).

36. See, for example, Shmuel N. Eisenstadt, *Multiple Modernities* (London and New York: Routledge, 2002).

37. Immanuel Wallerstein, *World-Systems Analysis: An Introduction* (Durham, NC: Duke University Press, 2004).

38. Jürgen Kocka, *Capitalism: A Short History* (Princeton: Princeton University Press, 2016), 26–35.

39. Karl Marx, *Capital: Volume 1* (London: Penguin Books, 1992), chapter 26.

40. Kocka, *Capitalism*, 57.

41. Stephen R. Bown, *Merchant Kings: When Companies Ruled the World, 1600–1900* (New York: St. Martin's Press/Thomas Dunne Books, 2009), 285–86.

42. Kocka, *Capitalism*, 56.

43. Ellen Meiksins Wood, *The Origin of Capitalism: The Longer View* (London: Verso, 2017), 11–33.

44. Wood, *The Origin of Capitalism*, 194.

45. Philip D. Curtin, *The World & the West: The European Challenge and the Overseas Response in the Age of Empire* (Cambridge, UK: Cambridge University Press, 2000), xii.

46. Harold James, *The War of Words: A Glossary of Globalization* (New Haven, CT: Yale University Press, 2021), 4.

47. Pomeranz, *The Great Divergence*.

48. Sven Beckert, *Empire of Cotton: A Global History* (New York: Vintage, 2014).

49. Sachs, *The Ages of Globalization*, 138.

50. Jeffry A. Frieden, *Global Capitalism: Its Fall and Rise in the Twentieth Century* (New York: W. W. Norton, 2020), 16.

51. John Maynard Keynes, *The Economic Consequences of Peace* (New York: Harcourt, Brace and Howe, 1920), 6.

52. Nayan Chanda, *Bound Together* (New Haven, CT: Yale University Press, 2007).

53. See Vanessa Ogle, *The Global Transformation of Time: 1870–1950* (Cambridge, MA: Harvard University Press, 2015), 12.

54. For an accessible account of major pro- and antiglobalist social currents during the interwar period, see Tara Zahra, *Against the World: Anti-Globalism and Mass Politics Between the World Wars* (New York: W. W. Norton, 2023).

55. J. R. McNeill and William H. McNeill, *The Human Web: A Bird's-Eye View of World History* (New York: W. W. Norton, 2003), 270.

56. Manuel Castells, *The Information Age: The Rise of the Network Society*, 3 vols. (Cambridge, UK: Blackwell Publishers, 1996–1998).

57. Marshall McLuhan, *Understanding Media: The Extensions of Man* (Boston, MA: MIT Press, 2004).

58. William I. Robinson, *A Theory of Global Capitalism: Production, Class, and State in a Transnational World* (Baltimore, MD: Johns Hopkins University Press, 2004), 9–10.

59. Kofi Annan, "The Politics of Globalization," Address to Harvard University at the Weatherhead Center for International Affairs, September 17, 1998, https://academy.wcfia.harvard.edu/politics-globalization-hon-kofi-annan, accessed December 28, 2022.

60. Donna Haraway, *Modest_Witness@Second_Millennium* (London and New York: Routledge, 1997), 58–59.

CHAPTER 3

1. Jan Aart Scholte, "Whither Global Theory?" *Protosociology* 33 (2016), 223.

2. See Manfred B. Steger and Paul James, "Disjunctive Globalization in the Era of the Great Unsettling," *Theory Culture & Society* 37, no. 7–8 (2020), 187–203; and Barrie Axford, *Populism vs The New Globalization* (London: Sage, 2021).

3. Scholte, "Whither Global Theory?"; and Sara Curran, "Green- or Rose-Colored Lenses for *Globalization Matters*? Transdisciplinary Epistemic Practices and Paradigmatic Transformations in Ecologies and Equalities," *Globalizations* 18, no. 5 (2021), 738–49.

4. See Paul Hirst and Grahame Thompson, *Globalization in Question* (Cambridge, UK: Polity Press, 1996); Justin Rosenberg, *The Follies of Globalisation Theory* (London: Verso, 2000); Justin Rosenberg, "Globalization Theory: A Post Mortem," *International Politics* 42 (2005), 2–74; Justin Rosenberg, "And the Definition of Globalization Is . . . ? A Reply to 'In the Death' by Barrie Axford," *Globalizations* 4, no. 3 (2007), 417–21; Andrew Jones, *Globalization: Key Thinkers* (Cambridge, UK: Polity, 2010); Scholte, "Whither Global Theory?"; Barrie Axford, *Theories of Globalization* (Cambridge, UK: Polity, 2013); Barrie Axford, "A Modest Proposal: Global Theory for Tough—and Not So Tough—Times," *Globalizations* 18, no. 5 (2021), 684–94; Manfred B. Steger and Paul James, "Globalization in Question: Why Does Engaged Theory Matter?" *Globalizations* 18, no. 5 (2021), 794–809.

5. Saskia Sassen, "How to Theorize Globalization: A Comment." *Globalizations* 18, no. 5 (2021), 792–93; and Axford, "A Modest Proposal."

6. See Boaventura de Sousa Santos, "Globalizations," *Theory Culture & Society* 23, nos. 2 and 3 (2006), 393–99; Raewyn Connell, *Southern Theory: The Global Dynamics of Knowledge in Social Science* (Crow's Nest, NSW: Allen & Unwin, 2007); Julian Go, *Postcolonial Thought and Social Theory* (Oxford and New York: Oxford University Press, 2016); Eve Darian-Smith and Philip McCarty, *The Global Turn: Theories, Research Designs, and Methods of Global Studies* (Berkeley, CA: University of California Press, 2017); Benjamin P. Davis, "Globalization/Coloniality: A Decolonial Definition and Diagnosis," *Transmodernity* 8, no. 4 (2018), 1–20; Walter Mignolo, "Coloniality and Globalization: A Decolonial Take," *Globalizations* 18, no. 5 (2021), 720–37.

7. Jan Nederveen Pieterse, *Connectivity and Global Studies* (Cham, Switzerland: Palgrave Macmillan, 2021), 55.

8. David Harvey, *The Condition of Postmodernity: An Enquiry into the Origins of Cultural Change* (Cambridge, MA: Blackwell, 1990).

9. See Chamsy El-Ojeili and Patrick Hayden, eds., *Critical Theories of Globalization: An Introduction* (Houndmills, UK: Palgrave Macmillan, 2006); Gary Browning, *Global Theory from Kant to Hardt and Negri* (Houndmills, UK: Palgrave Macmillan, 2011); and Axford, *Theories of Globalization*.

10. See David Held, Anthony McGrew, David Goldblatt, and Jonathan Perraton, *Global Transformations* (Cambridge: Polity Press, 1999); Colin Hay and David Marsh, eds., *Demystifying Globalization* (Houndmills, UK: Palgrave Macmillan,

2000); Luke Martell, "The Third Wave in Globalization Theory," *International Studies Review* 9 (2007), 173–96.

11. Kenichi Ohmae, *The Borderless World: Power and Strategy in the Interlinked World Economy* (New York: Harper Business, 1990); and Kenichi Ohmae, *The End of the Nation-State: The Rise of Regional Economies* (New York: Free Press, 1995).

12. Susan Strange, *The Retreat of the State* (Cambridge University Press, 1996), 4.

13. Hirst and Thompson, *Globalization in Question*, 2.

14. Immanuel Wallerstein, *World-Systems Analysis: An Introduction* (Durham: Duke University Press, 2004); Rosenberg, *The Follies of Globalisation Theory*; Leo Panitch and Sam Gindin, *The Making of Global Capitalism: The Political Economy of American Empire* (London: Verso, 2014); and Clyde W. Barrow and Michelle Keck, "Globalization Theory and State Theory: The False Antinomy, *Studies in Political Economy* 98, no. 2 (2017), 177–96.

15. Dani Rodrik, *Has Globalization Gone Too Far?* (Washington, DC: Peterson Institute for International Economics, 1997); and Alan Scott, ed., *The Limits of Globalization: Cases and Arguments* (London: Routledge, 1997).

16. Jan Aart Scholte, *Globalization: A Critical Introduction*, 2nd ed. (Houndmills, UK: Palgrave Macmillan, 2005).

17. Held et al., *Global Transformations*, 7.

18. James Rosenau, *Distant Proximities: Dynamics Beyond Globalization* (Princeton, NJ: Princeton University Press, 2003), 11.

19. Anthony McGrew and Andrew Jones, for example also offer mappings of globalization literature according to similar categories they call "modes of inquiry" and "forms of thinking." However, their perspectives remain deeply embedded in the conventional "wave & camps" framework and thus focuses on differences, disagreements, and fractures among "key thinkers." See Anthony McGrew, "Globalization in Hard Times: Contention in the Academy and Beyond," in Georg Ritzer, ed., *The Blackwell Companion to Globalization* (Oxford, UK: Blackwell Publishing, 2007), 32; and Andrew Jones, *Globalization: Key Thinkers* (Cambridge, UK: Polity, 2010), 9–11.

20. Anthony Giddens, *The Consequences of Modernity* (Redwood City, CA: Stanford University Press, 1990); Roland Robertson, *Globalization: Social Theory and Global Culture* (London: Sage, 1992); Held et al., *Global Transformations*; Scholte, *Globalization*.

21. Held et al., *Global Transformations*, 1.

22. Held et al., *Global Transformations*, 12.

23. Giddens, *The Consequences of Modernity*.

24. In addition to some previously referenced works, see, for example, Saskia Sassen, *The Global City: London, Paris, New York* (Princeton, NJ: Princeton University Press, 1991); Eric Helleiner, *States and the Reemergence of Global Finance* (Ithaca: Cornell University Press, 1994); Jagdish Bhagwati, *In Defense of Globalization* (New York: Oxford University Press, 2007); Peter Dicken, *Global Shift: Mapping the Contours of the World Economy*, 7th ed. (New York: Guilford Press, 2015); and Joseph Stiglitz, *Globalization and Its Discontents Revisited: Anti-Globalization*

in the Era of Trump (New York: W. W. Norton, 2018); William I. Robinson, *Global Civil War: Capitalism Post-Pandemic* (Oakland, CA: PM Press, 2022).

25. In addition to some previously referenced works, for example, Saskia Sassen, *Losing Control: Sovereignty in the Age of Globalization* (New York: Columbia University Press, 1996); Linda Weiss, *The Myth of the Powerless State: Governing the Economy in a Global Era* (Ithaca: Cornell University Press, 1998); Andrew Hurrell and Ngaire Woods, eds., *Inequality, Globalization, and World Politics* (Oxford: Oxford University Press, 1999); Ian Clark, *Globalization and International Relations Theory* (Oxford: Oxford University Press, 1999); Martin Shaw, *Theory of the Global State: Globality as an Unfinished Revolution* (Cambridge, UK: Cambridge University Press, 2000); John Baylis and Steve Smith, *The Globalization of World Politics*, 7th ed. (Oxford: Oxford University Press, 2017).

26. In addition to some previously referenced works, for example, Mike Featherstone, ed., *Global Culture* (London: Sage, 1990); Nestor Garcia Canclini, *Hybrid Cultures: Strategies for Entering and Leaving Modernity* (Minneapolis: University of Minnesota Press, 1995); Benjamin Barber, *Jihad vs. McWorld* (New York: Ballantine Books, 1996); Serge Latouche, *The Westernization of the World* (Cambridge: Polity Press, 1996); Arjun Appadurai, *Modernity at Large: Cultural Dimensions of Globalization* (Minneapolis: University of Minnesota Press, 1996); John Tomlinson, *Globalization and Culture* (Cambridge: Polity Press, 1999); Jan Nederveen Pieterse, *Globalization and Culture: The Global Mélange,* 4th ed. (Lanham, MD: Rowman & Littlefield, 2019).

27. In addition to some previously referenced works, see, for example, Robert Cox, *Approaches to World Order* (Cambridge, UK: Cambridge University Press, 1996); Pierre Bourdieu, *Acts of Resistance: Against the Tyranny of the Market* (New York: New Press, 1998); Mark Rupert, *Ideologies of Globalization: Contending Visions of a New World Order* (New York: Routledge, 2000); James Mittelman, *Whither Globalization? The Vortex of Knowledge and Ideology* (London: Routledge, 2004); Paul James, *Globalism Nationalism Tribalism: Bringing the State Back In* (London: Sage, 2006); Jamie Peck, *Constructions of Neoliberal Reason* (Oxford, UK: Oxford University Press, 2010); Manfred B. Steger, *Globalisms: Facing the Populist Challenge* (Lanham, MD: Rowman & Littlefield, 2019).

28. See, for example, Andrew Jorgenson and Edward Lee Kick, eds., *Globalization and the Environment* (Leiden: Brill, 2006); Anthony Giddens, *The Politics of Climate Change* (Cambridge, UK: Polity Press, 2009); Peter Newell, *Globalization and the Environment: Capitalism, Ecology, and Power* (Cambridge, UK: Polity Press, 2012); Robyn Eckersley and Peter Christoff, *Globalization and the Environment* (Lanham, MD: Rowman & Littlefield, 2013).

29. See the book series edited by Manfred B. Steger and Terrell Carver with Rowman & Littlefield, https://rowman.com/Action/SERIES/_/GLO/Globalization; and the book series edited by Barry Gills with Routledge, https://www.routledge.com/Rethinking-Globalizations/book-series/RG.

30. Michael Hardt and Antonio Negri, *Empire* (Cambridge, MA: Harvard University Press, 2000), 353 and 413.

31. Hardt and Negri, *Empire*, xii–xv.

32. Hardt and Negri, *Empire*, 210.

33. Hardt and Negri, *Empire*, 396–413.

34. Major globalization theorists writing in the complexity style include Ulf Hannerz, *Cultural Complexity: Studies in the Social Organization of Meaning* (New York: Columbia University Press, 1992); Manuel Castells, *The Rise of the Network Society*, Vol. 1–3 (Cambridge, UK: Blackwell Publishers, 1996–1998); Zygmunt Bauman, *Globalization: The Human Consequences* (New York: Columbia University Press, 1998); Neil Brenner, "Globalisation as Reterritorialisation: The Re-Scaling of Urban Governance in the European Union," *Urban Studies* 36, no. 3 (1999), 431–51; George Ritzer, *The Globalization of Nothing* (Thousand Oaks, CA: Sage, 2004); John Urry, *Mobilities* (Cambridge, UK: Polity, 2007); Scott Lash and Celia Lury, *Global Culture Industry: The Mediation of Things* (Cambridge, UK: Polity, 2007); Saskia Sassen, *Territory, Authority, Rights: From Medieval to Global Assemblages* (Princeton, NJ: Princeton University Press, 2008); Jens Bartelson, "The Social Construction of Globality," *International Political Sociology* 4 (2010), 219–35; Victor Roudometof, *Glocalization: A Critical Introduction* (London and New York: Routledge, 2016).

35. As noted in the acknowledgments, I am grateful to Margie Walkover for providing this short summary of complexity theory. For the social application of complexity theory, see David Byrne and Gillian Callaghan, *Complexity Theory and the Social Sciences*, 2nd ed. (London and New York: Routledge, 2023).

36. Tomlinson, *Globalization and Culture*, 1–2.

37. Axford, *Theories of Globalization*, 8.

38. Castells, *The Rise of the Network Society*.

39. Castells, *The Rise of the Network Society*, 6.

40. Castells, *The Rise of the Network Society*, xxxii.

41. John Urry, *Global Complexity* (Cambridge, UK: Polity, 2003), 15 and 39.

42. Urry, *Global Complexity*, 14.

43. Urry, *Global Complexity*, 56–9.

44. Urry, *Global Complexity*, 60–1.

CHAPTER 4

1. For a useful summary of the main functions of ideology, see Paul Ricoeur, *Lectures on Ideology and Utopia* (New York: Columbia University Press, 1986). A short summary of Ricoeur's arguments can be found in Steger, *Globalisms*, chapter 1.

2. Michael Freeden, *Ideology: A Very Short Introduction* (Oxford: Oxford University Press, 2003), 54–55. See also Michael Freeden, *Ideologies and Political Theory* (Oxford, UK: Oxford University Press, 1996). The ideological function of "fixing" the process of signification around certain meanings was discussed as early as the 1970s by the French linguist Michel Pecheux and intellectuals associated with the French semiotic journal *Tel Quel*. See Terry Eagleton, *Ideology: An Introduction* (London: Verso, 1991), 195–97.

3. Harold D. Lasswell, *Politics: Who Gets What, When and How* (New York: Meridian Books, 1958).

4. Charles Taylor, *Modern Social Imaginaries* (Durham and London: Duke University Press, 2004), 2, 23–26; and *A Secular Age* (Cambridge, MA: The Belknap Press of Harvard University Press, 2007), chapter 4. As employed throughout this chapter, my key concepts of the "national" and "global" imaginary draw on relevant arguments presented in the works of Charles Taylor, Benedict Anderson, Pierre Bourdieu, and Arjun Appadurai.

5. See Cornelius Castoriadis, *The Imaginary Institution of Society* (Cambridge, UK: Polity Press, 1987), 148.

6. Anderson, *Imagined Communities*, 6–7.

7. Michael Billig, *Banal Nationalism* (London: Sage, 1995), 6.

8. See Roland Robertson, *Globalization: Social Theory and Global Culture* (Thousand Oaks, CA: Sage, 1992), 6.

9. See Anthony Elliott and Charles Lemert, *The New Individualism: The Emotional Costs of Globalization* (London: Routledge, 2006), 90.

10. For a detailed discussion of these neoliberal policy initiatives, see John Micklethwait and Adrian Woolridge, *A Future Perfect: The Challenge and Hidden Promise of Globalization* (New York: Crown Publishers, 2000), 22–54, and John Ralston Saul, *The Collapse of Globalism: And the Reinvention of the World* (London: Penguin, 2005).

11. Friedman, *The Lexus and the Olive Tree*, 112–13.

12. Robert Rubin, "Reform of the International Financial Architecture," *Vital Speeches* 65, no. 15 (1999), 455.

13. William I. Robinson, *Promoting Polyarchy: Globalization, U.S. Intervention, and Hegemony* (Cambridge: Cambridge University Press, 1996), 56–62.

14. Subcomandante Marcos, "First Declaration of La Realidad," August 3, 1996, https-//schoolsforchiapas.org/wp-content.

15. See Mazur, "Labor's New Internationalism," 79–93. See also Dimitris Stevis and Terry Boswell, *Globalization and Labor: Democratizing Global Governance* (Lanham, MD: Rowman & Littlefield, 2007).

16. See Alexander Cockburn, Jeffrey St. Clair, and Allan Sekula, *Five Days That Shook the World: Seattle and Beyond* (London: Verso, 2000).

17. See, for example, Jackie Smith, *Social Movements for Global Democracy* (Baltimore: Johns Hopkins University Press, 2007).

18. For a more detailed discussion of these five claims of justice globalism, see Manfred B. Steger, James Goodman, and Erin Wilson, *Justice Globalism: Ideology, Crises, Policy* (London: Sage, 2013).

19. Ernst Bloch, *The Principle of Hope*, 2 vols. (Cambridge, MA: MIT Press, 1995).

20. Osama bin Laden, "The Invasion of Arabia" (c. 1995/1996), in *Messages to the World*, 15. See also Osama bin Laden, "The Betrayal of Palestine" (December 29, 1994), in *Messages to the World*, 3–14.

21. Bruce Lawrence, "Introduction," in Osama bin Laden, *Messages to the World: The Statements of Osama Bin Laden*, edited by Bruce Lawrence and translated by James Howarth (London: Verso, 2005), xvii and xi. See also Bernard Lewis, "License to Kill," *Foreign Affairs* (November–December 1998).

22. Osama bin Laden, "Under Mullah Omar" (April 9, 2001), in Bin Laden, *Messages to the World*, 96, and "The Winds of Faith" (7 October 2001), 104–5.

23. See, for example, bin Laden, "The Saudi Regime," 32–33.

24. Mohammed Bamyeh, "Global Order and the Historical Structures of *dar al Islam*," in Manfred B. Steger, ed., *Rethinking Globalism* (Lanham, MD: Rowman & Littlefield, 2004), 225.

25. Bin Laden, "The Betrayal of Palestine," in *Messages to the World*, 9.

26. Osama bin Laden, "A Muslim Bomb" (December 1998), in bin Laden, *Messages to the World*, 88.

27. Ayman al-Zawahiri, "I Am among the Muslim Masses" (2006), in *The Al Qaeda Reader*, 227–28.

28. Roy, *Globalized Islam*, 19.

29. Osama bin Laden, "Moderate Islam Is a Prostration to the West" (2003), in Ibrahim, *The Al Qaeda Reader*, 22–62. For a readable overview of the history and meanings of jihad, see David Cook, *Understanding Jihad* (Berkeley: University of California Press, 2005).

30. Osama bin Laden, "The World Islamic Front" (February 23, 1998), in *Messages to the World*, 61; "To the Americans" (October 6, 2002), 166.

31. Bin Laden, "A Muslim Bomb," 73 and 87; and "The Winds of Faith," in *Messages to the World*, 105.

32. Osama bin Laden, "Among a Band of Knights" (February 14, 2003), in bin Laden, *Messages to the World*, 202; "Resist the New Rome" (January 4, 2004), in *Messages to the World*, 218; and "A Muslim Bomb," in *Messages to the World*, 69.

33.Bin Laden, "Moderate Islam Is a Prostration to the West," in Ibrahim, *The Al Qaeda Reader*, 30–31 and 51–52.

34. Osama bin Laden, untitled transcript of the videotaped message (September 6, 2007), https://publicintelligence.net/osama-bin-laden-september-7-2007-video-with-transcript/.

35. Bin Laden, "To the Americans," 167–68, and "Resist the New Rome," in *Messages to the World*, 214.

36. Bin Laden, "A Muslim Bomb," in *Messages to the World*, 91.

37. Joseph S. Nye, *Soft Power: The Means to Success in World Politics* (New York: PublicAffairs, 2004).

38. Walter Russell Mead argues that the military and economic dimensions of Nye's "hard power" concept are sufficiently different to warrant separate terms. Thus, he refers to military power as "sharp power" and to economic power as "sticky power," which he defines as a more coercive "sort of soft power" comprised of "a set of economic institutions and policies that attracts others toward US influence and then traps them in it." See Walter Russell Mead, "America's Sticky Power," *Foreign Policy* (March/April 2004), 46–53.

39. Chalmers Johnson, *The Sorrows of Empire: Militarism, Secrecy, and the End of the Republic* (New York: Metropolitan Books, 2004), 24 and 288.

40. Thomas P. M. Barnett, *The Pentagon's New Map: War and Peace in the Twenty-First Century* (New York: G. P. Putnam's Sons, 2004). The sequel to this

book is *Blueprint for Action: A Future Worth Creating* (New York: G. P. Putnam's Sons, 2005).

41. Barnett, *The Pentagon's New Map*, 31–32 and 294–302.

42. Barnett, *The Pentagon's New Map*, chapters 3 and 4.

43. Barnett, *The Pentagon's New Map*, 245.

CHAPTER 5

1. Dani Rodrik, *The Globalization Paradox: Democracy and the Future of the World Economy* (New York: W. W. Norton, 2012).

2. Heikki Patomäki, *Disintegrative Tendencies in the Global Political Economy: Exits and Conflicts* (London and New York: Routledge, 2018), 122.

3. See Karl Jackson, ed., *Asian Contagion: The Causes and Consequences of a Financial Crisis* (New York, Perseus, 1999).

4. David M. Kotz, "The Financial and Economic Crisis of 2008: A Systemic Crisis of Neoliberal Capitalism," *Review of Radical Political Economies* 41, no. 3 (2009), 307.

5. See Joseph Stiglitz, *Freefall: America, Free Markets, and the Sinking of the World Economy* (New York: W. W. Norton, 2010).

6. See David M. Kotz, *The Rise and Fall of Neoliberalism* (Cambridge: Harvard University Press, 2015).

7. Stiglitz, *Freefall.*

8. Eliot Dickinson, *Globalization and Migration: A World in Motion* (Lanham, MD: Rowman & Littlefield, 2016), 121–26.

9. See Pierre-Andre Taguieff, "The Revolt against the Elites, or the New Populist Wave: An Interview," *TelosScope* (June 25, 2016), http://www.telospress.com/the-revolt-against-the-elites-or-the-new-populist-wave-an-interview, accessed July 23, 2019; John Judis, *The Populist Explosion: How the Great Recession Transformed American and European Politics* (New York: Columbia Global Reports, 2016); Rogers Brubaker, "Why Populism?" *Journal of Theoretical Social Psychology* 46 (2017), 357–85; and Barry Eichengreen, *The Populist Temptation: Economic Grievance and Political Reaction in the Modern Era* (New York: Oxford University Press, 2018).

10. Pierre-Andre Taguieff, "La rhétoric du national-populisme," *Mots: Les Langues du politique* 9 (1984), 113–39.

11. Anton Jäger, "The Semantic Drift: Images of populism in post-war American historiography and their relevance for (European) political science," *Populismus Working Papers*, no. 3 (2016), 16.

12. Jean-Yves Camus and Nicolas Lebourg, *Far Right Politics in Europe* (Cambridge, MA: Belknap Press, 2017), 13; and Ruth Wodak, *The Politics of Fear: What Right-Wing Populist Discourses Mean* (London: Sage, 2015).

13. See, for example, Paolo Gerbaudo, *The Mask and the Flag* (Cambridge, UK: Cambridge University Press, 2017); and Chantal Mouffe, *For a Left Populism* (London: Verso, 2018).

14. Benjamin Moffitt, *The Global Rise of Populism: Performance, Political Style, and Representation* (Redwood City, CA: Stanford University Press, 2016); Dani Rodrik, "Populism and the Economics of Globalization," *Journal of International Business Policy* 1, nos. 1–2 (2018), 13.

15. Guy Standing, *The Precariat: The New Dangerous Class* (London: Bloomsbury, 2011).

16. Pankaj Ghemawat, "Globalization in the Age of Trump," *Harvard Business Review* (July/August 2017), https://hbr.org/2017/07/globalization-in-the-age-of -trump.

17. Pippa Norris and Ronald Inglehart, *Cultural Backlash: Trump, Brexit, and Authoritarian Populism* (Cambridge, UK: Cambridge University Press, 2019), 12–13 and 16.

18. The critical discourse analysis in this chapter draws on a dataset of formal speeches made by then Republican Party candidate Donald J. Trump during the US electoral campaign between March and October 2016. Most citations appearing in this chapter are taken from transcripts accessible via the Factbase website at http://factba.se. A useful online source for the study of Trump's speeches, Factbase also contains a massive collection of his campaign-relevant tweets, deleted tweets, and video materials, including his deleted video log from 2011–2014. Factbase does not engage in news or interpretation but focuses on the entire available corpus of Donald Trump's public statements and recordings in unedited form.

19. Although this chapter does not focus on the racial and gendered aspects of Trumpism, these categories are crucial in the drawing of exclusive boundaries to racial and religious minorities, women, and other social groups that are seen as lower in the social pecking order and thus might not qualify as "real Americans." For an examination of such "boundary work" in Trump's discourse, see Michèle Lamont, Bo Yun Park, and Elena Ayala-Hurtado, "Trump's Electoral Speeches and His Appeal to the American White Working Class," *The British Journal of Sociology* 68, no. S1 (Nov 8, 2017), 153–80.

20. Donald J. Trump, "Remarks at a Rally in Fredericksburg" in Fredericksburg, PA (August 20, 2016).

21. Benjamin Moffitt, "How Do Populists Visually Represent 'the People'? Visual Content Analysis of Donald Trump and Bernie Sanders' Instagram Accounts," *The International Journal of Press/Politics* (2022), https://doi.org/10.1177 /19401612221100418.

22. Donald J. Trump, "Remarks on American Economic Independence" in Monessen, PA (June 28, 2016).

23. Donald J. Trump, "Remarks on American Economic Independence"; "Address Accepting the Presidential Nomination" at the Republican National Convention in Cleveland, OH (July 21, 2016); "Remarks at a Rally in Fredericksburg" in Fredericksburg, PA (August 20, 2016); "Remarks at the Mississippi Coliseum" in Jackson, MS (August 21, 2016); and "Remarks at the South Florida Fair Expo Center" in West Palm Beach, FL (October 13, 2016).

24. Donald J. Trump, "Remarks at Luedecke Arena" in Austin, TX (August 23, 2016), and "Address Accepting the Presidential Nomination."

25. Donald J. Trump, "Remarks at Trump SoHo" in New York City (June 22, 2016).

26. Donald J. Trump, "Remarks at Trump SoHo"; "Remarks at the South Florida Fair Expo Center"; and "Remarks on American Economic Independence."

27. Donald J. Trump, "Remarks Announcing Candidacy for President" in New York City (June 16, 2015), and "Remarks at a Rally" in Toledo, OH (September 21, 2016).

28. Donald J. Trump, "Remarks at the Mississippi Coliseum" in Jackson, MS (August 24, 2016); "Remarks at a Rally"; "Remarks on American Economic Independence"; and "Remarks at a Rally at Berglund Center" in Roanoke, VA (September 24, 2016).

29. Donald J. Trump, "Remarks at the South Florida Fair Expo Center."

30. Donald J. Trump, "Remarks Announcing Candidacy for President."

31. Donald J. Trump, "Remarks on American Economic Independence."

32. Donald J. Trump, "Remarks on American Economic Independence"; "Remarks Introducing Governor Mike Pence as the 2016 Republican Vice-Presidential Nominee" in New York City (July 16, 2016); "Address Accepting the Presidential Nomination at the Republican National Convention"; "Remarks to the Detroit Economic Club" in Detroit, MI (August 8, 2016); "Remarks at a Rally in Fredericksburg" in Fredericksburg, PA (August 20, 2016); "Remarks at Luedecke Arena"; "Remarks at the Mississippi Coliseum"; and "Remarks to the American Legion" in Cincinnati, OH (September 1, 2016).

33. Donald J. Trump, "Remarks on Foreign Policy at the National Press Club" in Washington, DC (April 27, 2016).

34. Donald J. Trump, "Remarks at a Rally"; "Remarks at Trump SoHo"; "Remarks at the South Florida Fair Expo Center"; and "Address Accepting the Presidential Nomination at the Republican National Convention."

35. Donald J. Trump, "Remarks on American Economic Independence" in Monessen, PA (June 28, 2016); "Remarks at Trump SoHo" in New York City (June 22, 2016); and "Remarks at a Rally at Berglund Center" in Roanoke, VA (September 24, 2016).

36. Donald J. Trump, "Remarks on American Economic Independence"; and "Remarks at Trump SoHo."

37. Donald J. Trump, "Address Accepting the Presidential Nomination"; "Remarks at the South Florida Fair Expo Center"; "Remarks to the American Legion"; "Remarks at the Cleveland Arts and Social Sciences Academy" in Cleveland, OH (September 8, 2016);

38. Donald J. Trump, "Remarks at a Rally at Berglund Center" in Roanoke, VA (September 24, 2016).

39. Donald J. Trump, "Remarks at the AIPAC Policy Conference" in Washington, DC (March 21, 2016); and "Remarks at a Rally at Berglund Center."

40. Donald J. Trump, "Remarks at Trump SoHo."

41. Donald J. Trump, "Remarks at a Rally at Berglund Center."

42. Donald J. Trump, "Remarks at the South Florida Fair Expo Center."

43. Donald J. Trump, "Remarks by Donald J. Trump to the United Nations General Assembly," https://www.whitehouse.gov/briefings-statements/remarks-president

-trump-73rd-session-united-nations-general-assembly-new-york-ny, accessed December 26, 2018.

44. Trump cited in Peter Baker, "'Use that word'! Trump embraces the 'Nationalist' label," *New York Times* (October 23, 2018), https://www.nytimes.com/2018/10/23/us/politics/nationalist-president-trump.html.

45. Most current national populist leaders share Trump's antiglobalist rhetoric. For example, RN leader Marine Le Pen identifies "globalism" as the "second enemy" next to "Islamism." For Le Pen, globalism consists of two principal elements: transnational capitalism and multiculturalism. In fact, in a 2017 speech in Lyon that kicked off her presidential campaign, Le Pen went so far as to characterize "Islamic fundamentalism" as "another form of globalization." See William Galston, *Anti-Pluralism: The Populist Threat to Liberal Democracy* (New Haven, CT: Yale University Press, 2018), 56, and Nicholas Vinocur, "Marine Le Pen makes globalization the enemy," *Politico* (February 6, 2017), https://www.politico.eu/article/marine-le-pen-globalization-campaign-launch-french-politics-news-lyon-islam, accessed December 31, 2018.

46. For an insightful analysis of how Trump's metaphor of "The Wall" has been used in his populist storytelling to closely interlink existential crises of the people to the more abstract dangers of globalization, see Katja Freistein, Frank Gadinger, and Christine Unrau, "From the Global to the Everyday: Anti-Globalization Metaphors in Trump's and Salvini's Political Language," *Centre for Global Cooperation Research, Global Cooperation Research Papers 24 (Duisburg: Universität Duisburg Essen, 2020), https://www.gcr21.org/publications/gcr/research-papers/from-the-global-to-the-everyday-anti-globalization-metaphors-in-trumps-and-salvinis-political-language.*

47. "Remarks by President Trump and Prime Minister Abe of Japan in Joint Press Conference" (June 7, 2018), https://trumpwhitehouse.archives.gov/briefings-statements/remarks-president-trump-prime-minister-abe-japan-joint-press-conference-2.

48. Adriano Cozzolino, "Trumpism as Nationalist Neoliberalism: A Critical Inquiry into Donald Trump's Political Economy," *Interdisciplinary Policy Studies* 4, no. 1 (2018), 47–73.

49. Karl Polanyi, *The Great Transformation: The Political and Economic Origins of Our Time* (1944; reprint, Boston: Beacon Press, 1957).

50. To be fair, Stiglitz has gradually radicalized his reformist approach by including part of the justice-globalist agenda. See Joseph E. Stiglitz, *Globalization and Its Discontents Revisited: Anti-Globalization in the Era of Trump* (New York: W. W. Norton, 2018); *The Price of Inequality: How Today's Divided Society Endangers Our Future* (New York, W. W. Norton, 2012); and *People, Power, and Profits: Progressive Capitalism for an Age of Discontent* (New York: W. W. Norton, 2019).

51. James H. Mittelman, "Ideologies and the Globalization Agenda," in Manfred B. Steger, ed., *Rethinking Globalism* (Lanham, MD: Rowman & Littlefield, 2004), 22.

52. Klaus Schwab, "The New Architecture for the Fourth Industrial Revolution," *Foreign Affairs* (January 16, 2019), https://www.foreignaffairs.com/articles/world/2019-01-16/globalization-40.

53. Schwab, "The New Architecture for the Fourth Industrial Revolution."

54. Klaus Schwab, "Climate Change—Arguably Humanity's Most Existential Challenge—Requires Urgent Global Action," *World Economic Forum*, January 22, 2019, https://naturalcapitalcoalition.org/klaus-schwab-founder-executive-chairman-of-the-world-economic-forum-climate-change-is-arguably-humanitys-most-existential-challenge.

CHAPTER 6

1. See Manfred B. Steger and Amentahru Wahlrab, *What Is Global Studies?* (London and New York: Routledge, 2016); and Eve Darian-Smith and Phillip McCarty, *The Global Turn: Theories, Research Designs, and Methods for Global Studies* (Berkeley, CA: University of California Press, 2017).

2. Fredric Jameson, "Preface," in Fredric Jameson and Masao Miyoshi, eds., *The Cultures of Globalization* (Durham, NC: Duke University Press, 1998), xi–xvi.

3. Manfred B. Steger, *The Rise of the Global Imaginary: Political Ideologies from the French Revolution to the Global War on Terror* (Oxford and New York: Oxford University Press, 2008).

4. John Lie, "Asian Studies/Global Studies: Transcending Area Studies in the Social Sciences," *Cross-Currents: East Asian History and Culture Review* 2 (March 2012), https://escholarship.org/uc/item/7cw2b7nf, 9.

5. For a history of the first decades of the International Studies Association, see Henry Teune, "The International Studies Association" (1982) at: http://www.isanet.org/Portals/0/Documents/Institutional/Henry_Teune_The_ISA_1982.pdf.

6. Stephen Rosow, "Toward an Anti-Disciplinary Global Studies," *International Studies Perspectives* 4 (2003), 7.

7. Robert O. Keohane, *After Hegemony: Cooperation and Discord in the World Political Economy* (Princeton, NJ: Princeton University Press, 1984).

8. Barrie Axford, *Theories of Globalization* (Cambridge: Polity, 2013), 38.

9. James Mittelman, "Globalization: An Ascendant Paradigm?" *International Studies Perspectives* 3, no. 1 (February 2002), 1.

10. See Brendan Cantwell, Ilkka Kauppinen, and Sheila Slaughter, eds., *Academic Capitalism in the Age of Globalization* (Baltimore, MD: John Hopkins University Press, 2014).

11. Isaac Kamola, *Making the World Global: U.S. Universities and the Production of the Global Imaginary* (Durham, NC: Duke University Press, 2019).

12. Paul James, "Globalization, Approaches To," in Helmut K. Anheier and Mark Juergensmeyer, eds., *Encyclopedia of Global Studies*, 4 vols. (Thousand Oaks, CA: Sage, 2012), vol. 2, 753.

13. Jan Nederveen Pieterse, "What Is Global Studies?" *Globalizations* 10, no. 4 (2013), 499.

14. For a listing of these colleges and universities, see https://bigfuture.collegeboard.org/college-search.

15. Author's interview with Richard Appelbaum, Santa Barbara, CA, February 13, 2015.

16. Mark Juergensmeyer, "Interview Mark Juergensmeyer," *Globalizations* 11, no. 4 (2014), 541.

17. Pieterse, "What Is Global Studies?" 499.

18. See, for example, Nayef R. F. Al-Rodhan and Gerard Stoudmann, "Definitions of Globalization: A Comprehensive Overview and a Proposed Definition," *GCSP Program on the Geopolitical Implication of Globalization and Transnational Security* (June 19, 2006), 1–21.

19. Michel Foucault, *Discipline and Punish: The Birth of Prison* (New York: Vintage, 1995).

20. See, for example, David Alvargonzález, "Multidisciplinarity, Interdisciplinarity, Transdisciplinarity, and the Sciences," *International Studies in the Philosophy of Science* 25, no. 4 (2011), 387–403; Alice Wendy Russell, "No Academic Borders? Transdisciplinarity in University Teaching and Research," *Australian University Review* 48, no. 1 (2005), 35–41; Manfred A. Max-Neef, "Foundations of Transdisciplinarity," *Ecological Economics* 53 (2005), 35–41; Bernard C. K. Choi and Anita W. P. Pak, "Multidisciplinarity, Interdisciplinarity, and Transdisciplinarity, Education and Policy: Definitions, Objectives, and Evidence of Effectiveness," *Clinical Investigative Medicine* 29, no. 6 (2006), 351–64; and Allen F. Repko, *Interdisciplinary Research: Process and Theory*, 2nd ed. (London: Sage, 2011).

21. Christian Pohl and Gertrude Hirsch Hadorn, "Methodological Challenges of Transdisciplinary Research," *Natures Sciences Sociétés* 16 (2008), 111–21; and Christian Pohl, "From Transdisciplinarity to Transdisciplinary Research," *Transdisciplinary Journal of Engineering & Science* 1, no. 1 (December 2010), 65–73.

22. Marshall McLuhan, *Understanding Media: The Extension of Man*, reprint ed. (Cambridge, MA: MIT Press, 1994), 3.

23. Henri Lefebvre, *The Production of Space* (Oxford, UK: Blackwell Publishing, 1991), 12.

24. Robertson, *Globalization*, 6–7; and Roland Robertson, "The Conceptual Promise of Glocalization: Commonality and Diversity," *Art-e-Fact* 4 (2003), https://www.scribd.com/document/259061451/THE-CONCEPTUAL-PROMISE-OF-GLOCALIZATION-docx, accessed September 29, 2023.

25. Appadurai, *Modernity at Large*, 188.

26. Harvey, *The Condition of Postmodernity*, 137, 265, 270–73, and 293.

27. Giddens, *The Consequences of Modernity*, 52–53.

28. Martin Albrow, *The Global Age: State and Society Beyond Modernity* (Redwood City, CA: Stanford University Press, 1996).

29. Saskia Sassen, "The Places and Spaces of the Global: An Expanded Analytic Terrain," in David Held and Anthony McGrew, eds., *Globalization Theory: Approaches and Controversies* (Cambridge, UK: Polity, 2007), 86; and Saskia Sassen, "Globalization or Denationalization?" *Review of International Political Economy* 10, no. 1 (February 2003), 3.

30. See, for example, Richard P. Appelbaum and William I. Robinson, eds., *Critical Globalization Studies* (New York and London: Routledge, 2005); and Chamsy

El-Ojeili and Patrick Hayden, eds., *Critical Theories of Globalization: An Introduction* (Houndmills, UK: Palgrave Macmillan, 2006).

31. See James H. Mittelman, "What Is a Critical Globalization Studies?" in Appelbaum and Robinson, *Critical Globalization Studies*, 19 and 24–25.

32. William I. Robinson, "Critical Globalization Studies," in Appelbaum and Robinson, *Critical Globalization Studies*, 14.

33. William I. Robinson, *A Theory of Global Capitalism* (Baltimore, MD: Johns Hopkins University Press, 2004), 17 and 32; and William I. Robinson, *Global Civil War: Capitalism Post-Pandemic* (Oakland, CA: PM Press, 2022).

34. Thomas Piketty, *Capital in the Twenty-First Century* (Cambridge, MA: Belknap Press, 2017); and Branko Milanovic, *Global Inequality: A New Approach for the Age of Globalization* (Cambridge, MA: Belknap Press, 2018).

35. See Hans Schattle, *Globalization and Citizenship* (Lanham, MD: Rowman & Littlefield, 2012), 44–45.

36. Mark Juergensmeyer, "What Is Global Studies," *global-e: A Global Studies Journal* 5 (2012), https://globaljournal.org/global-e/may-2011/what-global-studies.

37. Razmig Keucheyan, *The Left Hemisphere: Mapping Critical Theory Today* (London: Verso, 2013), 3–21.

38. Keucheyan, *The Left Hemisphere*, 20–21.

39. Pieterse, "What Is Global Studies?"

40. See Darian-Smith and McCarty, *The Global Turn.*

41. Ramón Grosfoguel, "The Implications of Subaltern Epistemologies for Global Capitalism: Transmodernity, Border Thinking, and Global Coloniality," in Appelbaum and Robinson, *Critical Globalization Studies* (2005), 284.

42. Robert McCrum, *Globish: How English Became the World's Language* (New York: W. W. Norton, 2011).

43. See Michael Kennedy, *Globalizing Knowledge: Intellectuals, Universities, and Publics in Transformation* (Redwood City, CA: Stanford University Press, 2015), xv.

CHAPTER 7

1. See Manfred B. Steger and Paul James, "Disjunctive Globalization in the Era of the Great Unsettling," *Theory, Culture & Society* 37, nos. 7–8 (2020), 187–203.

2. See Karl Polanyi, *The Great Transformation: The Political and Economic Origins of Our Time,* 2nd ed. (Boston: Beacon Press, 2001).

3. Finbarr Livesay, *From Global to Local: The Making of Things and the End of Globalization* (New York: Vintage, 2017); Stephen D. King, *Grave New World: The End of Globalization: The Return of History* (New Haven, CT: Yale University Press, 2017); Michael O'Sullivan, *The Levelling: What's Next After Globalization* (New York: PublicAffairs, 2019); Henry Farrell and Abraham Newman, "Will the Coronavirus End Globalization as We Know It?" *Foreign Affairs* (March/April 2020); Rana Foroohar, *Homecoming: The Path to Prosperity in a Post-Global World* (New York: Crown, 2022).

4. Richard Baldwin, *The Great Convergence: Information Technology and the New Globalization* (Cambridge, MA: Belknap Press, 2016); and *The Globotics Upheaval: Globalization, Robotics, and the Future of Work* (New York: Oxford University Press, 2019); Kati Suominen, *Revolutionizing World Trade: How Disruptive Technologies Open Opportunities for All* (Redwood City: Stanford University Press, 2019); Klaus Schwab and Thierry Malleret, *COVID 19: The Great Reset* (Geneva: World Economic Forum, 2020); Steven A. Altman and Caroline R. Bastian, DHL Global Connectedness Index 2022, https://www.dhl.com/content/dam/dhl/global/delivered/documents/pdf/dhl-global-connectedness-index-2022-complete-report.pdf; McKinsey Global Institute, "Global Flows: The Ties that Bind in an Interconnected World" (November 15, 2022), https://www.mckinsey.com/capabilities/strategy-and-corporate-finance/our-insights/global-flows-the-ties-that-bind-in-an-interconnected-world.

5. See, for example, Peter A. G. Van Bergeijk, *Deglobalization 2.0: Trade and Openness during the Great Depression and the Great Recession* (Cheltenham, UK: Edward Elgar Publishing, 2019); and Alicia Garcia Herrero, *From Globalization to Deglobalization: Zooming into Trade,* Bruegel.org/wp-content/uploads/2020/02/Globalization-desglobalization.pdf.

6. Arjun Appadurai, "Disjuncture and Difference in the Global Cultural Economy," in Mike Featherstone, ed., *Global Culture: Nationalism and Modernity* (London: Sage, 1990), 295–310.

7. Neil Selwyn, *What Is Digital Sociology?* (Cambridge, UK: Polity, 2019), 23–24.

8. Colin Crouch, *The Globalization Backlash* (Cambridge, UK: Polity, 2019); Joseph Stiglitz, *Globalization and Its Discontents Revisited: Anti-Globalization in the Era of Trump* (New York: W. W. Norton, 2018); James Bridle, *The New Dark Age: Technology and the End of the Future* (London: Verso, 2018).

9. Azeem Azhar, *The Exponential Age: How Accelerating Technology is Transforming Business, Politics, and Society* (New York: Diversion Books, 2021), 232.

10. Daniele Schillirò, "Towards Digital Globalization and the COVID-19 Challenge," *International Journal of Business Management and Economic Research* 11, no. 2 (2020), 1711.

11. Azhar, *The Exponential Age*, 15.

12. Azhar, *The Exponential Age*, xvi.

13. Klaus Schwab, *The Fourth Industrial Revolution* (Geneva: World Economic Forum, 2016); Bernard Marr, *Tech Trends in Practice: The 25 Technologies that Are Driving the 4th Industrial Revolution* (Chichester, UK: Wiley, 2020); and Selwyn, *What Is Digital Sociology?* 30.

14. Richard Susskind and Daniel Susskind, *The Future of the Professions: How Technologies will Transform the Work of Human Experts* (Oxford, UK; Oxford University Press, 2022), 62–71.

15. Susskind and Susskind, *The Future of the Professions*, 115–23; and Azhar, *The Exponential Age*, 176.

16. Elisa Shearer, "More Than Eight-in-Ten Americans Get News from Digital Devices," Pew Research Center, January 12, 2021, https://www.pewresearch.org/fact-tank/2021/01/12/more-than-eight-in-ten-americans-get-news-from-digital-devices.

17. Susskind and Susskind, *The Future of the Professions*, 95.

18. Susskind and Susskind, *The Future of the Professions*, 71–77; Selwyn, *What Is Digital Sociology?* 49; and Azhar, *The Exponential Age*, 49.

19. Elsevier AI Author Policy (2023), https://www.elsevier.com/about/policies /publishing-ethics/the-use-of-ai-and-ai-assisted-writing-technologies-in-scientific -writing.

20. See, for example, Aaron Benanav, *Automation and the Future of Work* (London: Verso, 2020); Phil Jones, *Work Without the Worker: Labour in the Age of Platform Capitalism* (London: Verso, 2021); and McKinsey Global Institute, *The Future of Work after COVID-19* (February 18, 2021), https://www.mckinsey.com/featured -insights/future-of-work/the-future-of-work-after-covid-19.

21. Cade Metz, "What is the future for A.I.?" *New York Times* (March 31, 2023), https://www.nytimes.com/2023/03/31/technology/ai-chatbots-benefits-dangers.html. See also Noam Chomsky, Ian Roberts, and Jeffrey Watumull, "The false promise of Chat GPT," *New York Times* (March 8, 2023), https://www.nytimes.com/2023/03/08/ opinion/noam-chomsky-chatgpt-ai.html.

22. Yuval Harari, Tristan Harris, and Aza Raskin, "You can have the blue pill or the red pill, and we're out of blue pills," *New York Times* (March 24, 2023), https://www .nytimes.com/2023/03/24/opinion/yuval-harari-ai-chatgpt.html.

23. Jonathan Haskel and Stian Westlake, *Capitalism without Capital: The Rise of the Intangible Economy* (Princeton, NJ: Princeton University Press, 2018).

24. William I. Robinson, *Global Civil War: Capitalism Post-Pandemic* (Oakland, CA: PM Press, 2022), 58–59.

25. Baldwin, *The Globotics Upheaval*, 10.

26. Baldwin, *The Globotics Upheaval*, 139.

27. Livesay, *From Global to Local*, 171.

28. McKinsey Global Institute, "Global Flows."

29. Nick Srnicek, *Platform Capitalism* (Cambridge, UK: Polity Press, 2017); Timothy E. Ström, *Globalization and Surveillance* (Lanham, MD: Rowman & Littlefield, 2019); and Shoshanna Zuboff, *The Age of Surveillance Capitalism: The Fight for a Human Future at the New Frontier of Power* (New York: PublicAffairs, 2019).

30. Zuboff, *The Age of Surveillance Capitalism*, 516–20.

31. Barrie Axford, "Where Globalities Are Made," *global-e* 13, no. 12 (2020), https://globaljournal.org/global-e/february-2020/where-globalities-are-made.

32. Zuboff, *The Age of Surveillance Capitalism*, 94.

33. Saima Salim, "More than Six Hours of Our Day Is Spent Online," *Digital Information World* (February 4, 2019), https://www.digitalinformationworld.com/2019/02/ internet-users-spend-more-than-a-quarter-of-their-lives-online.html.

34. Pankaj Ghemawat, *The Laws of Globalization and Business Applications* (Cambridge, UK: Cambridge University Press, 2017), 40.

35. Statista, "Leading Countries Based on Facebook Audience Sizes as of July 2023," https://www.statista.com/statistics/268136/top-15-countries-based-on-number -of-facebook-users/.

36. Anthony Elliott and Charles Lemert, *The New Individualism: The Emotional Costs of Globalization* (London and New York: Routledge, 2005); Steve Melluish,

"Globalization, Culture, and Psychology," *International Review of Psychiatry* 26, no. 5 (2014), 538–43; Richard Sutcliffe, "Subjective Globalization," in Ali Farazmand, ed., *Global Encyclopedia of Public Administration, Public Policy, and Governance* (New York: Springer, 2017); https://doi.org/10.1007/978-3-319-31816-5_3155-1.

37. Georg W. F. Hegel, *Phenomenology of Spirit*, trans. A. V. Miller (New York: Oxford University Press, 1977).

38. Hegel, *Phenomenology of Spirit*, 126.

39. Peter Singer, *Hegel: A Very Short Introduction* (Oxford: Oxford University Press), 84.

40. Jonathan Allen, *Hegel's "Unhappy Consciousness"* (2013), https://jonathanrexallen.wordpress.com/2013/06/30/hegels-unhappy-consciousness/#:~:text=The%20unhappy%20consciousness%20can%20be,and%20finite%20aspects%20of%20itself.

41. Herbert Marcuse, *One-Dimensional Man* (Boston, MA: Beacon Press, 1991).

42. Stephen Eric Bronner, *Critical Theory: A Very Short Introduction* (Oxford: Oxford University Press, 2017), 79–82.

43. Zygmunt Bauman, *Wasted Lives: Modernity and Its Outcasts* (Cambridge, UK: Polity, 2004).

44. Anthony Giddens, *A Contemporary Critique of Historical Materialism* (London: MacMillan, 1981), 13.

45. Kenneth J. Gergen, *The Challenge of the Absent Present*, in J. E. Katz, M. Aakhus (eds.), *Perpetual Contact: Mobile Communication, Private Lives, Public Performance* (Cambridge, UK: Cambridge University Press, 2002), 227–41.

46. Guy Standing, *The Precariat: The New Dangerous Class* (London: Bloomsbury, 2016).

47. Le Lin and Manfred B. Steger, "Sailing around the World or Sinking with the Ship? Disjunctive Globalization and Transnational Education Platforms," *Global Perspectives* 3, no. 1 (2022), https://doi.org/10.1525/gp.2022.35734.

48. Lin and Steger, "Sailing around the World or Sinking with the Ship?"

49. DMR Business Statistics, "Zoom Statistics and User Count (2023)," https://expandedramblings.com/index.php/zoom-statistics-facts, accessed August 17, 2020.

50. Anthony Cuthbertson, "Coronavirus tracked: Internet use hits record high," *Independent* (June 25, 2020), https://www.independent.co.uk/life-style/gadgets-and-tech/news/coronavirus-internet-use-uk-lockdown-facebook-google-a9583701.html.

51. Azeem Azhar, *The Exponential Age*, 252.

52. Abigal Hess, "Harvard Business School Professor: Half of American Colleges Will be Bankrupt in 10 to 15 Years," *CNBC* (August 30, 2018), https://www.cnbc.com/2018/08/30/hbs-prof-says-half-of-us-colleges-will-be-bankrupt-in-10-to-15-years.html.

53. Scott Galloway, *Post Corona: From Crisis to Opportunity* (New York: Penguin, 2020), 146–47.

54. *Chronicle of Higher Education*, "Rethinking Campus Spaces: How to Prepare for the Future of Learning and Work" (December 2020), https://store.chronicle.com/products/rethinking-campus-spaces?variant=37725108633797?cid=SectionfrontstorefooterFY20.

55. Roland Benedikter, "The Dawn of Digitized Religion: A New Business Model—Or More?" *Challenge* 63, no. 3 (2020), 165–76.

56. Stan Choe, Alex Veiga, and Christopher Rugaber, "Wall Street flourishing, Main Street struggling," *Honolulu Star-Advertiser* (August 13, 2020), B5.

57. Youngrong Lee, Ye Jin Jeon, Sunghyuk Kang, Jae Il Shin, Young-Chul Jung, and Sun Jae Jung, "Social Media Use and Mental Health during the COVID-19 Pandemic in Young Adults: A Meta-Analysis of 14 Cross-Sectional Studies," *BMC Public Health* 22, no. 995 (2022), https://doi.org/10.1186/s12889-022-13409-0; and Nirmita Panchal, Heather Saunders, Robin Rudowitz, and Cynthia Cox, "The Implications of COVID-19 for Mental Health and Substance Use," *Kaiser Family Foundation* (March 20, 2023), https://www.kff.org/coronavirus-covid-19/issue-brief /the-implications-of-covid-19-for-mental-health-and-substance-use.

58. Matt Steen cited in Vicky Schaubert, "My disabled son's amazing gaming life in the World of Warcraft," *BBC* (February 7, 2019), https://www.bbc.com/news/ disability-47064773.

59. Yanqiu Rachel Zhou, "Vaccine Nationalism: Contested Relationships between COVID-19 and Globalization," *Globalizations* 19, no. 3 (2022), 454.

60. Stiglitz, *Globalization and Its Discontents Revisited*; and Schwab and Malleret, *COVID-19: The Great Reset.*

61. Joe Hollier cited in Liam Mays, "Dumb phones are on the rise in the U.S. as Gen Z looks to limit screen time," *CNBC* (March 29, 2023), https://www.cnbc .com/2023/03/29/dumb-phones-are-on-the-rise-in-the-us-as-gen-z-limits-screen-time .html.

62. Schwab and Malleret, *COVID-19: The Great Reset*, 244.

CHAPTER 8

1. McKinsey Global Institute, "Global Flows"; and Jeanna Smialek and Ana Swanson, "The death of globalization? You won't find that in New Orleans," *New York Times* (January 23, 2023), https://www.nytimes.com/2023/01/20/business/economy/ globalization-new-orleans.html.

2. The discussion in this chapter has greatly benefited from empirical data and information provided by the US National Intelligence Council, *Global Trends 2040* (March 2021), https://www.dni.gov/files/ODNI/documents/assessments/ GlobalTrends_2040.pdf. Additional sources containing empirical data used in this chapter include: *KOF Swiss Economic Institute Globalization Index* (2023), https:// kof.ethz.ch/en/forecasts-and-indicators/indicators/kof-globalisation-index.html; *Bertelsmann Stiftung Globalization Report 2020*, https://www.bertelsmann-stiftung.de /fileadmin/files/user_upload/GlobalizationReport2020_2_final_en.pdf; and McKinsey Global Institute Discussion Paper, *On the Cusp of a New Era?* (October 20, 2022); https://www.mckinsey.com/capabilities/risk-and-resilience/our-insights/on -the-cusp-of-a-new-era.

3. Bruno Latour, *We Have Never Been Modern* (Cambridge, MA: Harvard University Press, 1993).

4. Paul J. Crutzen and Eugene Stoermer, "The 'Anthropocene,'" *IGBP Newsletter* 41 (2000), 17–18.

5. Nigel Clark and Bronislaw Szerszynski, *Planetary Social Thought: The Anthropocene Challenge to the Social Sciences* (Cambridge, UK: Polity, 2021), 3–5; 93. Dipesh Chakrabarty emphasizes in his recent book, *The Climate of History in a Planetary Age* (Chicago, IL: University of Chicago Press, 2021), the importance of distinguishing the concept of the "global"—an anthropocentric construction—from the term "planetary," which decenters the human. I do not follow his distinction in this book because I see the "planetary" and "global" as exchangeable terms.

6. Ulrich Beck, *World Risk Society* (Cambridge, UK: Polity, 1999).

7. Ulrich Beck, *The Metamorphosis of the World: How Climate Change is Transforming our Concept of the World* (Cambridge, UK: Polity Press, 2017), xi.

8. UN Development Program, *Human Development Report 2021/2022*, https://hdr.undp.org/system/files/documents/global-report-document/hdr2021-22pdf_1.pdf.

9. Franz J. Broswimmer, *Ecocide: A Short History of the Mass Extinction of Species* (London: Pluto, 2002).

10. UN Intergovernmental Panel on Climate Change, *Climate Change Synthesis Report 2023: Summary for Policymakers*, https://www.ipcc.ch/report/ar6/syr/downloads/report/IPCC_AR6_SYR_SPM.pdf. This Assessment Report is the outcome of an eight-year-long undertaking from the world's most authoritative scientific body on climate change. Drawing on the findings of 234 scientists on the physical science of climate change; 270 scientists on impacts, adaptation, and vulnerability to climate change; and 278 scientists on climate change mitigation, the report provides the most comprehensive, best available scientific assessment of climate change.

11. Eve Darian-Smith, *Global Burning: Rising Antidemocracy and the Climate Crisis* (Redwood City, CA: Stanford University Press, 2022), 133–37.

12. US National Intelligence Council, *Global Trends 2040*.

13. Darian-Smith, *Global Burning*, 134.

14. Pope Francis, *Laudato Si* (2015), https://www.vatican.va/content/francesco/en/encyclicals/documents/papa-francesco_20150524_enciclica-laudato-si.html.

15. Bruno Latour, *Down to Earth: Politics in a New Climate Regime* (Cambridge, UK: Polity Press, 2018).

16. Institute for Economics & Peace, *Ecological Threat Report 2022*, https://www.economicsandpeace.org/wp-content/uploads/2022/10/ETR-2022-Web.pdf.

17. US National Intelligence Council, *Global Trends 2040*.

18. Steven A. Camarota and Karen Ziegler, "Estimating the Illegal Immigrant Population Using the Current Population Survey," Center for Immigration Studies (March 29, 2022), https://cis.org/Report/Estimating-Illegal-Immigrant-Population-Using-Current-Population-Survey.

19. Eliot Dickinson, *Globalization & Migration: A World in Motion* (Lanham, MD: Rowman & Littlefield, 2017), 116.

20. UN Development Program, *Human Development Report 2021/2022*.

21. Measure of America of the US Social Science Research Council, "About Human Development" (2023), https://measureofamerica.org/human-development/#:~:text

=Human%20development%20is%20defined%20as,by%20economist%20Mahbub%20ul%20Haq.

22. UN Development Program, *Human Development Report 2021/2022*.

23. UN General Assembly, *Transforming Our World: The 2030 Agenda for Sustainable Development*, Resolution A/RES/70/1 (October 21, 2015), https://www.un.org/en/development/desa/population/migration/generalassembly/docs/globalcompact/A_RES_70_1_E.pdf.

24. European Parliament, "Achieving the UN Agenda 2030: Overall Actions for the Successful Implementation of the Sustainable Development Goals Before and After the 2030 Deadline" (2022), https://www.europarl.europa.eu/RegData/etudes/IDAN/2022/702576/EXPO_IDA(2022)702576_EN.pdf.

25. Tony Pipa, Krista Rasmussen, and Kait Pendrak, "The State of the Sustainable Development Goals in the United States," Center for Sustainable Development at Brookings (March 16, 2022), https://www.brookings.edu/wp-content/uploads/2022/03/2022_Brookings_State-of-SDGs-in-the-US_Executive-Summary.pdf.

26. UN Development Program, *Human Development Report 2021/2022*; Pipa, Rasmussen, and Pendrak, "The State of the Sustainable Development Goals in the United States."

27. US National Intelligence Council, *Global Trends 2040*.

28. António Guterres, "Remarks to High-Level Political Forum on Sustainable Development" (September 24, 2019), https://www.un.org/sg/en/content/sg/speeches/2019-09-24/remarks-high-level-political-sustainable-development-forum.

Index

About the Author

Manfred B. Steger is professor of sociology at the University of Hawai'i at Mānoa. He has served as an academic consultant on globalization for the US State Department and as an advisor to the PBS television series *Heaven on Earth: The Rise and Fall of Socialism*. He has delivered many invited lectures on globalization for academic and public audiences around the world and is the author of more than thirty books and numerous articles on globalization and social and political theory. These include *The Rise of the Global Imaginary: Political Ideologies from the French Revolution to the Global War on Terror*; the award-winning *Globalisms: Facing the Populist Challenge*, 4th ed.; and the best-selling *Globalization: A Very Short Introduction*, 6th ed.

Made in United States
Orlando, FL
28 August 2024

50883275R00126